CFA® Level 1
3-Day Review
Slide Workbook

for the 2010 CFA Exam

Kaplan Schweser
1905 Palace Street
La Crosse, WI 54603
United States of America

Or visit our website at www.schweser.com.

Printed in the United States of America.

CFA® 2010 LEVEL 1 3-DAY REVIEW SLIDE WORKBOOK

Published in February 2010 by Kaplan Schweser.

Printed in the United States of America.

ISBN: 1-4277-2074-6

PPN: 4550-0172

3-DAY REVIEW SEMINAR SYLLABUS
FOR THE 2010 LEVEL 1 CFA® EXAM

This is a guideline syllabus; expect the instructor to make minor adjustments to the time blocks. Please note that lunch is not provided. In consideration of others, please return promptly from breaks and turn off cell phones and pagers. Thank you.

Date	Topic	Study Sessions	Book
FRIDAY			
8:30–9:00	Introduction, Exam Overview and Strategy		
9:00–10:00	Quantitative Methods	2	1
10:00–10:15	BREAK		
10:15–12:00	Quantitative Methods	2,3	1
12:00–1:00	LUNCH		
1:00–2:15	Portfolio Management	12	4
2:15–2:45	Economics	4	2
2:45–3:00	BREAK		
3:00–5:00	Economics	4,5,6	2
SATURDAY			
8:30–10:00	Financial Reporting and Analysis	7,8	3
10:00–10:15	BREAK		
10:15–12:00	Financial Reporting and Analysis	8,9	3
12:00–1:00	LUNCH		
1:00–2:15	Financial Reporting and Analysis	9,10	3
2:15–2:45	Corporate Finance	11	4
2:45–3:00	BREAK		
3:00–4:30	Corporate Finance	11	4
4:30–5:00	Equity Investments	13	4
SUNDAY			
8:30–10:00	Equity Investments	13,14	4
10:00–10:15	BREAK		
10:15–11:30	Derivatives	17	5
11:30–12:00	Alternative Investments	18	5
12:00–1:00	LUNCH		
1:00–1:30	Alternative Investments	18	5
1:30–2:45	Fixed Income	15,16	5
2:45–3:00	BREAK		
3:00–4:30	Fixed Income	15,16	5

Contents: CFA Level 1
3-Day Review Slide Workbook

Welcome to the Schweser 3-Day Review for the CFA Level I Exam

This slide workbook has been created specifically for the Schweser 3-Day Review Seminar. The 3-Day Review for Level I covers topics that we believe are central to the Level I curriculum and encompasses the great majority of the required Learning Outcome Statements. Our combination of review, instruction, and practice is designed to present an integrated view of the Level I curriculum and to prepare you for answering questions on the Level I CFA Exam.

Ideally, you will have covered the entire Level I curriculum in some way prior to attending the review. For the final phase of your exam preparation, please consider the six full-length exams contained in Schweser Practice Exams Volume 1 and Volume 2 and the Schweser Live Mock Exam on May 22, 2010.

CFA® LEVEL 1

3-Day Review Slide Workbook

INTRODUCTION

Welcome to the Schweser 3-Day Level I CFA Review Seminar

Introduction

Study Sessions, Readings, Topics, and Learning Outcome Statements

There are **10 Topics, 18 Study Sessions**, **74 Readings** and **482 Learning Outcome Statements** for the 2010 Level I CFA Exam.

Introduction

Exam Topics and Weights

SS	Topic	# of Q's	%
1	Ethics	36	15%
2 – 3	Quant. Methods	29	12%
4 – 6	Economics	24	10%
7 – 10	Financial Reporting and Analysis	48	20%
11	Corp. Finance	19	8%

Introduction

Exam Topics and Weights

SS	Topic	# of Q's	%
12	Portfolio	12	5%
13 – 14	Equity	24	10%
15 – 16	Fixed Income	29	12%
17	Derivatives	12	5%
18	Alternative Inv.	7	3%

Introduction

3-Day Review Seminar Schedule

- **Day 1** – Quantitative Methods, Portfolio Management, and Economics
- **Day 2** – Financial Reporting and Analysis, Corporate Finance, and begin Equity Investments
- **Day 3** – Equity Investments, Derivatives, Alternative Investments, and Fixed Income

Streaming online Ethics video included

Read the entire Standards of Practice Handbook and GIPS (one more time) the day before the exam

How hard is the exam?

Introduction

Pass Rates
(exam actually taken)

Exam	% Pass	Exam	% Pass
2002	44%	Dec 2006	39%
2003	44%	June 2007	40%
June 2004	34%	Dec 2007	39%
Dec 2004	36%	June 2008	35%
June 2005	36%	Dec 2008	35%
Dec 2005	34%	June 2009	46%
June 2006	40%	Dec 2009	34%

About the 2010 Level I Exam

Introduction

2010 Exam

- All multiple choice – **3 choices**
- Morning session – covers all topics
  - 120 questions – 1½ minutes each
  - Old exams are NOT available
- Afternoon session – covers all topics
  - 120 questions – 1½ minutes each
  - Old exams are NOT available

Introduction

2010 Exam

Both the morning and afternoon sessions will cover all topics.

Questions are divided by topic, e.g., Ethics, Quant, Econ, FR&A, etc.

Final Preparation

Introduction

Do many timed practice exams

Practice Exams – Exam-like questions
3 full 6-hour exams – 240 questions each
Vol. 1 with SchweserNotes Package
Vol. 2 with Essential and Premium

Introduction

Schweser Live Mock Exam
May 22, 2010

Complete 6-hour Mock Exam
3-hour am Section + 3-hour pm Section

- Fully proctored live exam
- CFA Institute topic weightings
- Grading key and answer explanations
- Performance analysis by topic and Study Session
- Your score relative to other candidates

Add **multimedia tutorials** (10+ hours) for missed questions

- How to approach the question
- Review of the relevant CFA material
- How to focus in on the most important concept or technique

Introduction

Secret Sauce®

Your study companion for the final weeks:

- ✓ All topics/readings
- ✓ Concise to-the-point explanations
- ✓ Formulas, examples
- ✓ The most concentrated explanation of the Level I curriculum ever made

Getting Ready for Exam Day

Introduction

The Day Before the Exam

DO – reread Standards of Practice and GIPS

DON'T – wear your brain out and create a high level of stress

DO – relax the night before the exam

DON'T – cram the evening/night before the exam

DO – get some exercise and a good night's sleep

DO – approach the exam as a test of mental agility and mental and physical endurance

Introduction

Exam Day

- Get an early start, arrive early, review key concepts to warm up your brain
- Start with a topic area you are comfortable with
- Follow the directions of the proctor
- DO NOT allow your eyes to wander around the room

Introduction

Exam Day

The following items must be kept on your desk during the exam:

- Exam admission ticket
- **Current** government-issued photo identification
- Approved calculator(s), including calculator case(s)
- Writing instruments (pencils for Levels I and II, pens and pencils for Level III)

Introduction

Exam Day

The following items may be kept on your desk, if needed:

- Erasers, calculator batteries (and screwdriver for battery replacement), pencil sharpeners (no knives), eyeglasses, earplugs, and wristwatches (analog and digital) are acceptable; however, audible alarms and/or timers must be turned off

Introduction

Exam Day

The following items are permitted in the testing room but must remain in your pockets or under your chair when not in use:

- Wallet (money purse)
- Medicine, tissues, and other necessary medical or personal items

Introduction

Exam Day Tips

- Ticket, ID, pens and pencils with fresh erasers, calculator
- Personal items – take your lunch
- Read each question carefully
- Start out with something easy
- Watch the time (no audible timers)

Introduction

Exam Day Tips

- Don’t leave anything blank
- Be neat and organized
- Expect the unexpected—earplugs?
- Stay calm and focused

Introduction

Things Not Permitted at the Exam!

- Food and drinks
- Baggage of any kind including transparent bags, backpacks, handbags, tote bags, briefcases, luggage, carrying cases, or pencil cases
- Study materials including SchweserNotes, papers, textbooks, or study guides
- Scratch paper, present/future value tables, or calculator manuals
- Highlighters, correction fluid, correction tape, or rulers
- Knives of any type, including box cutter and X-ACTO® knives for use as pencil sharpeners
- Cellular telephones, cameras, pagers, headsets, computers, electronic organizers, personal data assistants, or any other remote communication or photographic devices
- Wristwatches with engaged audible alarms/timers or any type of desk clock/timer

CFA® LEVEL 1

3-Day Review Slide Workbook

QUANTITATIVE METHODS

Quantitative Methods

Quantitative Methods - Book 1

Quantitative Methods

Interest Rates

Equilibrium interest rates are:

- the **required rate of return** for a particular investment
- the **discount rate** to value future cash flows
- the **opportunity cost** of current consumption

2

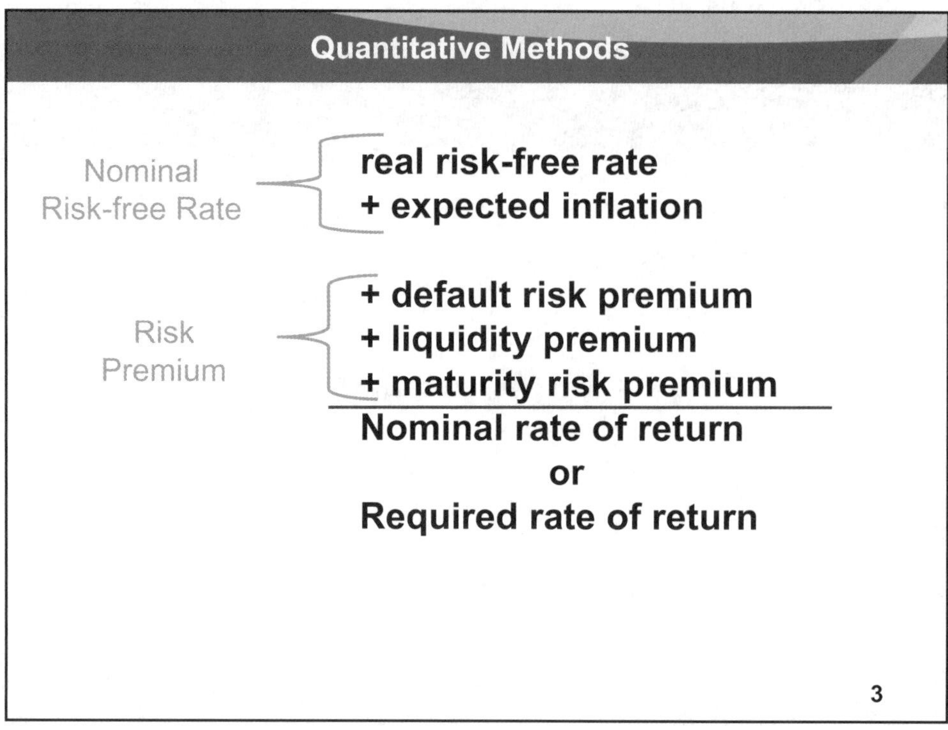

Quantitative Methods
Nominal Risk-free Rate
real risk-free rate
+ expected inflation
Risk Premium
+ default risk premium
+ liquidity premium
+ maturity risk premium
Nominal rate of return
or
Required rate of return
3

Quantitative Methods

If **Stated annual rate** is 12% with monthly compounding

Monthly effective rate is 12 / 12 = 1%

Effective annual rate is $1.01^{12} - 1 = 12.68\%$

4

Quantitative Methods

Two years from today Dimitri will make the first of 20 semiannual contributions of $500 to an account that has a stated rate of 8% and quarterly compounding. How much will be in the account 12 years from now?

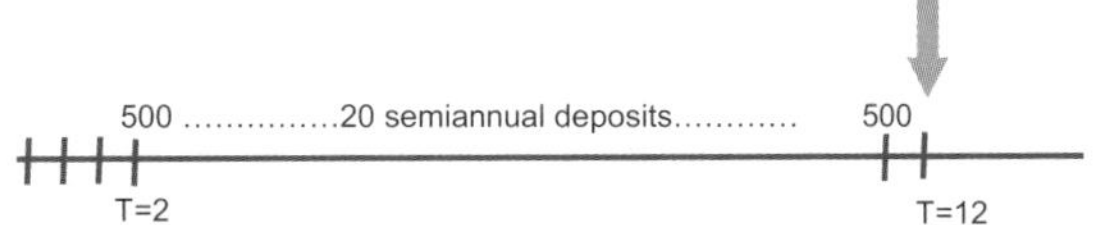

- Quarterly rate is 2%
- Effective semiannual rate is $1.02^2 - 1 = 4.04\%$
- PV = 0 N = 20 I/Y = 4.04 PMT = 500
- (bgn mode)CPT FV = $15,555
- (end mode)CPT FV = $14,951 (1.0404) =$15,555

5

Quantitative Methods

Value a Perpetuity

A preferred stock will pay $3/year forever and the rate of return is 8%.

$$PV = \frac{3}{0.08} = \$37.50$$

6

Quantitative Methods

Using Geometric Mean

A stock paid a dividend of $0.08 five years ago and now pays one of $0.42. What is the annual growth rate of dividends?

$$\left(\frac{42}{8}\right)^{\frac{1}{5}} - 1 = 39.3\% \text{ so that } 8 \times (1.393)^5 = 42$$

7

Quantitative Methods

Using Geometric Mean

The total returns on a mutual fund over the last 4 years were: + 13%, +17%, –21%.

What is the holding period return?

$$(1.13)(1.17)(0.79) - 1 = 4.45\%$$

What is the average annual compound return?

$$\left[(1.13)(1.17)(0.79)\right]^{\frac{1}{3}} - 1 = 1.46\%$$

Note that mean return, 3%, is higher than the geometric mean

8

Quantitative Methods

TWR and MWR – Problem

An account is opened with deposit of 1 million euros. At the end of one year, the account is worth 1.2 million euros and the account owner deposits 800,000 euros into the account. At the end of two years the account value is 2.2 million euros.

What is time-weighted annual return?

Is the annual money-weighted return higher or lower?

What is the annual money-weighted return?

Which is the better measure of manager performance?

9

Quantitative Methods

BDY, HPY, EAY, MMY

$$\text{Bank discount yield} = \frac{\text{Discount}}{\text{Face}} \times \frac{360}{\text{days to maturity}}$$

$$\text{Holding period yield} = \frac{\text{Ending value}}{\text{Beginning value}} - 1$$

$$\text{Effective annual yield} = (1 + \text{HPY})^{\frac{365}{\text{days}}} - 1$$

$$\text{Money market yield} = \text{HPY} \times \frac{360}{\text{days to maturity}}$$

10

Quantitative Methods

100-day T-bill priced at $975

What is the annualized discount yield?

$$\left(\frac{25}{1{,}000}\right)\left(\frac{360}{100}\right)=9\%$$

What is the HPY (100-day holding period yield)?

$$\frac{25}{975}=2.564\%$$

11

Quantitative Methods

100-day T-bill priced at $975

What is the money market yield?

$$\left(\frac{25}{975}\right)\left(\frac{360}{100}\right)=9.23\%$$

What is the effective annual yield?

$$\left(\frac{1{,}000}{975}\right)^{\frac{365}{100}}-1=\left(1+\text{HPY}\right)^{\frac{365}{100}}-1=9.68\%$$

12

Quantitative Methods

Converting among yields

The effective annual yield on a T-bill is 7.65%
What is the annual discount yield?

$7.65\% = EAY = (1 + HPY)^{365/100} - 1$

$HPY = 1.0765^{100/365} - 1 = 2.04\%$

$$MMY = HPY\left(\frac{360}{\#Days}\right) = 2.04\%\left(\frac{360}{100}\right) = 7.344\%$$

13

Quantitative Methods

Bond Equivalent Yield (BEY)

Annual effective yield is 9%, calculate BEY

Effective semi-annual yield is $1.09^{1/2} - 1 = 4.40\%$

BEY = 2 × 4.40 = 8.80%

14

Quantitative Methods

Statistics

- A sample is drawn from a population
- Descriptive statistics (true parameters)
- Inferential statistics (based on sample)
- Sampling error (deviation of sample statistic from parameter)

Central Limit Theorem

Distribution of sample errors approx. normal

Std. deviation of sample error gets smaller with larger samples = $s/\sqrt{n}$

15

Quantitative Methods

Measurement Scales (NOIR)

- Nominal
- Ordinal
- Intervals
- Ratio

The market share ranks of the five largest investment banks is what kind of scale?

An ordinal scale, intervals and ratios don't make sense.

16

Quantitative Methods

Statistics Terms

- A parameter describes a characteristic of a population
- A sample statistic describes a characteristic of a sample (drawn from a population)
- A relative frequency distribution shows the percentage of a distribution's outcomes in each interval
- A cumulative frequency distribution shows the percentage of observations less than the upper bound of each interval

17

Quantitative Methods

Presenting Data—A Histogram

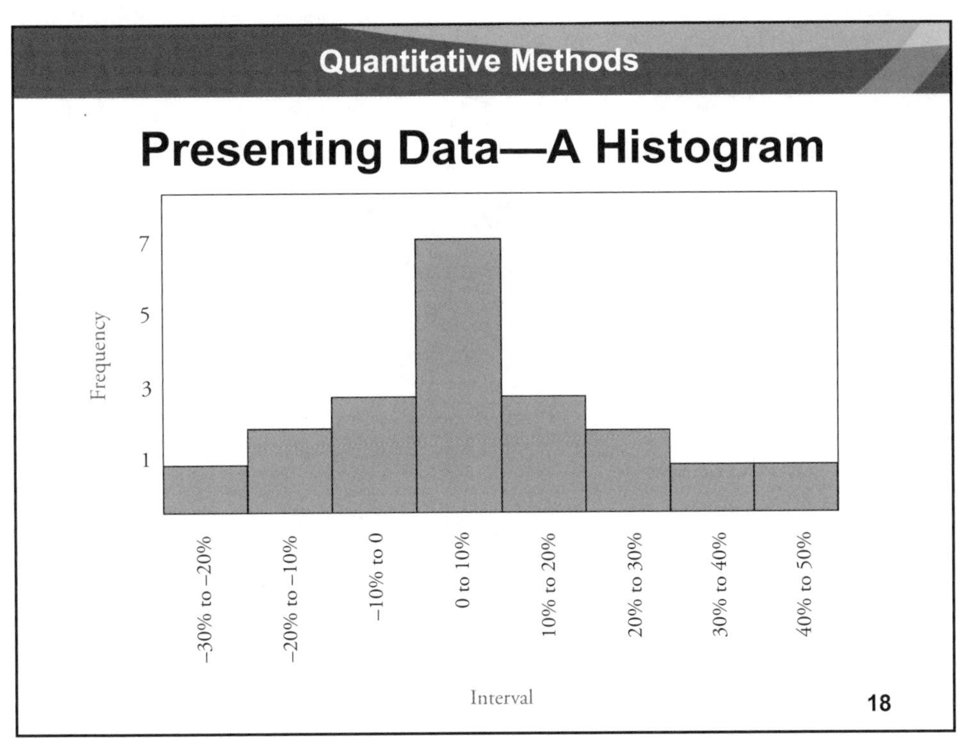

18

Quantitative Methods

Measures of Central Tendency: Mean, Median, Mode

Data (%): 5, 8, 2, 12, 8, 7, 5, 4, 8, 10

What is mean, median, and mode?

$$\text{Mean}: \mu = \frac{\sum_{i=1}^{N} X_i}{N} = \frac{69}{10} = 6.9$$

Mode

Ordered data: 2, 4, 5, 5, 7, *8, 8, 8,* 10, 12

Median = 7.5

19

Quantitative Methods

Negative Skew = Left Skew

- Negative skew has outliers in the left tail
- Mean is most affected by outliers

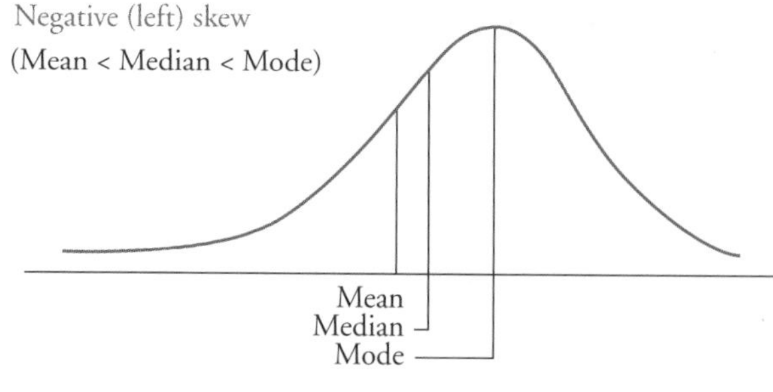

20

Quantitative Methods

Measures of Dispersion

Data (%): 5, 8, 2, 12, 8, 7, 5, 4, 8, 10

What is the range?

Ordered data: 2, 4, 5, 5, 7, *8, 8, 8*, 10, 12

Mean = 6.9%

Calculate Mean Absolute Deviation?

Average distance from mean

MAD = 2.32%

21

Quantitative Methods

Variance and Standard Deviation

Sample Data (%): 5, 8, 2, 12, 8, 7, 5, 4, 8, 10

Mean = 6.9% Compute the sample variance.

Sum squared deviations from the mean and divide by n–1 for sample variance

Variance = 8.77 (0.000877)

Std. Deviation = 2.96%

22

Quantitative Methods

Harmonic Mean - Example

Investor buys $1,000 of a stock at the end of month 1 at $20 a share, and $1,000 at the end of month 2 at $25 per share.

What is the average cost per share of stock?

$$\frac{2(1{,}000)}{1{,}000/20 + 1{,}000/25} = \frac{2}{1/20 + 1/25} = \$22.22 \text{ per share} = \frac{2{,}000}{90}$$

23

Quantitative Methods

Calculating Means – Example

Calculate the arithmetic, geometric, and harmonic means of 2, 3, and 4.

Arithmetic: $\frac{2+3+4}{3} = 3$

Largest

Geometric: $\sqrt[3]{2 \times 3 \times 4} = 2.88$

Harmonic: $\frac{3}{1/2 + 1/3 + 1/4} = 2.77$

Smallest

24

Quantitative Methods

Portfolio Expected Return

Dr. Hoover had the following portfolio at the beginning of the year: cash = \$4 million, bonds = \$6 million, equities = \$10 million.

Expected returns are 5% on cash, 7% on bonds, and 12% on equities, what is the expected portfolio return?

	Return		Weight		
Cash	5%	×	20%	=	1.00%
Bonds	7%	×	30%	=	2.10%
Stocks	12%	×	50%	=	6.00%
					9.10%

Use weighted average for expected portfolio return

25

Quantitative Methods

Chebyshev's Inequality

For any probability distribution, what is the minimum percentage of the observations within 3 std. dev. of the mean?

$$1-\frac{1}{3^2}=\frac{8}{9}=89\%$$ Minimum!

26

Quantitative Methods

Coefficient of Variation (CV)

A measure of <u>risk per unit of return</u>

Example:	Mean	Std. Dev.
Asset A	5%	10%
Asset B	8%	12%

Asset B has higher std. dev. and higher return

Lower CV is better, less risk per unit of return

$CV = \frac{s}{\overline{X}}$ or $\frac{\sigma}{\mu}$ $CV_A = \frac{10}{5} = 2$ $CV_B = \frac{12}{8} = 1.5$

27

Quantitative Methods

Sharpe Ratio

Excess Return per unit of risk; **higher is better**

Example: Mean portfolio return = 15%, standard deviation = 8%, average risk-free rate = 3%.

What is the Sharpe ratio for the portfolio?

$$\text{Sharpe ratio} = \frac{\overline{R}_P - \overline{R}_F}{\sigma_P} = \frac{15 - 3}{8} = 1.5$$

Sharpe Ratio is Safety-first with R_f for target return

28

Quantitative Methods

Skewness

- Skew measures the degree to which a distribution lacks symmetry
- A symmetrical distribution has skew = 0

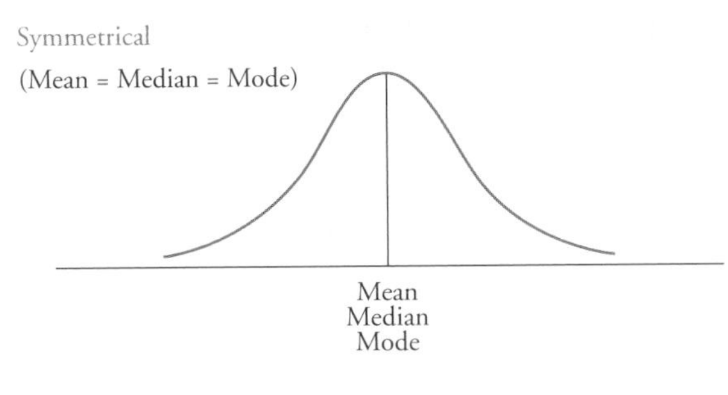

29

Quantitative Methods

Kurtosis

- Normal distribution kurtosis = 3
- *Leptokurtic* (kurtosis > 3, + *excess* kurtosis) is **more peaked** with **fatter tails (like *t*-dist)**

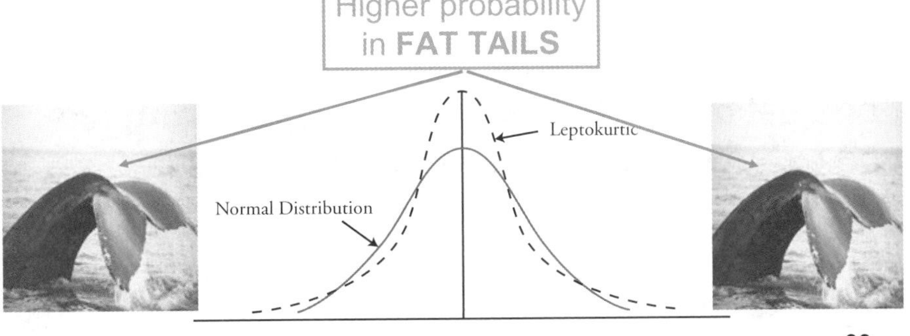

30

Quantitative Methods

Probability Terminology

Random variable: Uncertain number

Outcome: Realization of random variable

Event: Set of one or more outcomes

Mutually exclusive: Cannot both happen

Exhaustive: Set of events includes all possible outcomes

31

Quantitative Methods

Properties of Probability

Probability of an event, $P(E_i)$, is between 0 and 1

$$0 \leq P(E_i) \leq 1$$

For a set of events that are **mutually exclusive** and **exhaustive**, the sum of probabilities is 1

$$\Sigma P(E_i) = 1$$

32

Quantitative Methods

Types of Probability

- **Empirical**: Based on analysis of data
- **Subjective**: Based on personal perception
- **A priori**: Based on reasoning, not experience

33

Quantitative Methods

Odds For or Against

Probability of winning = 40%
Probability of losing = 60% → $\frac{2}{3}$

Odds for: 0.40 / 0.60 = 2/3 = two-to-three

Odds against: 0.60 / 0.40 = 3/2 = three-to-two

34

Quantitative Methods

Types of Probabilities

Given

Unconditional: **P(A)** Probability oil prices will fall the next trading day **(60%)**

Unconditional: **P(B)** Probability market index will rise next trading day **(40%)**

Conditional: **P(B|A),** Probability market will be up next trading day given a fall in oil prices **(80%)**

Calculate

Joint: **P(AB)** Probability that oil prices fall and the market is up P(A) P(B|A) = 0.6 × 0.8= **48%**

Addition rule: P(A or B) Probability either market index **or** oil prices (or both) will rise next trading day P(A) + P(B) – P(AB) = 0.6 + 0.4 – 0.48 = **52%**

35

Quantitative Methods

Independent Events

If (conditional) P(A|B) = Prob A (unconditional), then A and B are independent events

Joint probability of independent events A and B is Prob(A) × Prob(B)

Probability of coin coming up heads twice in a row is simply 0.5 × 0.5 = 25%

Probability of coin coming up tails 4 times in succession is 0.5^4 = 6.25%

36

Quantitative Methods

Total (unconditional) Probability

P (Interest rate increase) = P(I) = 0.4

P (No interest rate increase) = $P(I^C)$ = 1 – 0.4 = 0.6

P (Recession | Increase) = P(R|I) = 0.70

P (Recession | No Increase) = $P(R|I^C)$ = 0.10

What is the unconditional probability of recession?

Prob(RI) + Prob(RI^C)

$$P(R) = P(R|I) \times P(I) + P(R|I^C) \times P(I^C)$$
$$= 0.70 \times 0.40 + 0.10 \times 0.60 = 0.34$$

37

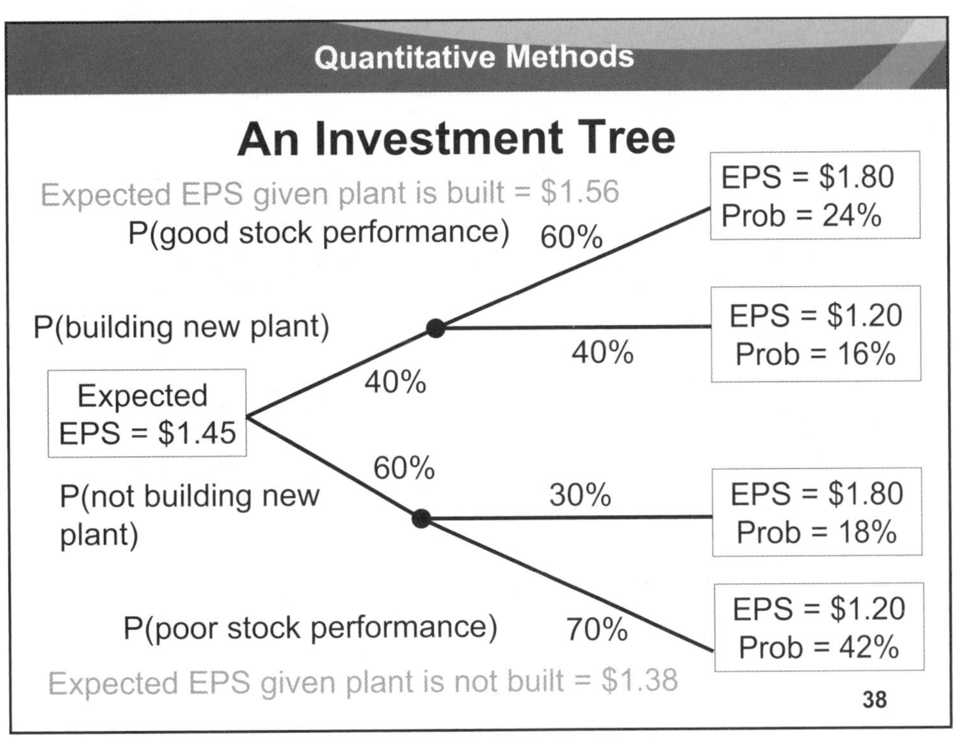

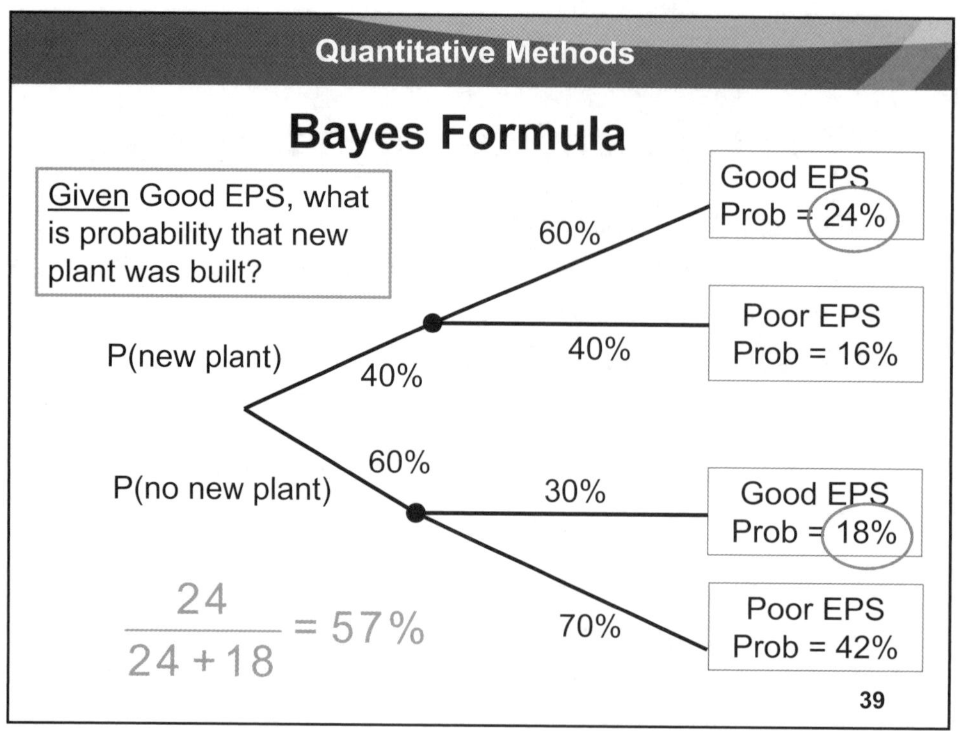

Quantitative Methods

Expected Value from a Probability Model

Economy	$P(x_i)$	Return (X_i)	$P(x_i)x_i$
Recession	0.25	–0.10	–0.025
Normal	0.50	0.08	0.040
Boom	0.25	0.22	0.055
			E(X) = 0.070

40

Quantitative Methods

Variance and Standard Deviation from a Probability Model

Economy	$P(x_i)$	Return (X_i)	$P(x_i)[x_i - E(X)]^2$
Recession	0.25	–0.10	0.00723
Normal	0.50	0.08	+ 0.00005
Boom	0.25	0.22	+ 0.00563
			$= 0.01290 = \sigma^2$

$\sigma^2 = 0.01290$ $\sigma = 0.1136$

41

Quantitative Methods

Portfolio Variance depends on:

Variance of the assets

How much of each asset

$$Var(R_p) = \sigma_A^2 w_A^2 + \sigma_B^2 w_B^2 + 2 w_A w_B Cov_{AB}$$

Asset returns covariance

Asset returns correlation

$$Var(R_p) = \sigma_A^2 w_A^2 + \sigma_B^2 w_B^2 + 2 w_A w_B \rho_{AB} \sigma_A \sigma_B$$

42

Quantitative Methods

Joint Probability Function

Returns	R_B = 40%	R_B = 20%	R_B = 0%
R_A = 20%	0.15		
R_A = 15%		0.60	
R_A = 4%			0.25

E(R_B) = 18%

Probabilities

E(R_A) = 13%

Cov_{AB} = 0.15 (0.20 – 0.**13**) (0.40 – 0.**18**)

+ 0.6 (0.15 – 0.**13**) (0.20 – 0.**18**)

+ 0.25 (0.04 – 0.**13**) (0 – 0.**18**) = 0.0066

43

Quantitative Methods

Discrete and Continuous Probability Distributions

- A discrete distribution has a finite number of possible outcomes e.g., binomial
- A continuous distribution has an infinite number of possible outcomes e.g., normal, Student's t-distribution

44

Quantitative Methods

Probability Distributions

- A **discrete uniform distribution** has a finite number of possible outcomes, all of which are equally likely
- A **binomial distribution** gives the probability of x successes in n trials
- A **binomial model** ties these probabilities to series of up moves and down moves
  - Need to know probability of upmove, **p**, and upmove factor, **U**, to construct a **binomial tree**

45

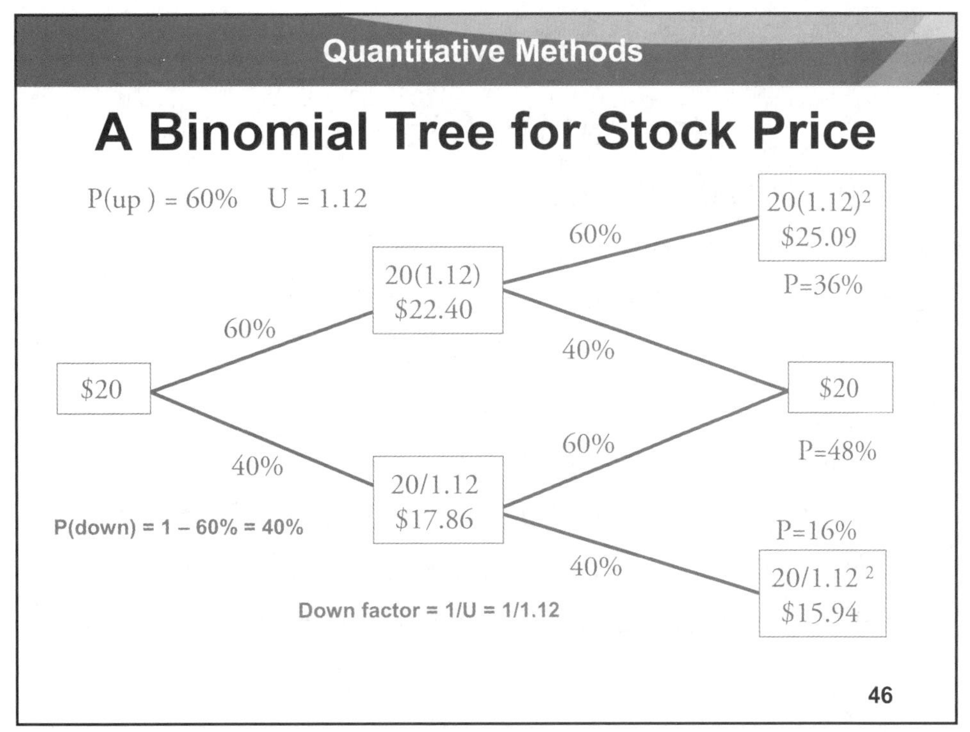

Quantitative Methods

Continuous Uniform Distribution

Probability distributed evenly over 1 to 9

What is Prob(2 ≤ x ≤ 8)?

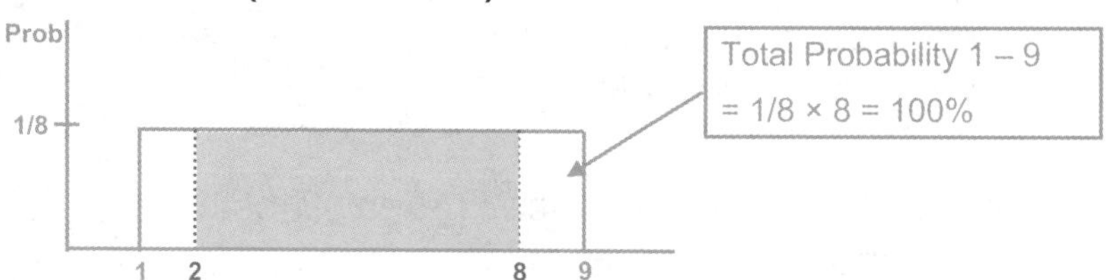

Prob(2 ≤ x ≤ 8) = 6/8 = 75%

47

Quantitative Methods

Normal Distribution

- Need to know mean and variance
- **Skew** = 0, symmetric
- **Kurtosis** = 3, Excess kurtosis = 0
- Unbounded, tails go on forever

- 68% of outcomes within 1 std. dev. of the mean
- 90% of outcomes within 1.65 std. dev. of the mean
- 95% of outcomes within 1.96 std. dev. of the mean
- 99% of outcomes within 2.58 std. dev. of the mean

48

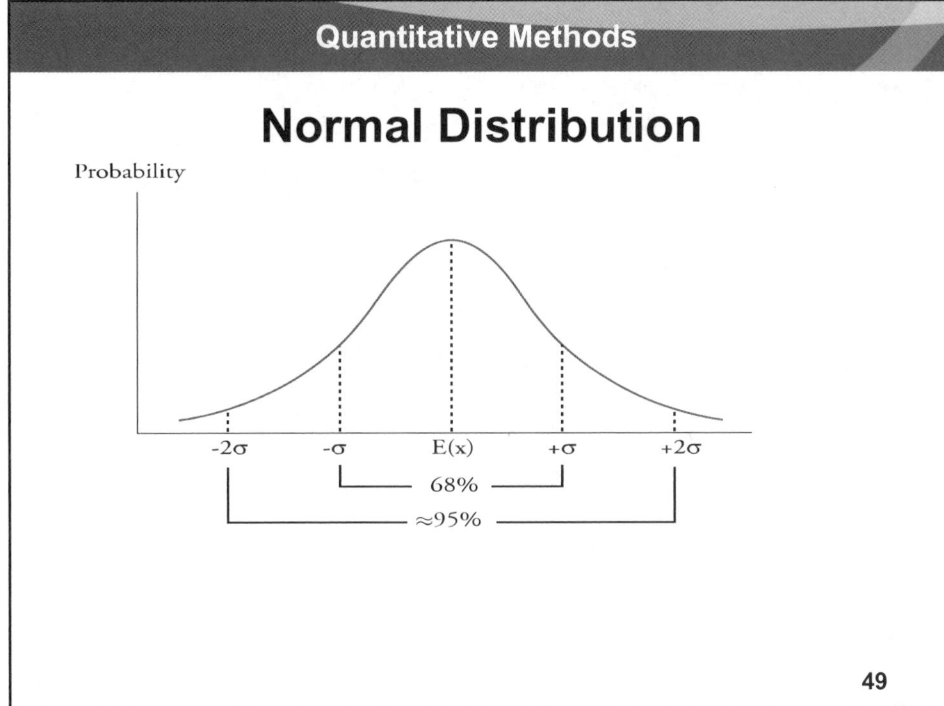

Quantitative Methods

Standard Normal Distribution

- A normal distribution that has **mean = 0 and standard deviation = 1**

Z is the number of standard deviations above or below the mean

$$z = \frac{X - \mu}{\sigma}$$

Security has an expected (mean) return of 6% and std. dev. of 10%. What is probability of a return **greater** than 23.1%?

$$z = \frac{23.1 - 6}{10} = 1.71$$

23.1% is 1.71 Std Dev above the mean

50

Quantitative Methods

Probability return is less than 23.1% *is same as*

Probability that return is less than 1.71 std dev above the mean *is same as*

Probability std normal r.v. is less than 1.71

Z	0.00	**0.01**	0.02
1.6	0.9452	0.9463	0.9474
1.7	0.9554	0.9564	0.9573
1.8	0.9641	0.9649	0.9664

Probability return is greater than 23.1% = 1 – 0.9564 = 0.0436 = 4.36%

51

Quantitative Methods

Probability of Shortfall

Expected EPS is $4 with std. dev. of $1.50

If target EPS is $3.70, what is Shortfall risk?

$$\frac{3.70-4.00}{1.50}=-0.20$$

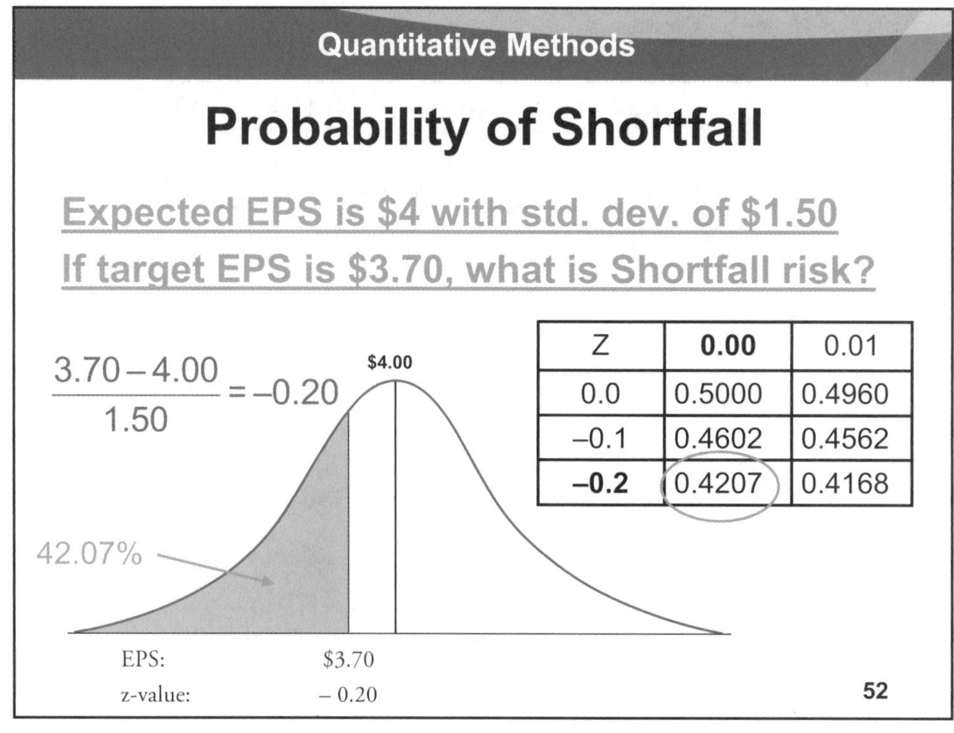

Z	**0.00**	0.01
0.0	0.5000	0.4960
–0.1	0.4602	0.4562
–0.2	0.4207	0.4168

52

Quantitative Methods

Expected EPS is $4 with std. dev. of $1.50

If target EPS is $3.70, what is Safety-first Ratio?

$$\text{SFRatio} = \frac{\left[E(R_P) - R_L\right]}{\sigma_P},\ R_L = \text{target / minimum return or value}$$

$$\text{SFR} = \frac{4.00 - 3.70}{1.50} = 0.20$$

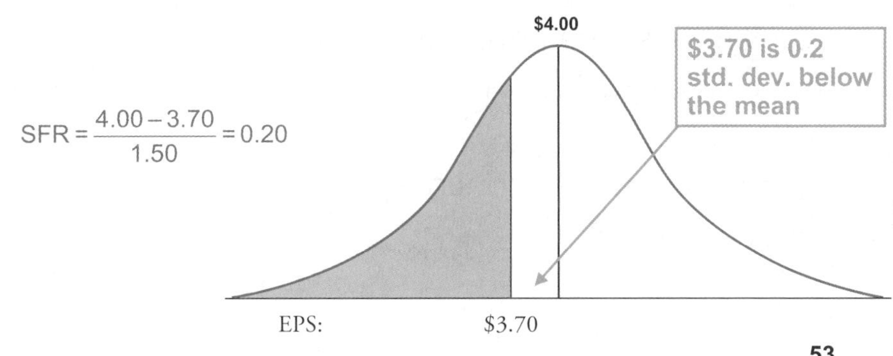

53

Quantitative Methods

Lognormal Distribution

- If x is normal, e^x is lognormal
- Lognormal is always positive, used for modeling price relatives→ (1 + return) = e^x and asset prices.

Normal Distribution

μ

Lognormal Distribution

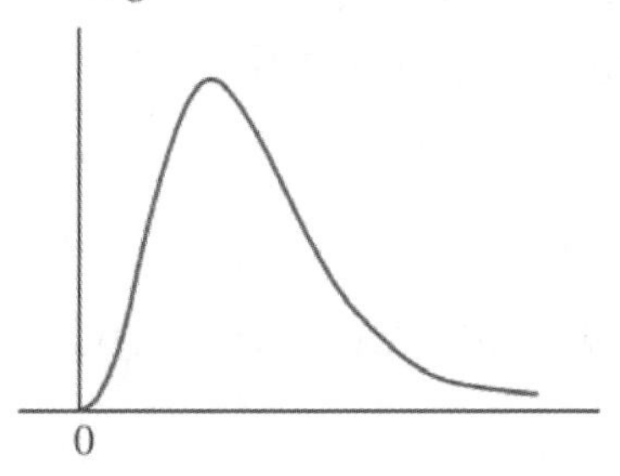

54

Quantitative Methods

Continuous Compounding

The 1-year holding period return on a security is 10%, what is the equivalent annual continuously compounded rate of return?

Continuously compounded rate of return =

$\ln(1+ 0.10) = 9.531\%$

9.531% rate with continuous compounding,

$EAY = e^{0.09531} - 1 = 10\%$

55

Quantitative Methods

Sampling

- A **simple random sample** is one where every population member has an equal chance of being selected
- A **sampling distribution** is the distribution of sample statistics for repeated samples of size *n*
- **Sampling error** is the difference between a sample statistic and true population parameter

56

Quantitative Methods

Standard Error of Mean of a Sample

When the population σ is **known**:

$$\sigma_{\overline{x}} = \frac{\sigma}{\sqrt{n}}$$

When the population σ is **unknown**:

$$s_{\overline{x}} = \frac{s}{\sqrt{n}}$$

57

Quantitative Methods

Confidence Interval for R.V.

The P/Es for a population of firms are normally distributed with a mean of **19.0**, with standard deviation of **6.6**.

What is a 90% confidence interval for the P/E of a firm chosen at random from this population?

+/– 1.65 std. dev.

$19 - (1.65)6.6 \leq EPS \leq 19 + (1.65)6.6$

$8.1 \leq EPS \leq 29.9$

58

Quantitative Methods

Confidence Interval for Sample Mean

The P/Es for a population of firms are normally distributed with a mean of **19.0**, with standard deviation of **6.6**.

What is a 90% confidence interval for the mean P/E of a sample of 25 firms chosen at random from this population?

+/– 1.65 Std errors **Std error = 6.6/√25 = 6.6/5 = 1.32**

19 – (1.65)**1.32** ≤ EPS ≤ 19 + (1.65)**1.32**

16.8 ≤ EPS ≤ **21.2** Bigger sample lower std error

59

Quantitative Methods

Student's *t*-Distribution

Properties of Student's *t*-Distribution

- Symmetrical (bell shaped)
- **Fatter tails than a normal distribution (leptokurtic)**
- Defined by single parameter, degrees of freedom (df), where df = n – 1
- As df increase, *t*-distribution approaches normal distribution (kurtosis declines)

60

Quantitative Methods

t-Distribution

The figure below shows the shape of the *t*-distribution with different degrees of freedom.

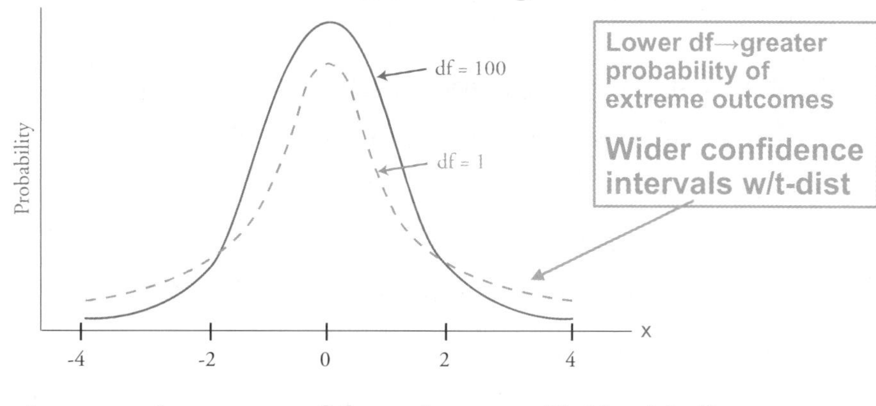

Lower degrees of freedom → 'fatter' tails

61

Quantitative Methods

Confidence Intervals for Mean

When sampling from a:		Reliability Factors	
Distribution	**Variance**	**Small Sample (n < 30)**	**Large Sample (n> 30)**
Normal	Known	*z*-statistic	*z*-statistic
Normal	Unknown	*t*-statistic	*t*-statistic*
Nonnormal	Known	Not available	*z*-statistic
Nonnormal	Unknown	Not available	*t*-statistic*

***The *z*-statistic is theoretically acceptable here, but use of the *t*-statistic is more conservative.**

62

Quantitative Methods

Confidence Interval for Sample Mean

The P/Es for a population of firms are normally distributed with a mean of **19.0** and unknown standard deviation.

What is a 90% confidence interval for the mean P/E of a random sample of 25 firms, if sample std. dev. is 6.6?

DF = 24, 5% in tails t-value = 1.711

Std error = 6.6/√25 = 6.6/5 = 1.32

19 – (1.711)**1.32** ≤ EPS ≤ 19 + (1.711)**1.32**

16.7 ≤ EPS ≤ **21.26** Wider interval with t-stat

63

Quantitative Methods

Types of Bias

- **Data-mining bias** – from repeatedly doing tests on same data sample
- **Sample selection bias** – sample not really random
- **Survivorship bias** – sampling only surviving firms, mutual funds, hedge funds
- **Look-ahead bias** – using information not available at the time to construct sample
- **Time-period bias** – relationship exists only during the time period of sample data

64

Quantitative Methods

Steps in Hypothesis Testing

- State the hypothesis—relation to be tested
- Select a test statistic
- Specify the level of significance
- State the decision rule for the hypothesis
- Collect the sample and calculate statistics
- Make a decision about the hypothesis
- Make a decision based on the test results

65

Quantitative Methods

Null and Alternative Hypotheses

- Null hypothesis (H_0)
  1. The hypothesis to be tested
  2. Researcher wants to reject it
  3. Always includes the equal sign (=, ≤, ≥)

- Alternative hypothesis (H_a)
  1. What the researcher would like to conclude
  2. What is concluded if the researcher rejects the null hypothesis

66

Quantitative Methods

Test Statistic

- A test statistic is (1) calculated from sample data and (2) compared to critical value(s) to test H_0
- If the test statistic exceeds the critical value (or is outside the range of critical values), the researcher rejects H_0
- Critical values are like a confidence interval

67

Quantitative Methods

Two-Tailed Test

Use when testing to see if a population parameter is different from a specified value

H_0: $\mu = 0$ versus H_a: $\mu \neq 0$

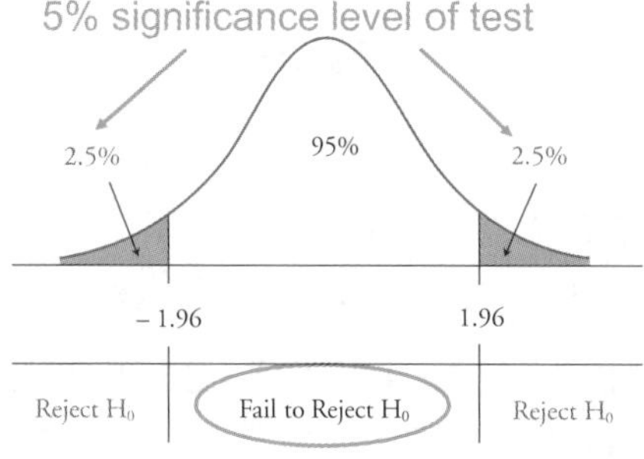

68

Quantitative Methods

One-Tailed Test

Use when testing to see if a parameter is above or below a specified value

H_0: $\mu \leq 0$ versus H_a: $\mu > 0$
H_0: $\mu \geq 0$ versus H_a: $\mu < 0$

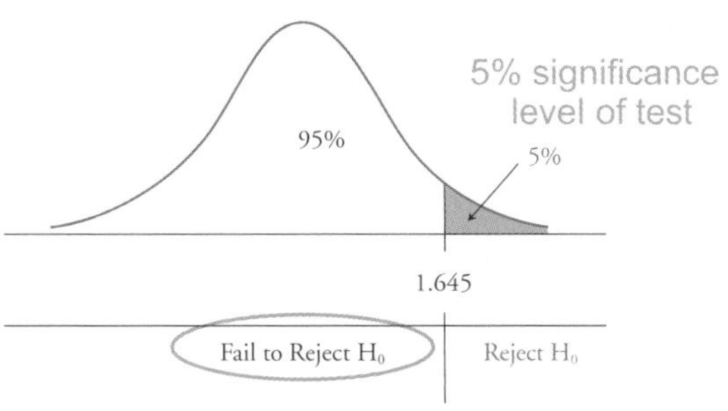

69

Quantitative Methods

Type I and Type II Errors

Type I Error:

- Rejecting H_0 when it is actually true
- Significance level is Prob. of Type I Error

Type II Error:

- Failing to reject H_0 when it is actually false
- Power of test is 1 – Prob. of Type II Error

70

Quantitative Methods

Statistically vs. Economically Meaningful Result

- **Statistical significance** does not necessarily imply **economic significance:**
  - Transactions costs
  - Taxes
  - Risk

71

Quantitative Methods

Hypothesis Test of Sample Mean

The P/Es for a population of firms are normally distributed with standard deviation of **6.6**.

Test whether the mean PE for the population = 19, 10% significance level, sample size = 25.

Null is μ = 19. Test statistic is sample mean.

+/– 1.65 Std errors **Std error = 6.6/√25 = 6.6/5 = 1.32**

Critical values are:

19 – (1.65)**1.32** =**16.82** and 19 + (1.65)**1.32** **= 21.18**

Like confidence interval. Reject null if sample mean is less than 16.82 or greater than 21.18

72

Quantitative Methods

Hypothesis Test of Sample Mean

Test statistic is usually a z- or t-statistic.

For the test on previous slide, z-statistic is:

$$z = \frac{X - \mu_0}{\sigma} \text{ which, here, is } z = \frac{\overline{X} - 19}{1.32}$$

Critical values for 10% significance are then +/– 1.65

Note that if sample mean is less than 16.8, test statistic will be less than –1.65

$$z = \frac{16.82 - 19}{1.32} = -1.65$$

73

Quantitative Methods

Hypothesis Test of Sample Mean

The P/Es for a population of firms are normally distributed with standard deviation of **6.6**.

Test whether the mean PE for the population > 19, 5% significance level, sample size = 25.

Null is μ > 19. Test statistic is $z = \frac{\overline{X} - 19}{1.32}$

Std error = 6.6/√25 = 6.6/5 = 1.32

Critical value (one-tail test) is –1.65, reject if z < –1.65

Which is the same as saying:

Reject null if sample mean is less than 16.8

74

Quantitative Methods

Hypothesis Testing – Problem

Researcher believes a fund's mean returns (μ_{FUND}) ***exceed*** 2% per month. Sample size is 36, sample mean is 2.5%, sample std. dev. is 1.8%, population normal. Use 5% significance level.

Hypotheses:

Type of Test:

Critical t-value:

Test Statistic:

75

Quantitative Methods

Test Statistics: Difference in Means

Test of whether the means of two normal populations are equal – **independent** samples

$$\text{t-stat} = \frac{\bar{x}_1 - \bar{x}_2}{\sqrt{\frac{s_P^2}{n_1} + \frac{s_P^2}{n_2}}}$$

$$\text{t-stat} = \frac{\bar{x}_1 - \bar{x}_2}{\sqrt{\frac{s_1^2}{n_1} + \frac{s_2^2}{n_2}}}$$

Calculation of std error depends on whether population variances are assumed to be equal or not.

Reject if t-stat is greater/less than critical values

76

Quantitative Methods

Test Statistics: Mean Differences

Test of the difference between the means of two normal populations – **dependent** samples
Paired Comparisons test

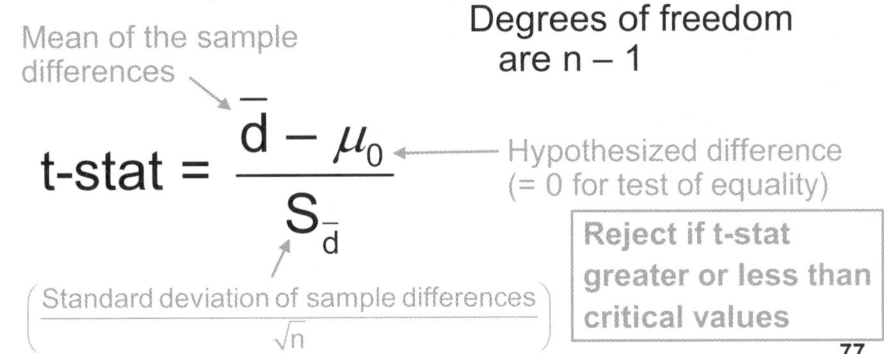

77

Quantitative Methods

Test Statistics: Variance

Test of whether the variance of a normal population equals σ_0^2 uses a **Chi-square** test statistic, two-tailed test, **reject if outside the critical values**

Degrees of freedom are n – 1

$$\chi^2_{n-1} = \frac{(n-1)S^2}{\sigma_0^2}$$

Sample variance

Reject if too high or too low

Hypothesized variance

78

Quantitative Methods

Test Statistics: Variance

Test of whether the variances of two normal populations are equal is an **F-test**

Putting the larger sample variance in the numerator allows us to **consider only upper critical value** – although F-test is a two-tailed test

$$F = \frac{S_1^2}{S_2^2}$$

S_1^2 ← Larger sample variance

S_2^2 ← Smaller sample variance

Degrees of freedom are $n_1 - 1$ and $n_2 - 1$

Reject if significantly greater than 1

79

Quantitative Methods

Nonparametric Tests

Nonparametric tests make few if any assumptions about the population distribution and test things other than parameter values (e.g., runs tests, rank correlation tests)

80

Quantitative Methods

Assumptions of Technical Analysis

- Stock values determined by **supply and demand**
- Supply and demand are **driven by both rational and irrational behavior**
- Security **prices move in trends** that persist for long periods
- While causes of changes in supply and demand are difficult to determine, the changes themselves can be **observed in market price behavior**

81

Quantitative Methods

Challenges to Technical Analysis

- The weak form **EMH** suggests that stock prices reflect all available trading information
- **Statistical tests** find no evidence of price trends or profitable trading rules
- If statistical trading rules worked, price changes would become **self-fulfilling prophecies**; its value would be neutralized

82

Quantitative Methods

Categories of Technical Indicators

1. **Contrarian indicators:** The majority is often wrong, do the opposite
2. **Smart money indicators:** "Smart" investors are right, do what they are doing
3. **Momentum indicators:** Direction and strength of market movement
4. **Stock price and volume techniques:** Identify patterns that repeat

83

Quantitative Methods

Contrary Opinion Rules

- **Mutual fund (cash) ratio** = cash / total assets
- **Investor credit balances** in brokerage accounts
- Opinions of **investment advisory services**
- OTC volume / NYSE volume
- CBOE **put/call ratio**
- Percentage of **bullish** stock index **futures traders**

84

Quantitative Methods

Smart Money Indicators

- **Confidence index** = $\frac{\text{high quality bond yields}}{\text{average bond yields}}$
- **T-bill yield to Eurodollar yield** spread
- **Margin debt** in brokerage accounts

85

Quantitative Methods

Momentum Indicators

- **Breadth of market**: Advance-decline line
- **Number of stocks > 200-day moving average**

86

Quantitative Methods

Price and Volume Techniques

- **Dow Theory** – major trends, intermediate trends, short-run movements
- **Ratio of upside to downside volume** (>1.75 is overbought, <0.75 is oversold)
- **Support and resistance levels** – movements through these levels on high volume, breakouts
- **Relative strength** – ratio of stock price to market index, increasing is bullish, decreasing is bearish, trend expected to continue

87

Quantitative Methods

Price and Volume Techniques

- **Moving averages** –
  - Stock price moves through the 50-day moving average on strong volume
  - 50-day moving average crosses the 200-day moving average on strong volume

To identify trends:

Bar charts – a bar from high to low price over a period with volume per period at the bottom

Point and figure charts – only record price movements of some minimum amount

88

Quantitative Methods

TWR and MWR – Solution

What is time-weighted annual return?

$[(1.2/1)(2.2/2)]^{1/2} - 1 = [(1 + 20\%)(1 + 10\%)]^{1/2} - 1 = 14.9\%$

Is the annual money-weighted return higher or lower?

Lower, more weight on lower (10%) second year returns.

What is the annual money-weighted return?

Cf0 = 1mill, CF1 = 0.8 mill, CF2 = – 2.2 mill; IRR = 13.6%

Which is the better measure of manager performance?

89

Quantitative Methods

Hypothesis Testing – Solution

Researcher believes a fund's mean returns (μ_{FUND}) ***exceed*** 2% per month. Sample size is 36, sample mean is 2.5%, sample std. dev. is 1.8%, population normal. Use 5% significance level.

Hypotheses: $H_0: \mu \leq 0.02$ $H_a: \mu > 0.02$

Type of Test: One-tailed *t*-test

Critical t-value: df = 35, 5% significance, = 1.69

Test Statistic:

$$t_{n-1} = \frac{\bar{x} - \mu_0}{s/\sqrt{n}} = \frac{0.025 - 0.020}{0.018/\sqrt{36}} = 1.667$$

Do not reject the null

90

CFA® LEVEL 1

3-Day Review Slide Workbook

PORTFOLIO MANAGEMENT

Portfolio Management

Portfolio Management - Book 4

Portfolio Management

Steps in the Portfolio Management Process

1. **Write a policy statement**
2. **Develop an investment strategy** consistent with the policy statement
3. **Implement the plan,** allocate assets, and choose securities based on market conditions
4. **Monitor and update** investor's needs and market conditions, rebalance portfolio as needed

92

Portfolio Management

Investment Policy Statement

- Identifies client objectives and constraints
- Clear statement of client risk tolerance
- Imposes investment discipline on both client and manager
- Identifies risks
- Identifies a benchmark portfolio consistent with client preferences

93

Portfolio Management

Investment Objectives

Investment objectives should include both risk and return objectives because of the trade-off between risk and expected return.

Factors affecting investor risk tolerance:

- Psychological factors
- Personal factors: age, family situation, existing wealth, insurance coverage, cash reserves, income

94

Portfolio Management

Four Return Objectives

- **Capital preservation**: Earning a return at least equal to the inflation rate
- **Capital appreciation**: Earning a return that exceeds the rate of inflation (most risky)
- **Current income**: Earning a return to generate income
- **Total return**: Meeting a future need through both capital appreciation and current income

95

Portfolio Management

Investment Constraints

- **Liquidity**: The potential need for cash
- **Legal and regulatory**: Mostly institutional investors, also affects IRAs
- **Time horizon**: The time until the proceeds of the investment will be required
- **Tax concerns**: Is the account taxable, tax-deferred, or tax exempt
- **Unique needs and preferences**: Anything that does not fit into the above categories

96

Portfolio Management

Importance of Asset Allocation

- 90% of differences in institutional portfolios' returns can be explained by **target asset allocations**
- Differences due to asset class weightings more important than differences from security selection
- Actual returns for actively managed accounts are less than target-asset-allocation returns

97

Portfolio Management

Risk Aversion

Risk aversion means investors prefer less risk to more risk

- When two investments have the same expected return, investors **prefer the lower risk investment**
- When two investments have the same risk, investors prefer the investment with the **higher expected return**

Investors do not "minimize" risk, it's a trade-off!

98

Portfolio Management

Expected Return Using a Probability Model

State	P_i	$E(R_i)$	$P_i R_i$
Expansion	**0.20**	**–0.05**	**–0.01**
Normal	**0.60**	**0.10**	**0.06**
Recession	**0.20**	**0.25**	**0.05**
			$E(R) = \Sigma P_i R_i = 0.10$

99

Portfolio Management

Variance Using a Probability Model

State	P_i	R_i	E(R)	$[(R_i) - E(R)]^2$	$P_i[(R_i) - E(R)]^2$
Expansion	0.20	–0.05	0.10	0.0225	0.0045
Normal	0.60	0.10	0.10	0.0000	0.0000
Recession	0.20	0.25	0.10	0.0225	0.0045
				Variance =	0.0090

Std. deviation = $\sqrt{0.0090} = 0.0949 = 9.49\%$

100

Portfolio Management

Expected Return on a Portfolio

$$E(R_p) = W_1E(R_1) + W_2E(R_2) + W_3E(R_3)$$

Asset	W_i	$E(R_i)$	$W_iE(R_i)$
Stock A	0.25	9.0%	2.25%
Stock B	0.45	19.0%	8.55%
Stock C	0.30	13.0%	3.90%
			$\sum W_iE(R_i)$ = 14.7%

101

Portfolio Management

Covariance of Rates of Return

$$\text{cov}_{1,2} = \frac{\sum_{t=1}^{n}\left[\left(R_{t,1} - \bar{R}_1\right)\left(R_{t,2} - \bar{R}_2\right)\right]}{n-1}$$

Example: Calculate the sample covariance for the two stocks in the table.

Year	Stock 1	Stock 2
1	+0.05	+0.07
2	–0.02	–0.04
3	+0.12	+0.18

102

Portfolio Management

Covariance of Sample

$$\text{cov}_{1,2} = \frac{\sum_{t=1}^{n}\left[\left(R_{t,1}-\bar{R}_1\right)\left(R_{t,2}-\bar{R}_2\right)\right]}{n-1}$$

Example: $\bar{R}_1 = (5 - 2 + 12) / 3 = 5\%$
$\bar{R}_2 = (7 - 4 + 18) / 3 = 7\%$

$$\frac{(5-5)(7-7) + (-2-5)(-4-7) + (12-5)(18-7)}{3-1} = 77 = 0.0077$$

103

Portfolio Management

Portfolio Standard Deviation $\rho_{1,2} = +1$

$$\sigma_P = \sqrt{w_1^2\sigma_1^2 + w_2^2\sigma_2^2 + 2w_1w_2\sigma_1\sigma_2} = w_1\sigma_1 + w_2\sigma_2$$

- Special case
- No diversification benefits
- Portfolio standard deviation is weighted average of asset standard deviations

104

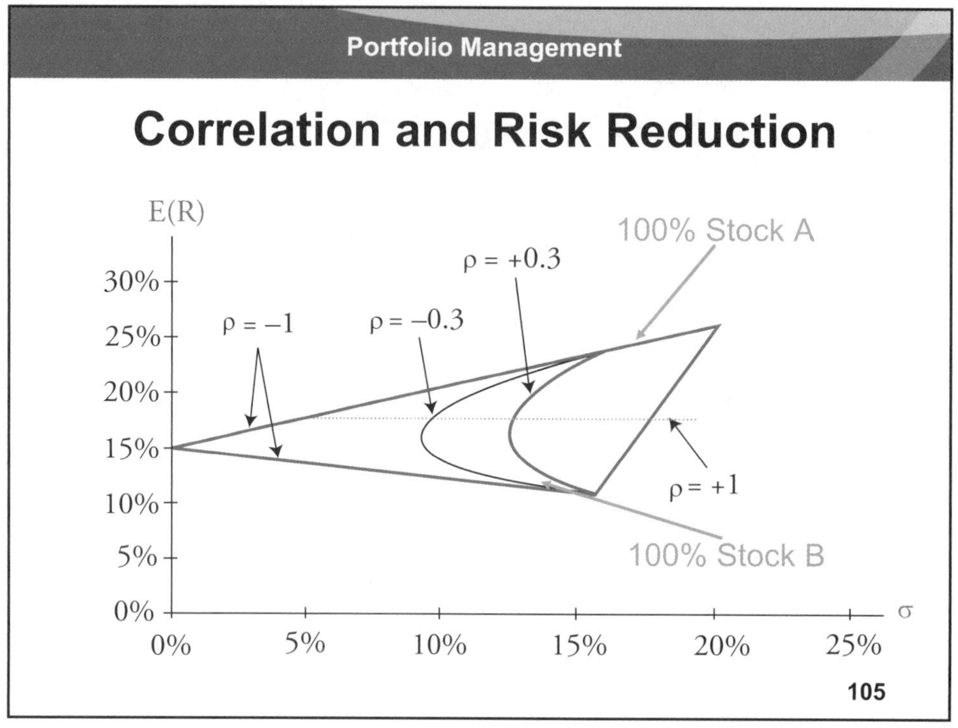

Portfolio Management

Efficient Frontier

Efficient frontier is the set of portfolios among all the possible portfolios of combinations of individual risky assets that offers:

The highest expected return for each level of risk (standard deviation)

106

Portfolio Management

Efficient Frontier

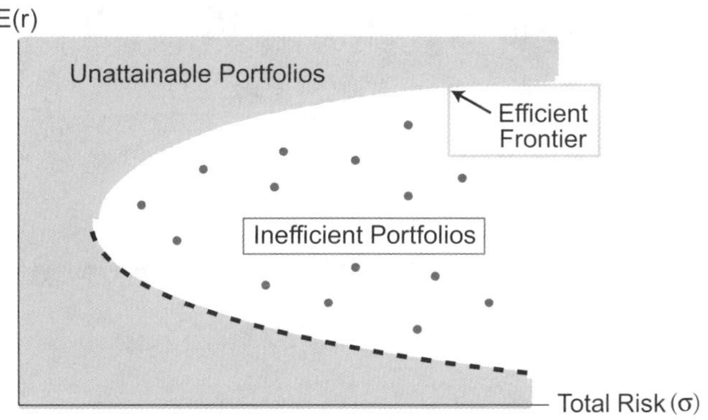

The efficient frontier is the upper boundary of the set of all possible portfolio risk/return combinations.

107

Portfolio Management

Assumptions of Capital Market Theory

- Investors use **mean-variance** framework
- Unlimited **lending and borrowing** at R_f
- Homogeneous **expectations**
- **One-period** time horizon
- **Divisible** assets
- **Frictionless** markets
- No inflation and **unchanging interest rates**
- Capital markets are in **equilibrium**

108

Portfolio Management

Combining Risk-free and Risky Assets

Portfolio expected return = $\mathbf{W_{risky}\,R_p + W_{Rf}\,R_f}$

Portfolio std. dev. = $\mathbf{W_{risky}\,\sigma_p}$

E(R)

$E(R_P)$

Risky Portfolio P

Combinations of R_f and Port. P

R_f

std. deviation

σ_P

109

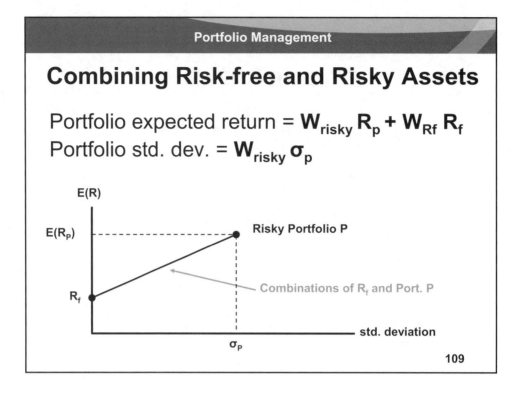

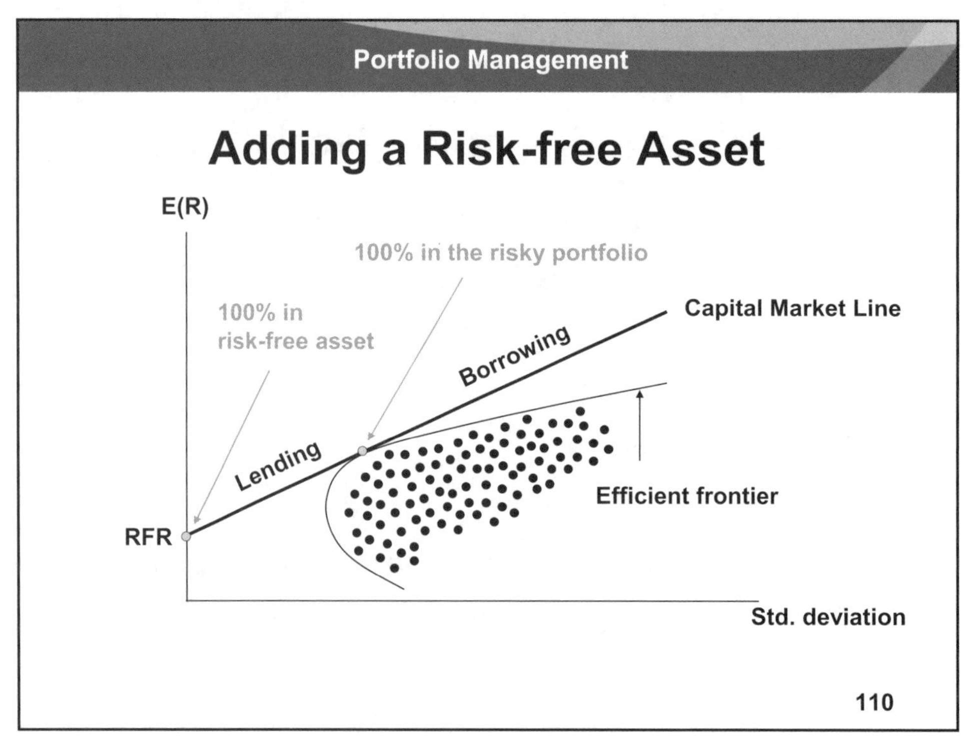

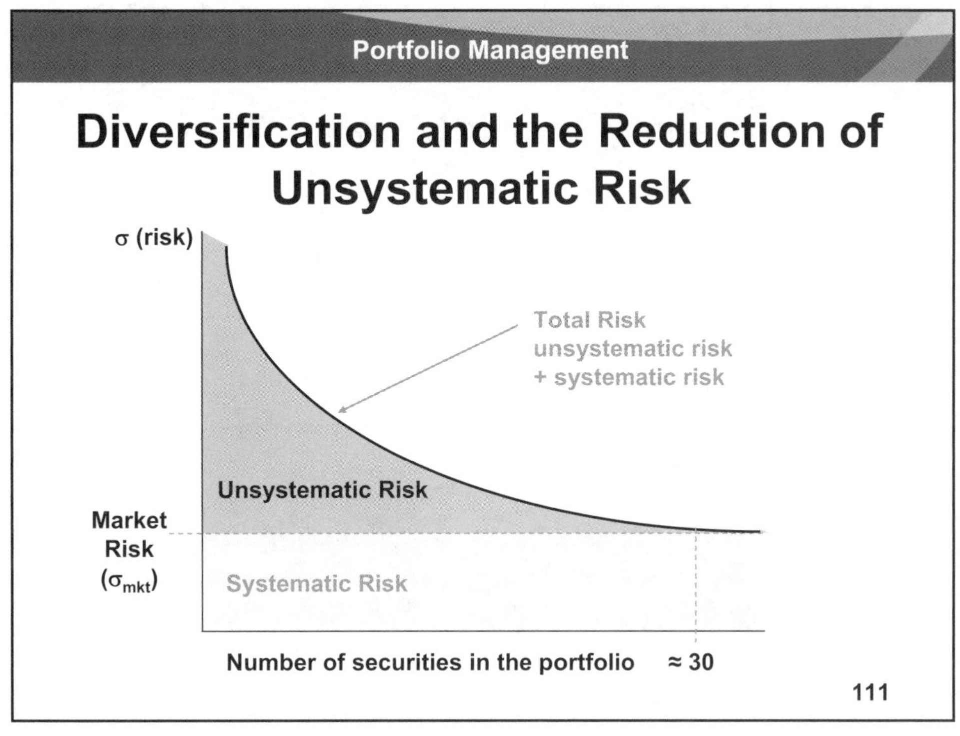

Portfolio Management

Systematic and Unsystematic Risk

Systematic risk (market risk)

- Caused by macro factors: interest rates, GDP growth, supply shocks
- Measured by covariance of returns with returns on the market portfolio

Unsystematic risk (firm-specific risk)

- Can be reduced/eliminated by holding well diversified portfolios

Only systematic (market) risk is rewarded with higher expected returns according to CAPM

112

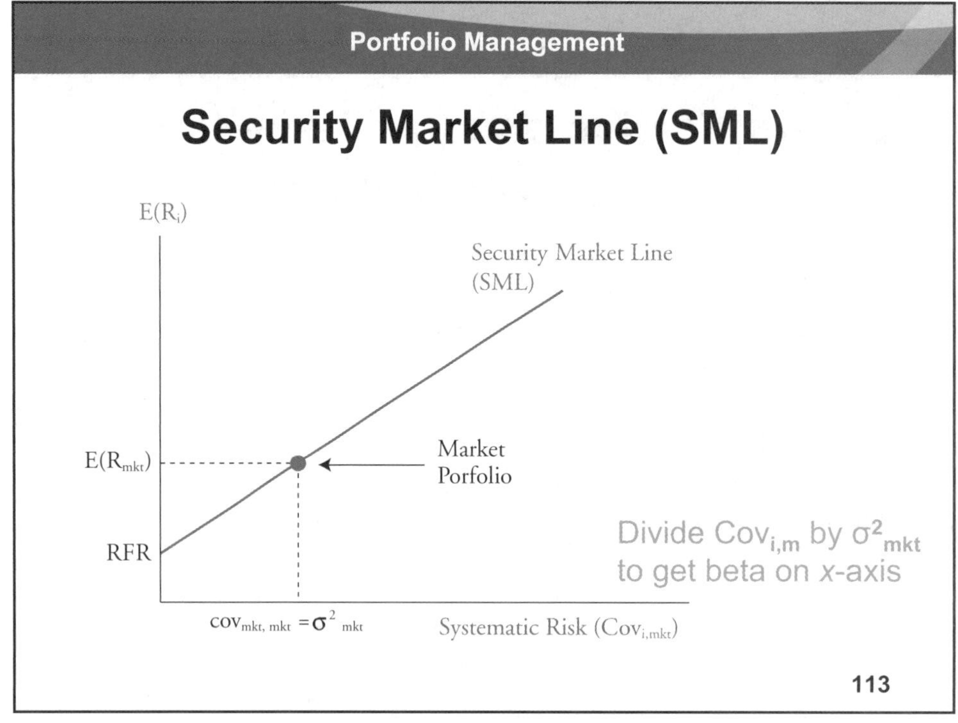

Portfolio Management

The Capital Asset Pricing Model

SML equation:

$$E(R_i) = RFR + \beta_i \, [E(R_{mkt}) - RFR]$$

- Beta is a standardized measure of systematic risk, beta of the market portfolio is 1
- Beta measures the covariance of an asset's returns with returns on the market portfolio
- Calculating beta of asset 'i': $\beta_i = \dfrac{Cov_{i,mkt}}{\sigma^2_{mkt}}$

114

Portfolio Management

Capital Asset Pricing Model (CAPM)

- CAPM: The expected return on an asset based (only) on the asset's systematic risk or beta
- CAPM is also used to determine the required return on an asset based on the asset's systematic risk (beta)
- Required return and expected return are the same in equilibrium

115

Portfolio Management

Relaxing the Assumptions of the SML

- **Different borrowing and lending rates:** Puts a kink in the CML; the CAPM can still be derived by assuming a **zero-beta portfolio**
- **Positive transaction costs, heterogeneous expectations, different planning horizons:** The SML becomes a band rather than a line
- **Taxes:** After-tax CAPM yields different SMLs and CMLs for investors with different tax rates

116

Portfolio Management

Forecast Returns and the CAPM – Example

An analyst has forecast the following for three stocks. $R_f = 7\%$ $E(R_{mkt}) = 15\%$

Stock	Price Today	E (price) in 1 year	E (dividend) in 1 year	Beta
A	$25	$27	$1.00	1.0
B	40	45	2.00	0.8
C	15	17	0.50	1.2

Are these stocks overpriced, underpriced, or at their equilibrium prices?

Show where they plot on the SML graph. 117

Portfolio Management

Forecast Returns and the CAPM – Example

Stock	Price Today	E (price) in 1 year	E (dividend) in 1 year	Beta
A	$25	$27	$1.00	1.0
B	40	45	2.00	0.8
C	15	17	0.50	1.2

$R_f = 7\%$ $E[R_{mkt}] = 15\%$

R_f

MRP

Stock	Forecast Return	Required Return
A	(27–25+1)/25 = 12.0%	0.07+1.0(0.15–0.07) = 15.0%
B	(45–40+2)/40 = 17.5%	0.07+0.8(0.15–0.07) = 13.4%
C	(17–15+0.50)/15 = 16.6%	0.07+1.2(0.15–0.07) = 16.6%

118

Portfolio Management

Forecast Returns and the CAPM – Example

When securities are priced at equilibrium values, they plot on the SML

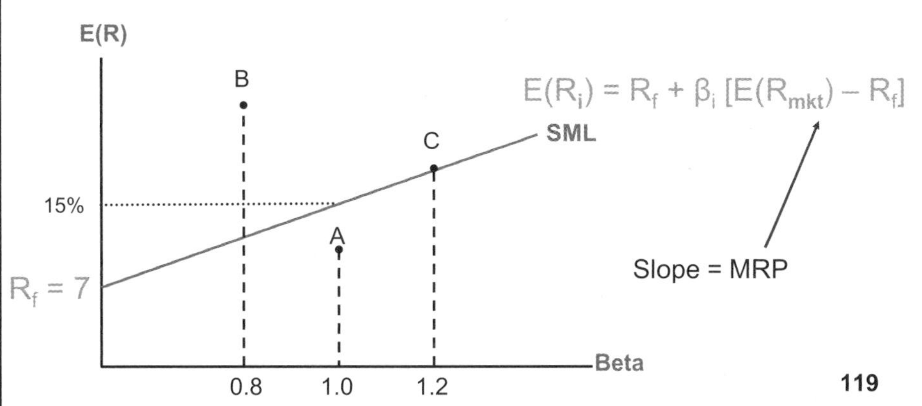

119

Portfolio Management

Forecast Returns and the CAPM

Stock	Forecast Return	Required Return
A	12.0%	15.0%
B	17.5%	13.4%
C	16.6%	16.6%

Stock A is overvalued (sell it or sell it short)

Stock B is undervalued (buy it)

Stock C is properly valued (indifferent)

120

CFA® LEVEL 1

3-Day Review Slide Workbook

ECONOMICS

Microeconomic Analysis

Economics - Book 2

Economic Concepts

Elasticity of Demand

$$\frac{\text{\% change in quantity demanded}}{\text{\% change in price}}$$

- **Elastic demand**: Percentage increase in price leads to a larger percentage decrease in quantity demanded, |Elasticity| > 1
- **Inelastic demand**: Percentage increase in price leads to a smaller percentage decrease in quantity demanded, |Elasticity| < 1

122

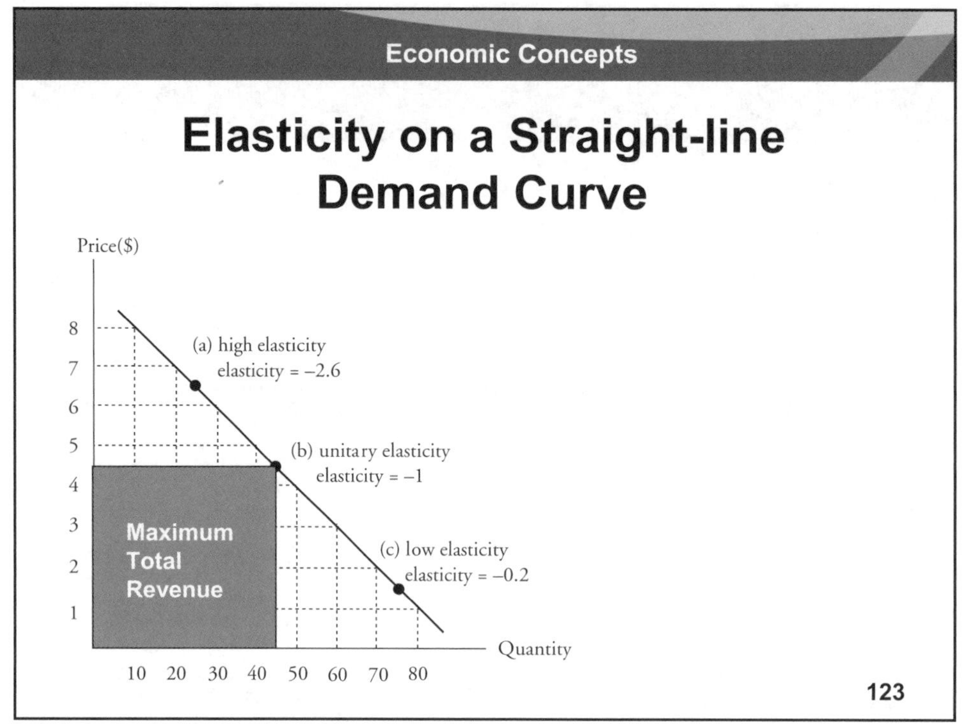

Economic Concepts

Factors That Influence the Elasticity of Demand

- Availability and closeness of **substitutes**
- **Proportion of income** spent on the item
- **Time** elapsed since previous price change

124

Economic Concepts

Cross Elasticity of Demand

$$\text{cross elasticity} = \frac{\%\ \Delta \text{ in quantity demanded}}{\%\ \Delta \text{ in price of substitute or complement}}$$

cross elasticity > 0: the goods are substitutes

cross elasticity < 0: the goods are complements

125

Economic Concepts

Income Elasticity of Demand

- The sensitivity of quantity demanded to changes in income

$$\text{income elasticity} = \frac{\%\ \text{change in quantity demanded}}{\%\ \text{change in income}}$$

- **Normal good**: Income↑ Demand↑ Elasticity > 0
  - **Necessity**: 0 < Income elasticity < 1
  - **Luxury good**: Income elasticity > 1
- **Inferior good**: Income↑ Demand↓ Elasticity < 0 (e.g., bus travel)

126

Economic Concepts

Elasticity of Supply

elasticity of supply

$$= \frac{\text{\% change in quantity supplied}}{\text{\% change in price}}$$

127

Economic Concepts

Determinants of Elasticity of Supply

$$\text{elasticity of supply} = \frac{\text{\% change in quantity supplied}}{\text{\% change in price}}$$

1. Availability of resource **substitutes**
2. Supply decision **time frame**
   - Momentary supply – grapes versus electricity
   - Short-term supply – succession of changes
   - Long-term supply – all possible adjustments, most elastic

128

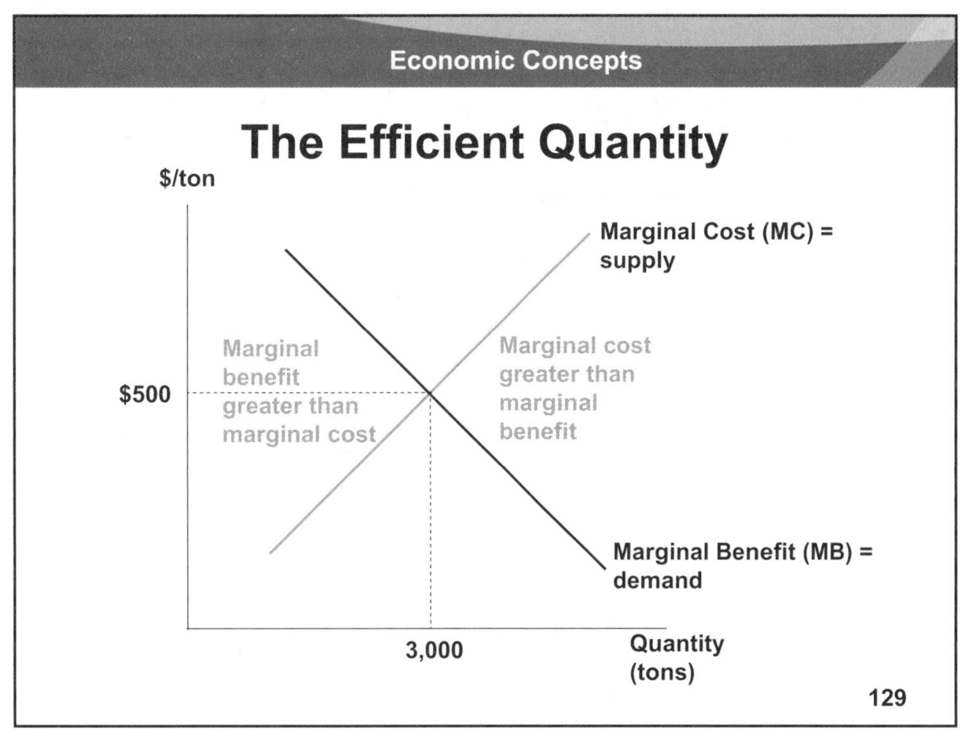
Economic Concepts
The Efficient Quantity
$/ton
Marginal Cost (MC) = supply
Marginal benefit greater than marginal cost
Marginal cost greater than marginal benefit
$500
Marginal Benefit (MB) = demand
3,000
Quantity (tons)
129

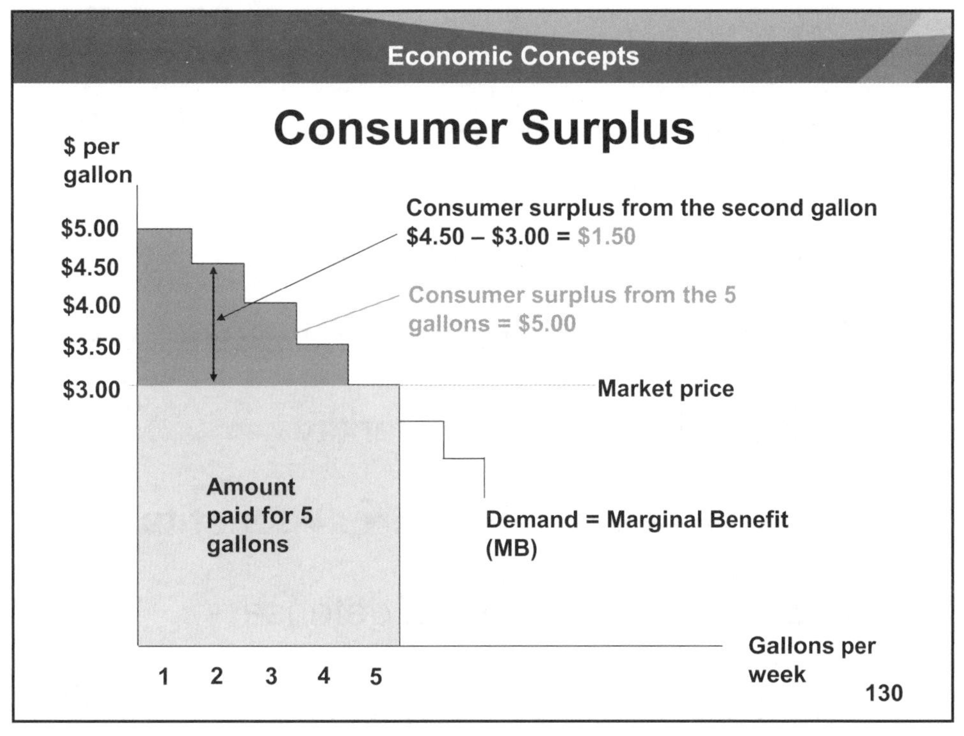
Economic Concepts
Consumer Surplus
$ per gallon
$5.00
$4.50
$4.00
$3.50
$3.00
Consumer surplus from the second gallon $4.50 – $3.00 = $1.50
Consumer surplus from the 5 gallons = $5.00
Market price
Amount paid for 5 gallons
Demand = Marginal Benefit (MB)
1 2 3 4 5
Gallons per week
130

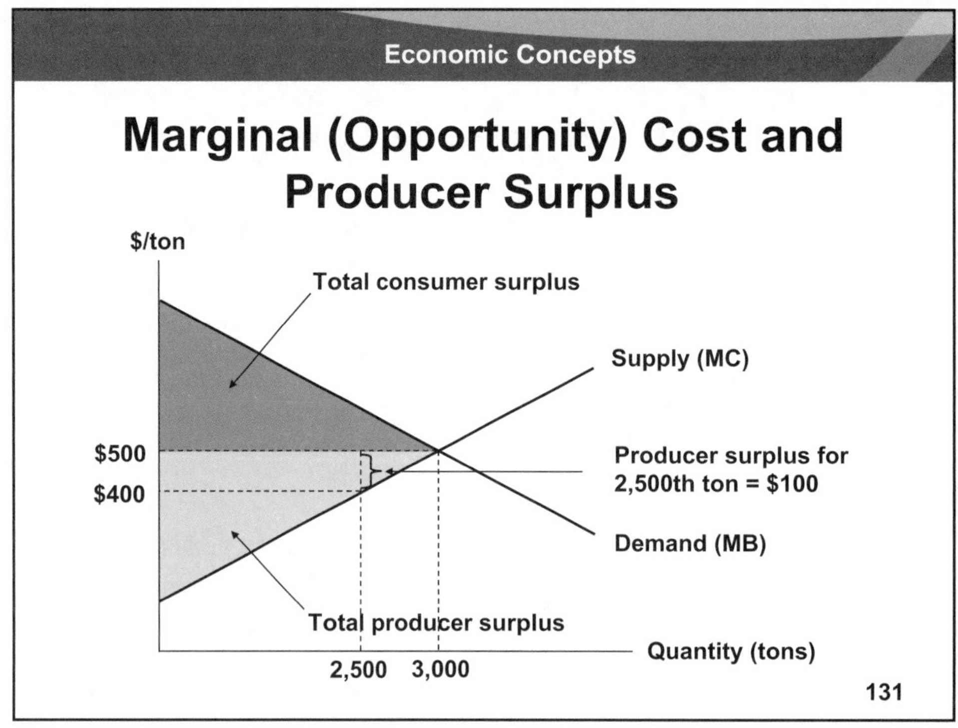

Economic Concepts

Obstacles to Efficient Allocation

- **Price controls** – ceilings, floors
- **Taxes and trade restrictions**
- **Monopolies** – restrict quantity
- **External costs and external benefits**
- **Public goods** – national defense

132

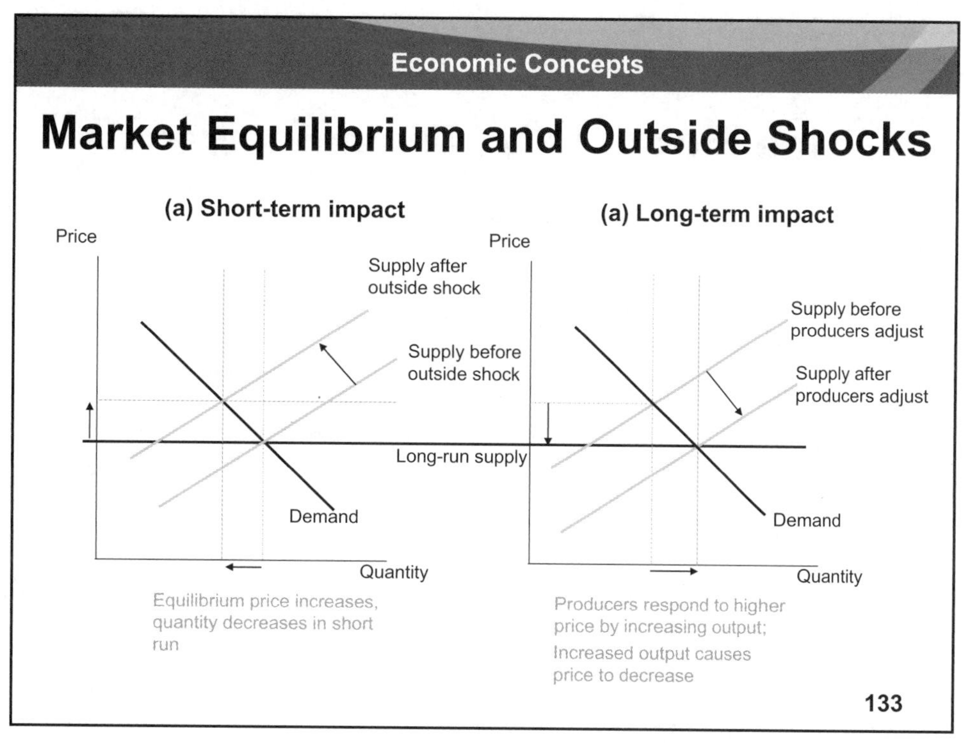
Economic Concepts
Market Equilibrium and Outside Shocks
(a) Short-term impact
Price
Supply after outside shock
Supply before outside shock
Long-run supply
Demand
Quantity
Equilibrium price increases, quantity decreases in short run
(a) Long-term impact
Price
Supply before producers adjust
Supply after producers adjust
Demand
Quantity
Producers respond to higher price by increasing output;
Increased output causes price to decrease
133

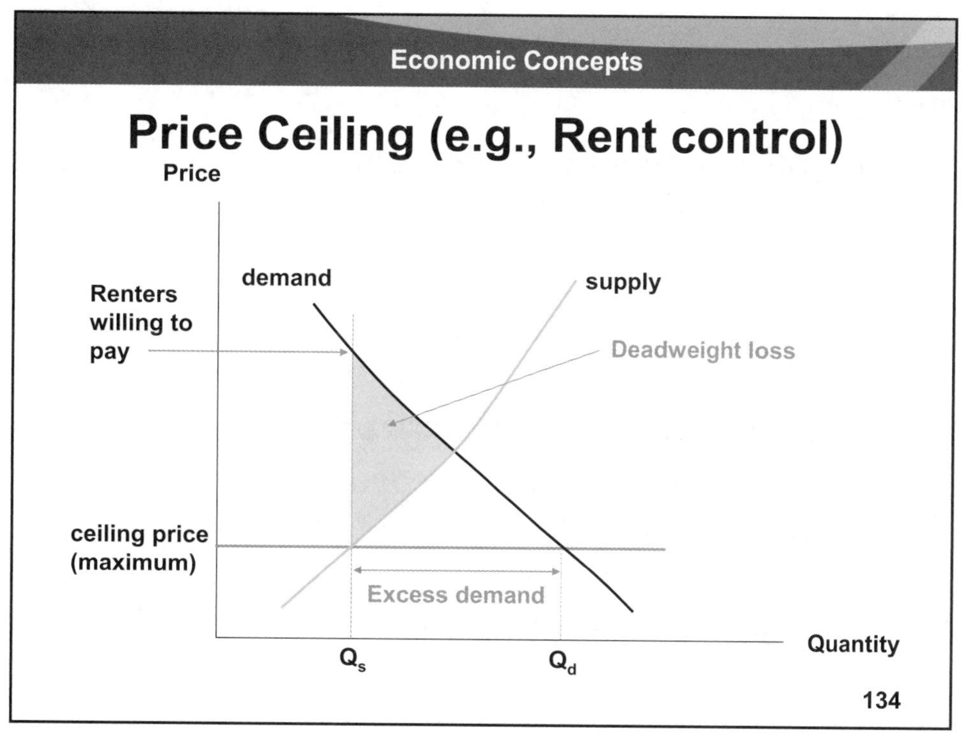
Economic Concepts
Price Ceiling (e.g., Rent control)
Price
Renters willing to pay
demand
supply
Deadweight loss
ceiling price (maximum)
Excess demand
Qs
Qd
Quantity
134

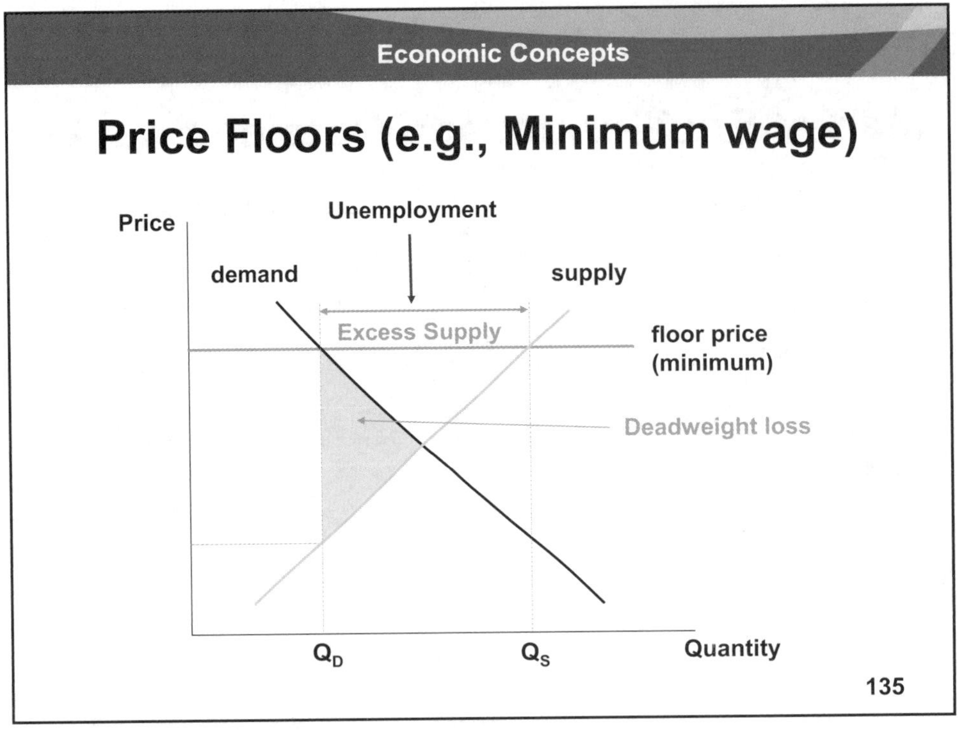

Economic Concepts

Long-Run Impact of Price Ceiling:

- Long waiting period to purchase
- Sellers discriminate
- Sellers take bribes
- Sellers reduce quality

Impact of Minimum Wage (price floor)

- Excess supply of labor increases unemployment
- Producers substitute capital for labor
- Non-monetary benefits, working conditions, on-the-job training all decrease

136

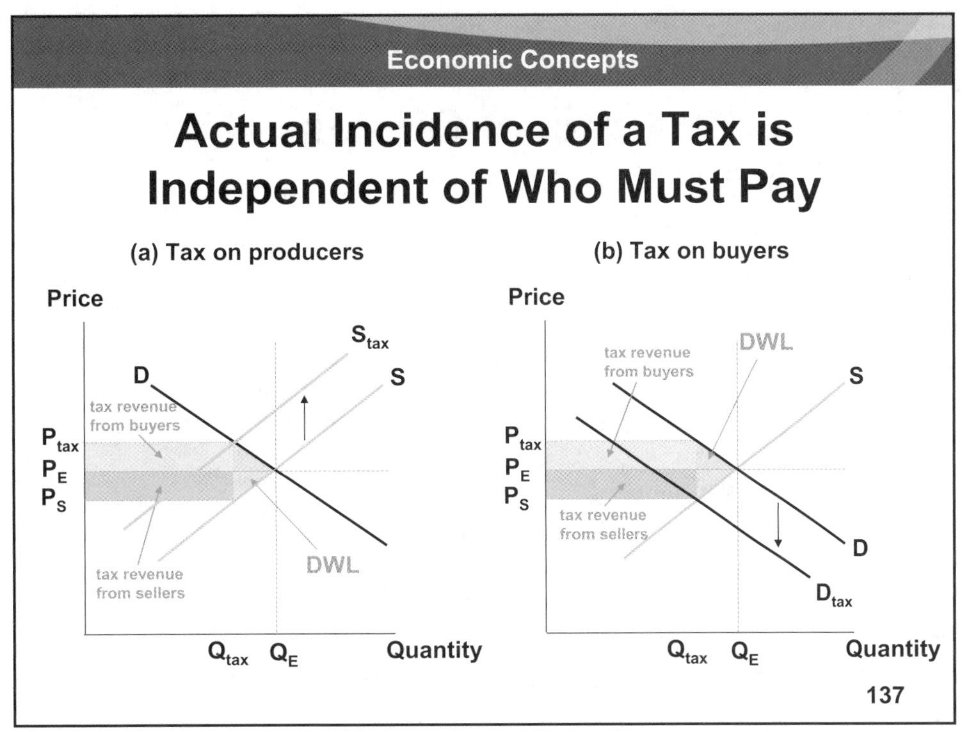
Economic Concepts
Actual Incidence of a Tax is Independent of Who Must Pay
(a) Tax on producers
Price
D
S tax
S
tax revenue from buyers
P tax
P E
P S
tax revenue from sellers
DWL
Q tax
Q E
Quantity
(b) Tax on buyers
Price
tax revenue from buyers
DWL
S
P tax
P E
P S
tax revenue from sellers
D
D tax
Q tax
Q E
Quantity
137

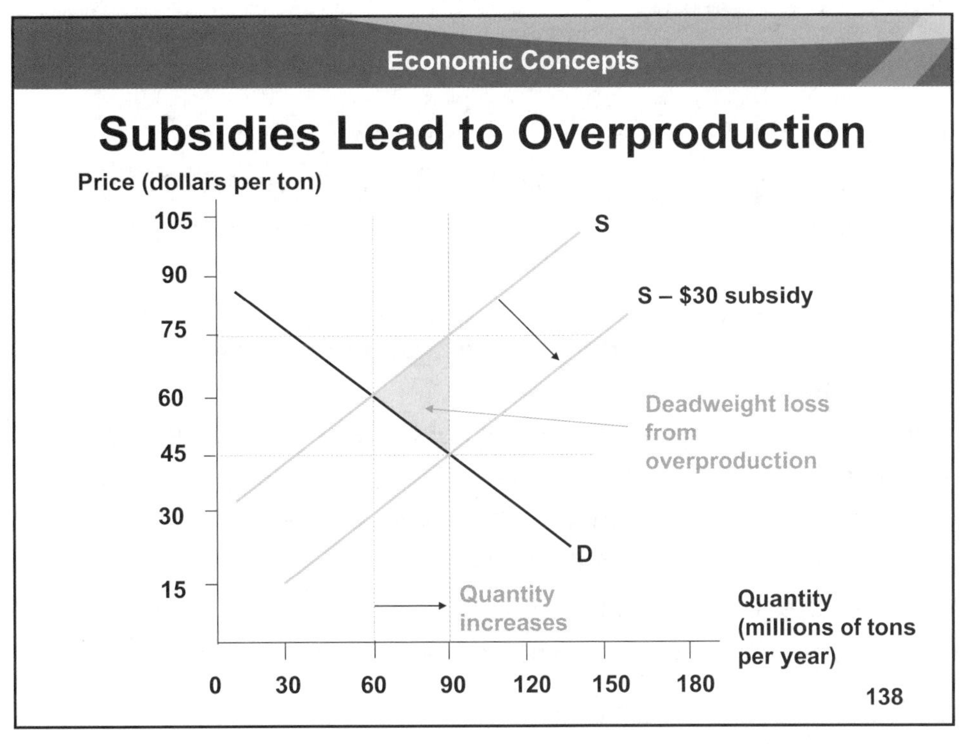
Economic Concepts
Subsidies Lead to Overproduction
Price (dollars per ton)
105
90
75
60
45
30
15
S
S – $30 subsidy
Deadweight loss from overproduction
D
Quantity increases
Quantity (millions of tons per year)
0
30
60
90
120
150
180
138

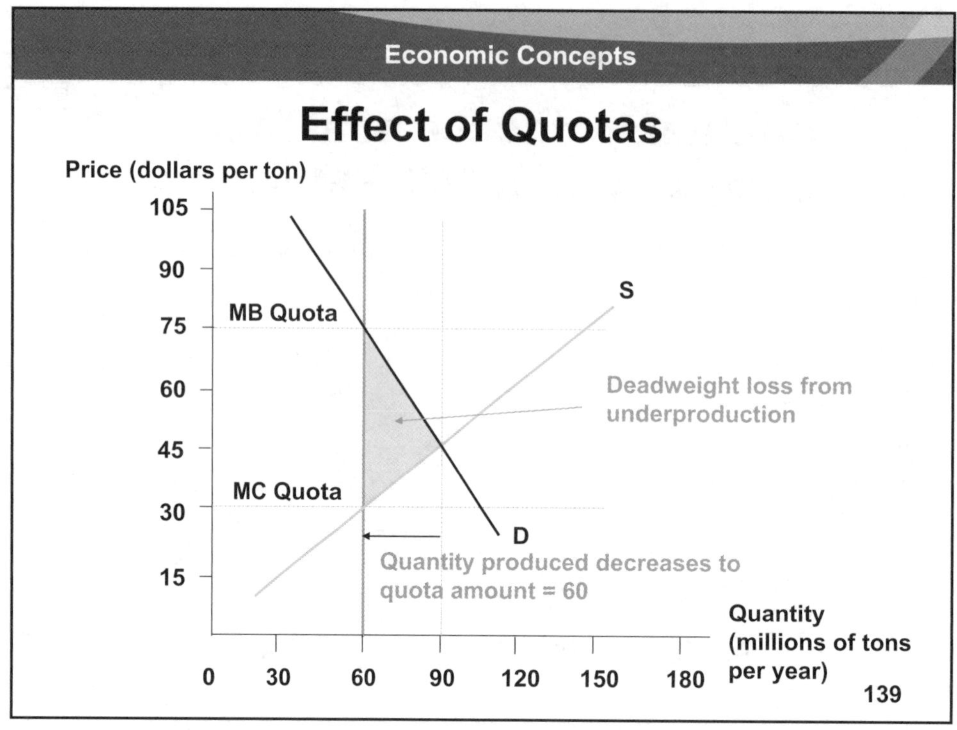

Economic Concepts

Economic profit considers both **explicit and implicit** costs. Economic profit is zero at competitive equilibrium.

Revenues
– Explicit costs
– Implicit costs (opportunity costs and normal profit)
= Economic profit

Implicit costs are returns that would have been earned from the next best use of resources

- Implied rental rate (use of firm's own capital)
  - Economic depreciation
  - Foregone interest
- Normal profit (use of owner's time or financial resources)

140

Economic Concepts

Technological and Economic Efficiency

	Input Quantities	
Method	Capital (machine-day equivalent)	Labor (worker-days)
Robotic manufacturing (RM)	5,000	5
Assembly line manufacturing (ALM)	50	50
Work station manufacturing (WSM)	50	500
Hand crafted manufacturing (HCM)	5	5,000

Not technologically efficient

141

Economic Concepts

Technological and Economic Efficiency

Method	*Capital Cost $250/unit*	*Labor Cost $75/unit*	*Total Cost*	*Cost Per Oven*
RM	$1,250,000	$375	$1,250,375	$12,503.75
ALM	**12,500**	**3,750**	**16,250**	**162.50**
WSM	12,500	37,500	50,000	500.00
HCM	1,250	375,000	376,250	3,762.50

Economically efficient

142

Economic Concepts

The Principal-Agent Problem

Principal-agent problem: Arises due to differences between the interests of a firm's owners (principals) and those of firm management (the owners' agents)

Methods to reduce the principal-agent problem:

- **Ownership** – senior managers
- **Incentive pay** – performance-based, stock options, promotions
- **Long-term contracts** – to give long horizon

143

Economic Concepts

Types of Business Organization

Proprietorship → Easy to establish, single taxation **but** → unlimited personal liability, limited life, difficult to raise capital

Partnership → can outlive partner, single taxation
but → unlimited personal liability, ability to raise capital still limited

Corporation → Limited liability, easy to raise large amounts of capital, separate entity with unlimited life **but** → cumbersome decision making, double taxation

144

Economic Concepts

Measures of Concentration

4-firm Concentration Ratio: Sum of the percentage market shares of four largest firms in an industry

- Ranges from near 0% for **perfect competition** to 100% for **monopoly**

Herfindahl-Hirschman Index (HHI) = sum of the squared market shares of the 50 largest firms in a market

- Ranges from near 0 for **perfect competition to** 10,000 for **monopoly**

145

Economic Concepts

Short Run and Long Run

- **Short run:** Technology of production and some resource quantities (e.g., plant size) are fixed
- **Long run:** Firm can adjust plant size, capital equipment, production methods

146

Economic Concepts

Total, Marginal, and Average Product

Workers	*Total Product*	*Marginal Product*	*Average Product*
1	8	8	8
2	20	12	10
3	26	6	8.7
4	30	4	7.5
5	32	2	6.4
6	33	1	5.5

33 ÷ 6 = 5.5

147

Economic Concepts

Output and Total Cost

Total costs = fixed costs + variable costs

- **Total fixed cost (TFC)** is the cost of fixed inputs, inputs that do not vary with output (e.g., rent)
- **Total variable cost (TVC)** is the cost of all inputs that vary with output (e.g., wages, raw materials)

148

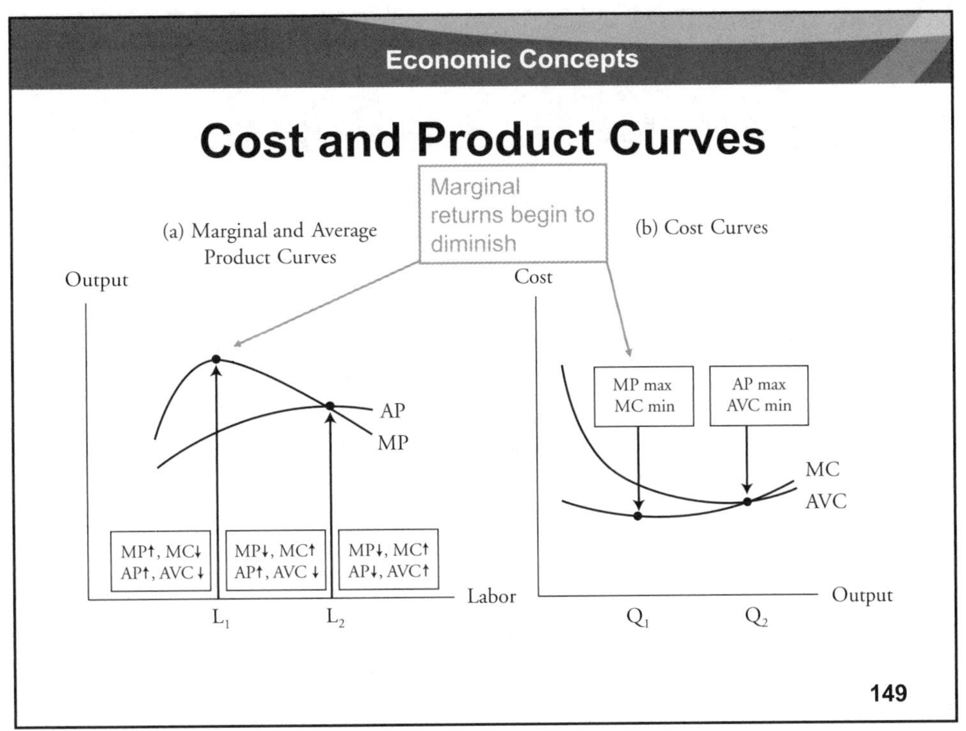

Economic Concepts
Cost and Product Curves
Marginal returns begin to diminish
(a) Marginal and Average Product Curves
Output
AP
MP
MP↑, MC↓ AP↑, AVC↓
MP↓, MC↑ AP↑, AVC↓
MP↓, MC↑ AP↓, AVC↑
Labor
L1
L2
(b) Cost Curves
Cost
MP max MC min
AP max AVC min
MC
AVC
Output
Q1
Q2
149

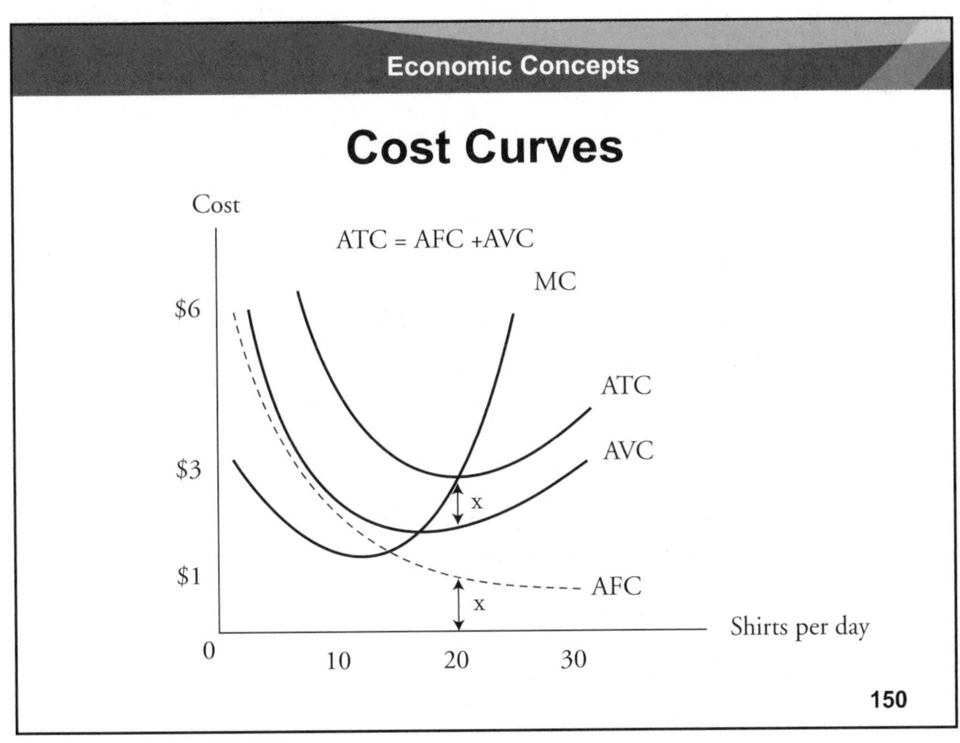

Economic Concepts
Cost Curves
Cost
ATC = AFC +AVC
MC
ATC
AVC
AFC
$6
$3
$1
0
10
20
30
x
x
Shirts per day
150

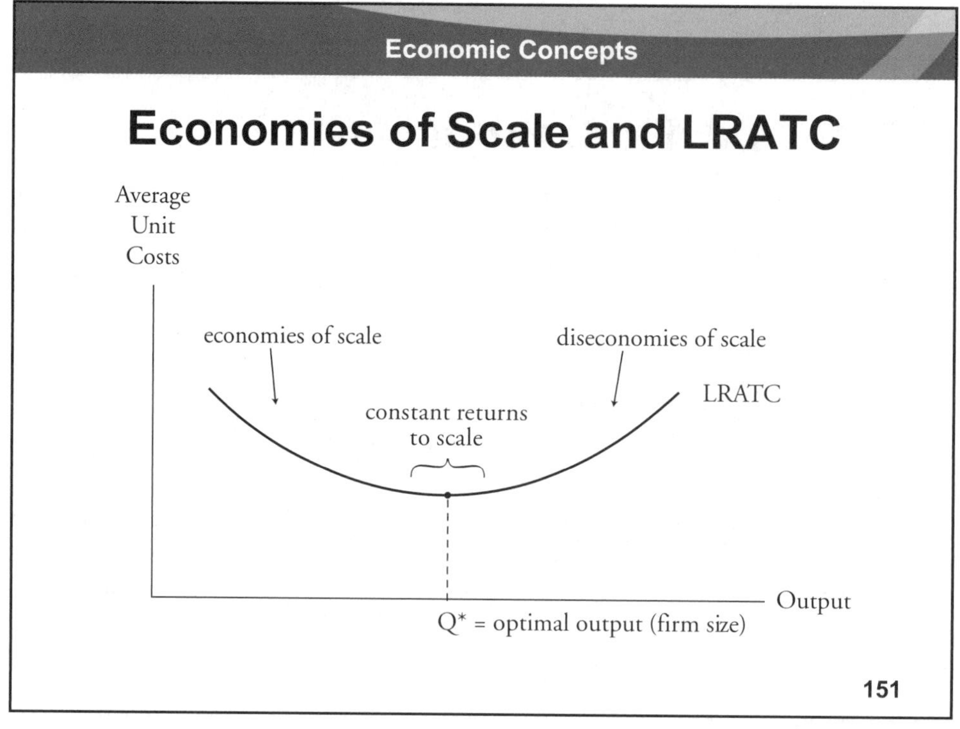

Economic Concepts

Types of Markets

1. **Perfect competition**
   - Same product
   - Many independent firms
   - No barriers to entry or exit
   - Competing prices are known
2. **Monopolistic competition**
   - Many competitors
   - Differentiated products
   - Low barriers to entry

152

Economic Concepts

Types of Markets

3. **Oligopoly**
   - Few sellers
   - Similar <u>or</u> differentiated products
   - Interdependence among competitors
   - Significant barriers to entry

4. **Monopoly**
   - One seller
   - Well-defined product, no good substitutes
   - High barriers to entry

153

Economic Concepts

Perfect Competition – Permanent Increase in Demand

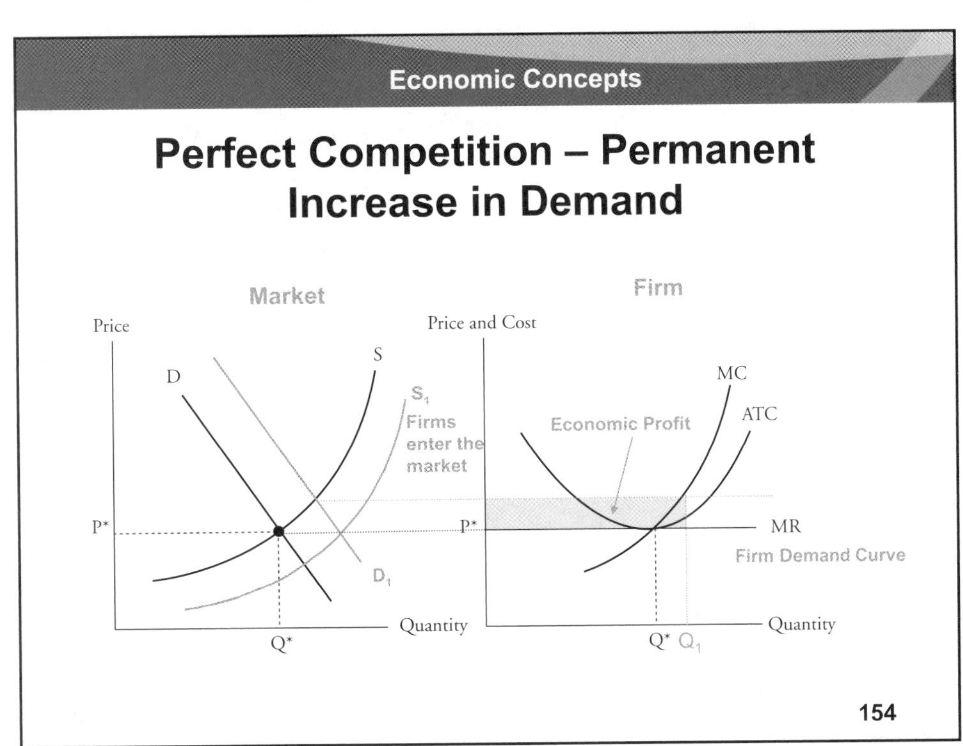

154

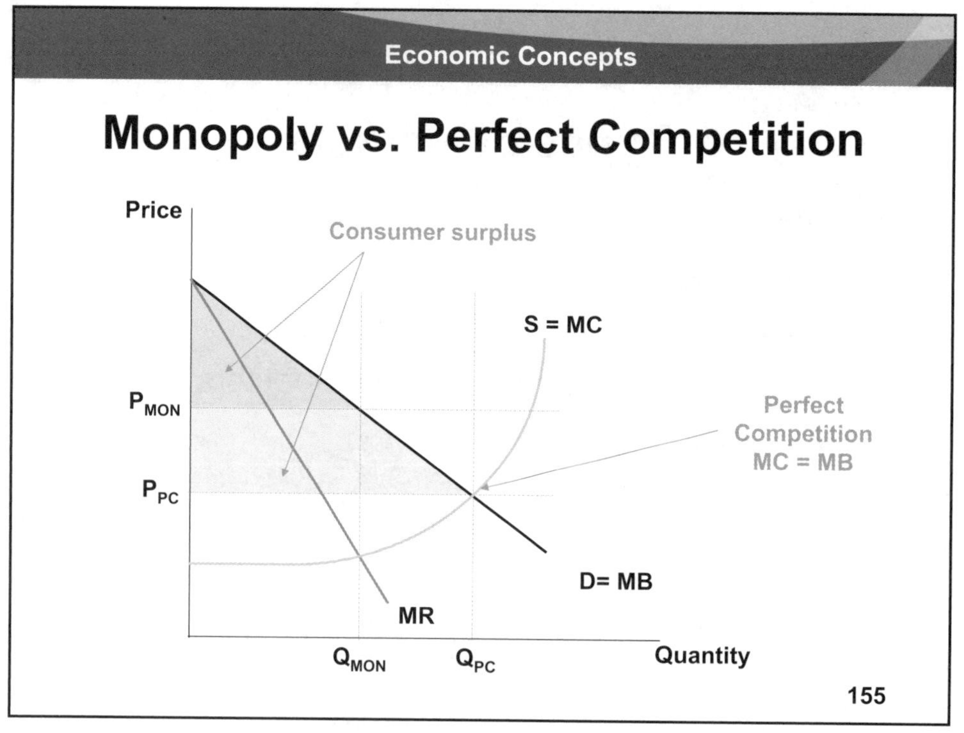
Economic Concepts
Monopoly vs. Perfect Competition
Price
Consumer surplus
S = MC
P MON
P PC
Perfect
Competition
MC = MB
D= MB
MR
Q MON
Q PC
Quantity
155

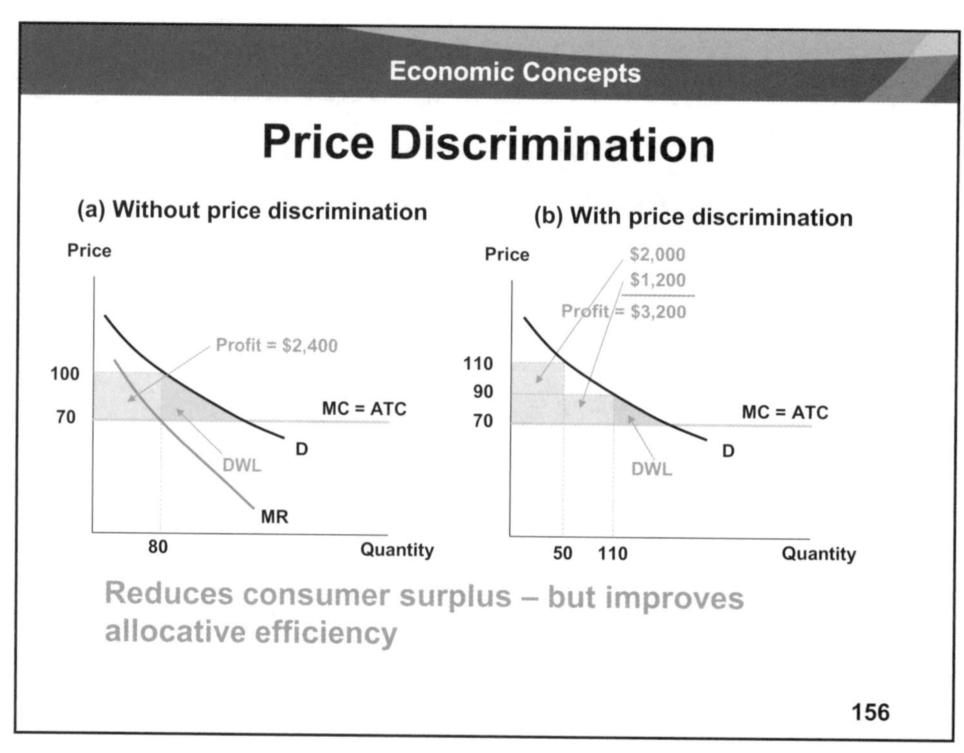
Economic Concepts
Price Discrimination
(a) Without price discrimination
Price
Profit = $2,400
100
70
MC = ATC
D
DWL
MR
80
Quantity
(b) With price discrimination
Price
$2,000
$1,200
Profit = $3,200
110
90
70
MC = ATC
D
DWL
50
110
Quantity
Reduces consumer surplus – but improves allocative efficiency
156

Economic Concepts

Sources and Regulation of Monopoly Power

- **Patents, copyrights, government license**
- **Significant economies of scale (natural monopoly)**
  - ATC declines as output increases
  - Utilities

Two types of regulation

- **Average cost pricing** → Increases output and social welfare, economic profit = 0
- **Marginal cost pricing** → May lead to a loss, require a government subsidy, if MC < ATC

157

Economic Concepts

Characteristics of Monopolistic Competition

- A large number of firms in industry
- Firms produce differentiated products
- Firms compete on price, quality, and marketing
- Low barriers to entry
- Relatively elastic demand

158

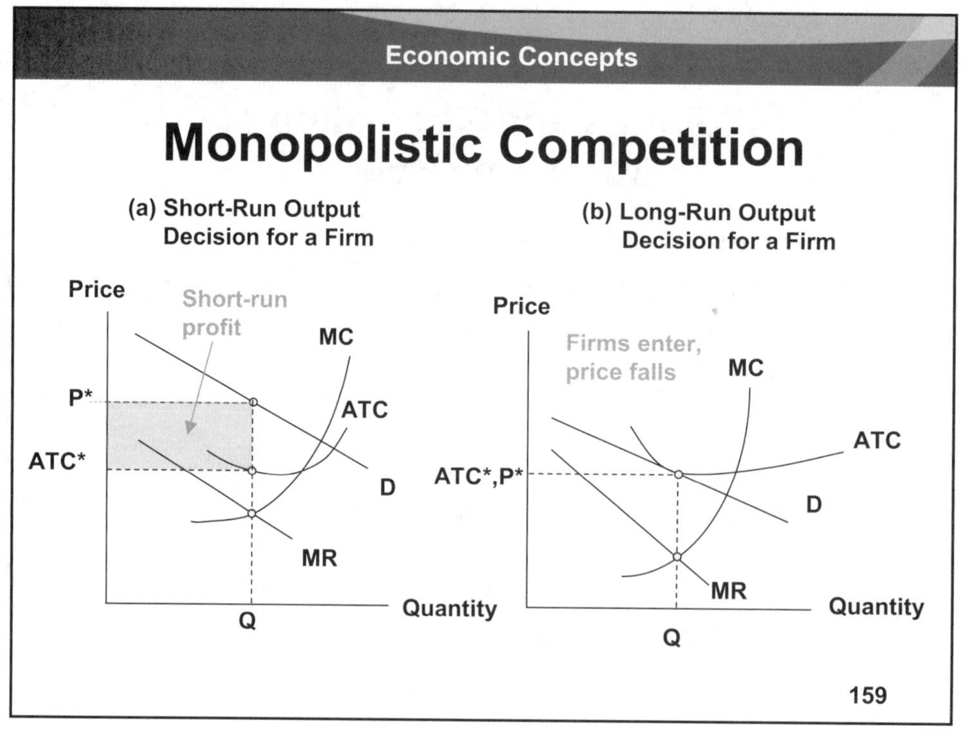

Economic Concepts

Efficiency of Monopolistic Competition

Brand names provide signals about quality

Product innovation and **differentiation** has value to consumers

Advertising provides valuable information to consumers

Efficiency unclear – the question is whether the resources devoted to advertising, innovation, and differentiation provide benefits at least equal to their costs

160

Oligopoly Characteristics

- **Small number** of sellers – downward sloping demand
- **Interdependence** among competitors
- Significant **barriers to entry** (e.g., scale of operations)
- Products may be similar *or* differentiated

161

Oligopoly Models

Dominant Firm Oligopoly

- One dominant firm has cost advantage
- Dominant firm produces most of the output
- Dominant firm **essentially sets market price**

Kinked Demand Curve

- Competitors **will not** follow a price increase
- Competitors **will** follow a price decrease

162

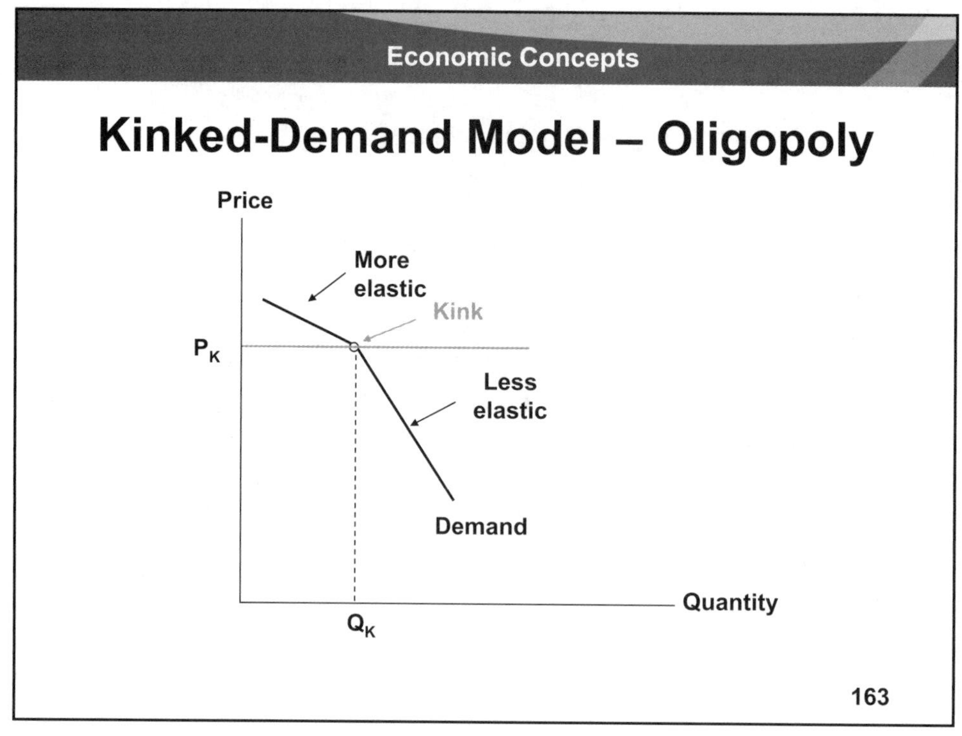

Economic Concepts
Kinked-Demand Model – Oligopoly
Price
More elastic
Kink
P_K
Less elastic
Demand
Quantity
Q_K
163

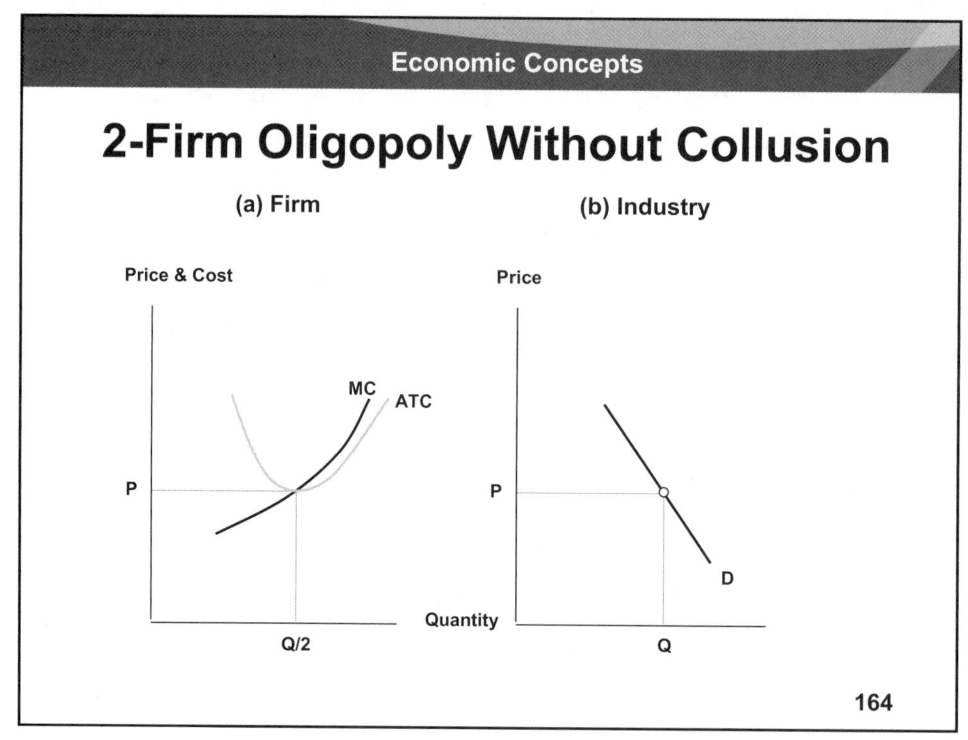

Economic Concepts
2-Firm Oligopoly Without Collusion
(a) Firm
(b) Industry
Price & Cost
Price
MC
ATC
P
P
D
Quantity
Q/2
Q
164

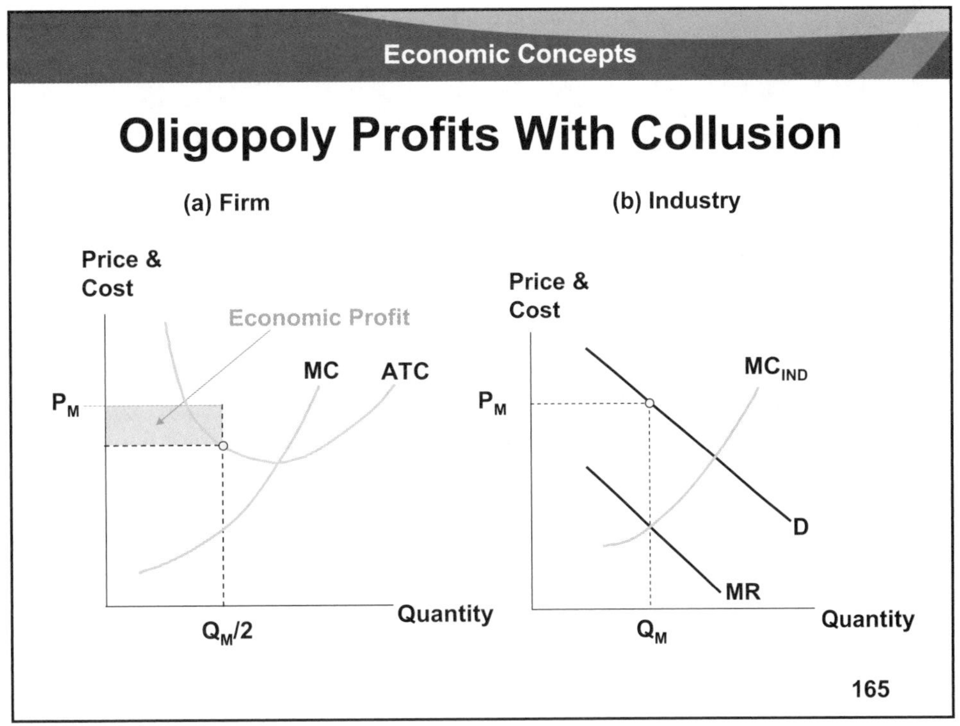

Economic Concepts

Prisoners' Dilemma and Oligopoly

Oligopoly firms can earn a greater profit if they **collude**, fix industry output at the monopoly (profit maximizing) quantity, and share the profits

Game theory suggests that if competitors cannot detect cheating, they will choose to violate the agreement and increase output

166

Economic Concepts

Marginal Product and Marginal Revenue

- **Marginal product:** The additional output from using one more unit of a productive input, holding the quantities of other inputs constant
- **Marginal revenue:** The addition to total revenue from selling one more unit of output
- **Marginal revenue product** (MRP): The addition to total revenue from selling an input's marginal product

167

Economic Concepts

Demand Curve for Labor

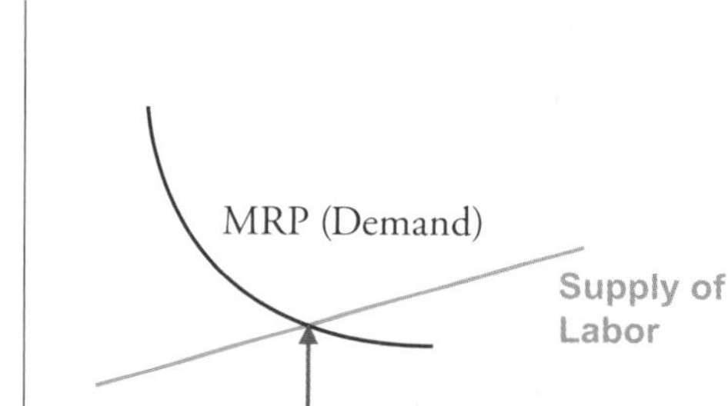

This downward-sloping MRP curve is the firm's short-run demand curve for the productive resource

168

Economic Concepts

Demand for Labor

- **Output** price up → Demand for labor up
- Price of a **substitute** (in production) down → demand for labor down (e.g., clerical workers and computers)
- Price of a **complement** (in production) down → demand for labor up (e.g., computers and IT professionals)

Advances in technology have increased the demand for labor on balance (rising real wage)

169

Economic Concepts

Factors Determining Elasticity of Demand for Labor

1. **Time** – demand for labor is **more elastic** in the long run
2. **Labor intensity** – the greater the reliance on labor in production, the **greater the elasticity** of labor demand
3. **Input substitution** – when substitution of inputs (capital for labor) is *easier*, labor demand will be **more elastic**

170

Economic Concepts

Unions and the Wage Rate

Unions restrict supply, increase wage

- Wage is above efficient wage
- Number employed is below competitive level

Unions attempt to increase demand for union labor by:

- Encouraging purchase of union-made goods
- Supporting trade restrictions on imported goods
- Supporting restrictions on immigrant labor
- Supporting minimum wage laws
- Training programs to increase MP of union labor

171

Economic Concepts

Monopsony in the Labor Market

- A monopsony is a market with a single **buyer**
- A monopsonist in the labor market can decrease wage and employment below competitive level – earn profits
- Success depends on elasticity of supply, just as monopoly power depends on elasticity of demand
- A bilateral monopoly is a market with a union and a monopsony – result depends on bargaining

172

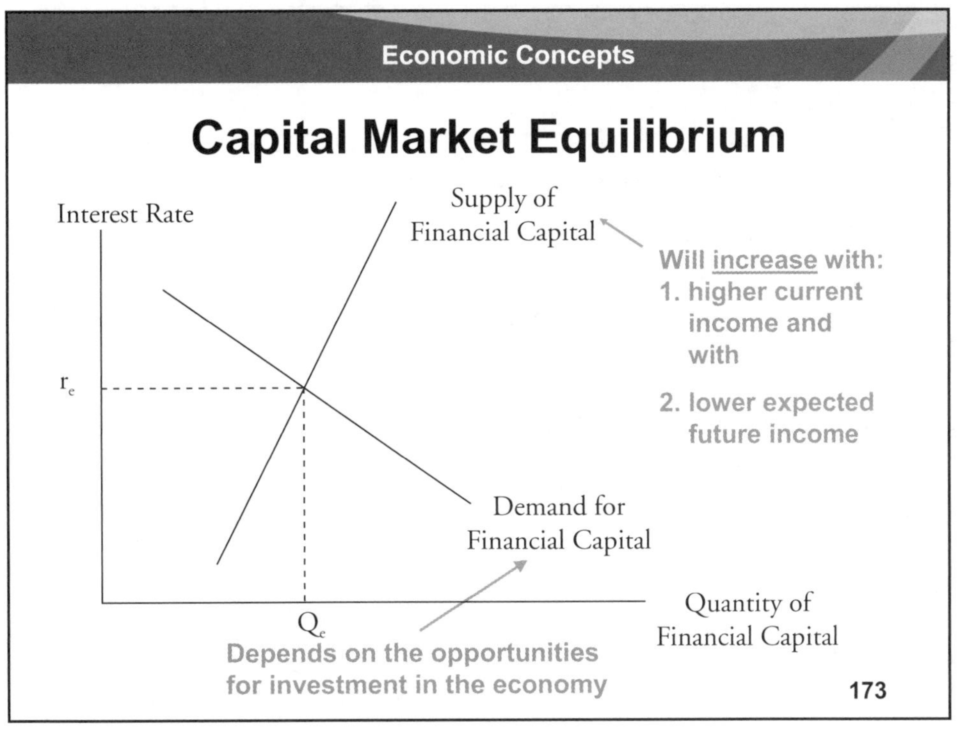
Economic Concepts
Capital Market Equilibrium
Interest Rate
Supply of Financial Capital
Will increase with:
1. higher current income and with
2. lower expected future income
r_e
Demand for Financial Capital
Q_e
Quantity of Financial Capital
Depends on the opportunities for investment in the economy
173

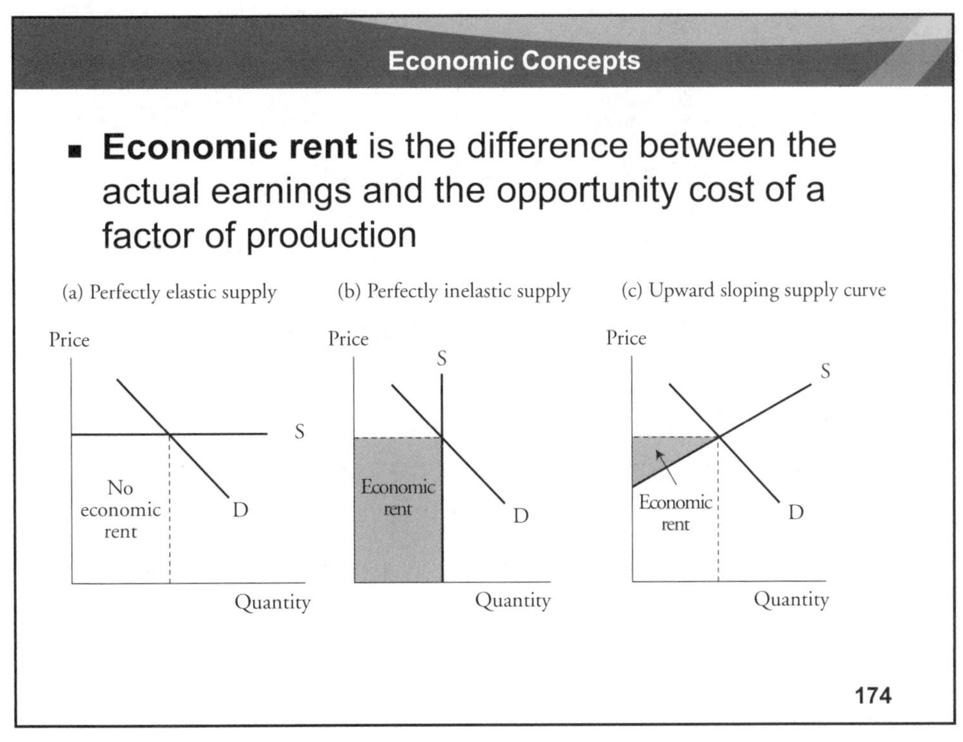
Economic Concepts
▪ Economic rent is the difference between the actual earnings and the opportunity cost of a factor of production
(a) Perfectly elastic supply
(b) Perfectly inelastic supply
(c) Upward sloping supply curve
Price
S
No economic rent
D
Quantity
Price
S
Economic rent
D
Quantity
Price
S
Economic rent
D
Quantity
174

Economic Concepts

To be counted as **unemployed** a person must be available for work and **either:**

- Be actively looking for work
- Laid off – waiting to be called back, or
- Starting a job within 30 days

$$\text{Unemployment rate} = \frac{\text{Number of unemployed}}{\text{Labor force}}$$

$$\text{Participation rate} = \frac{\text{Labor force}}{\text{Working - age population } (> 16)}$$

$$\text{Employment-to-population ratio} = \frac{\text{Number employed}}{\text{Working - age pop.}}$$

175

Economic Concepts

- **Aggregate hours** are the total hours worked in a year by all employed people

$$\frac{\text{GDP}}{\text{Aggregate Hours}} \text{ used to measure productivity}$$

- The more productive an hour of labor is (higher MRP) is, the higher **wage rate** labor can receive
- **Real wage rates** are money wage rates adjusted for changes in the price level
- Real wage rates include wages, salaries, and benefits (total compensation)

176

Economic Concepts

Types of Unemployment

- **Frictional** unemployment results from time it takes employers and employees to find each other
- **Structural** unemployment results from long-term changes in the economy that require workers to gain new skills to fill new jobs
- **Cyclical** unemployment results from changes in economic growth

177

Economic Concepts

"Full" Employment

- **Full employment** is when the economy has no *cyclical* unemployment
- **Structural** and **frictional** unemployment always exist
- 5% unemployment rate could be full employment (expert opinion differs)
- **Natural rate of unemployment** at full employment
- Full-employment GDP is **potential GDP**

178

Economic Concepts

Consumer Price Index

$$\text{CPI} = \frac{\text{cost of basket at current prices}}{\text{cost of basket at base year prices}} \times 100$$

$$\text{Inflation rate} = \frac{\text{current CPI} - \text{previous CPI}}{\text{previous CPI}} = \%\ \text{increase in CPI}$$

179

Economic Concepts

CPI Bias

- The CPI is widely believed to overstate the true rate of inflation by about 1% per year
- The most significant biases in the CPI data include:
  - **New goods** replace older, lower-priced products
  - Price increases due to **quality improvements**
  - **Commodity substitution** changes the typical consumer's basket of goods and services
  - **Outlet substitution** as consumers shift their purchases toward discount stores

180

KAPLAN
SCHWESER
Macroeconomics
Economics - Book 2

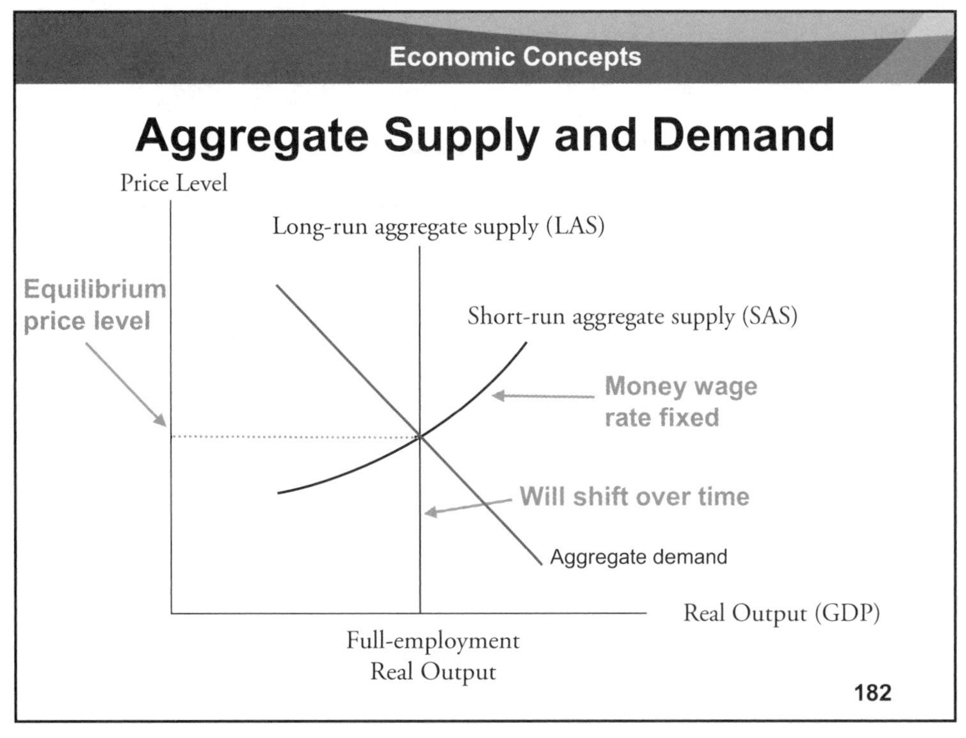
Economic Concepts
Aggregate Supply and Demand
Price Level
Long-run aggregate supply (LAS)
Equilibrium price level
Short-run aggregate supply (SAS)
Money wage rate fixed
Will shift over time
Aggregate demand
Real Output (GDP)
Full-employment Real Output
182

Economic Concepts

Factors that Increase Aggregate Demand

1. An expansion of money supply to **decrease interest rates**—Monetary Policy
2. An **increase in gov't spending** (G)—Fiscal Policy
3. A **tax cut** (C)—Fiscal Policy
4. An **increase in expected inflation** (C)
5. An **expectation of higher incomes** in the future (C)
6. An **increase in expected profits** (I)
7. An **increase in foreign incomes** (net X)
8. A **decrease in the exchange value of domestic currency** (net X)

Aggregate demand = C + I + G + $_{net}$X

183

Economic Concepts

Short-Run Disequilibrium

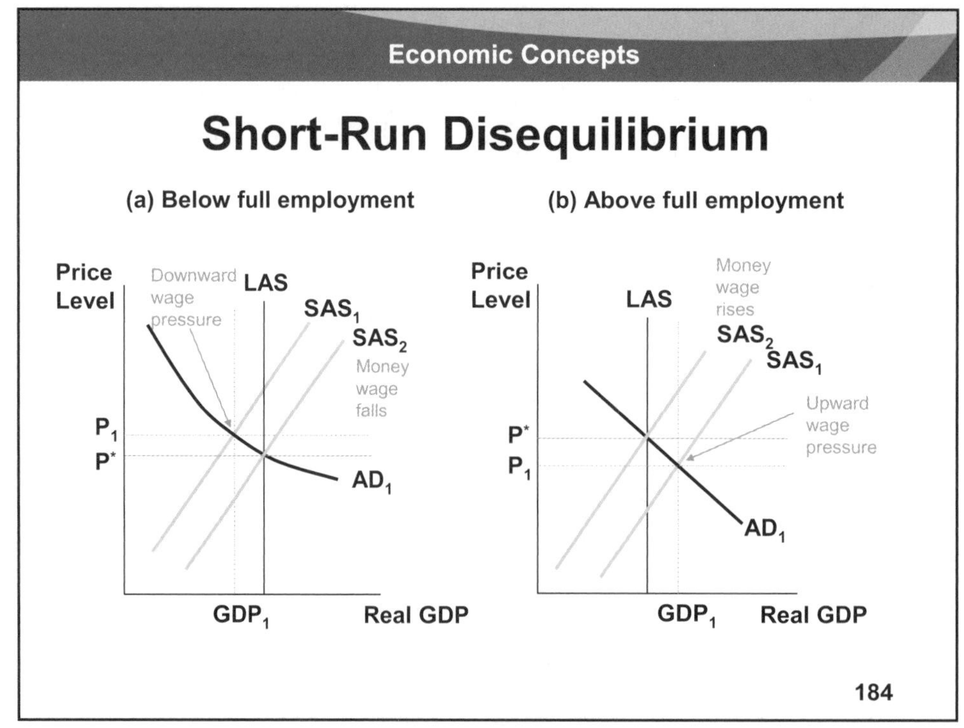

184

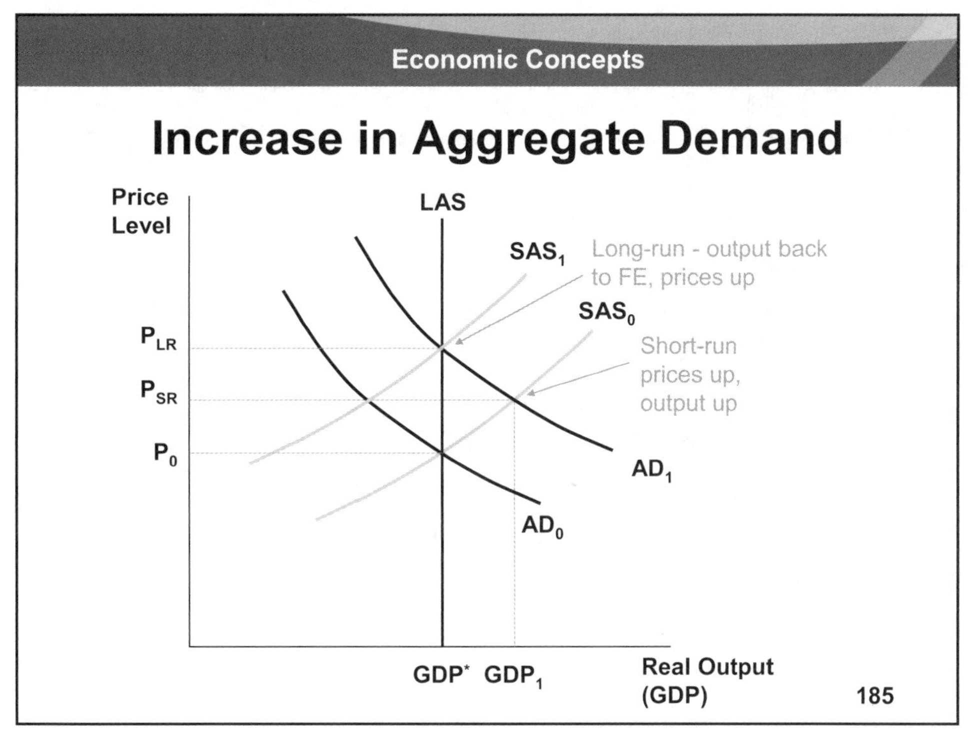
Economic Concepts
Increase in Aggregate Demand
Price Level
LAS
SAS1
Long-run - output back to FE, prices up
SAS0
Short-run prices up, output up
PLR
PSR
P0
AD1
AD0
GDP* GDP1
Real Output (GDP)
185

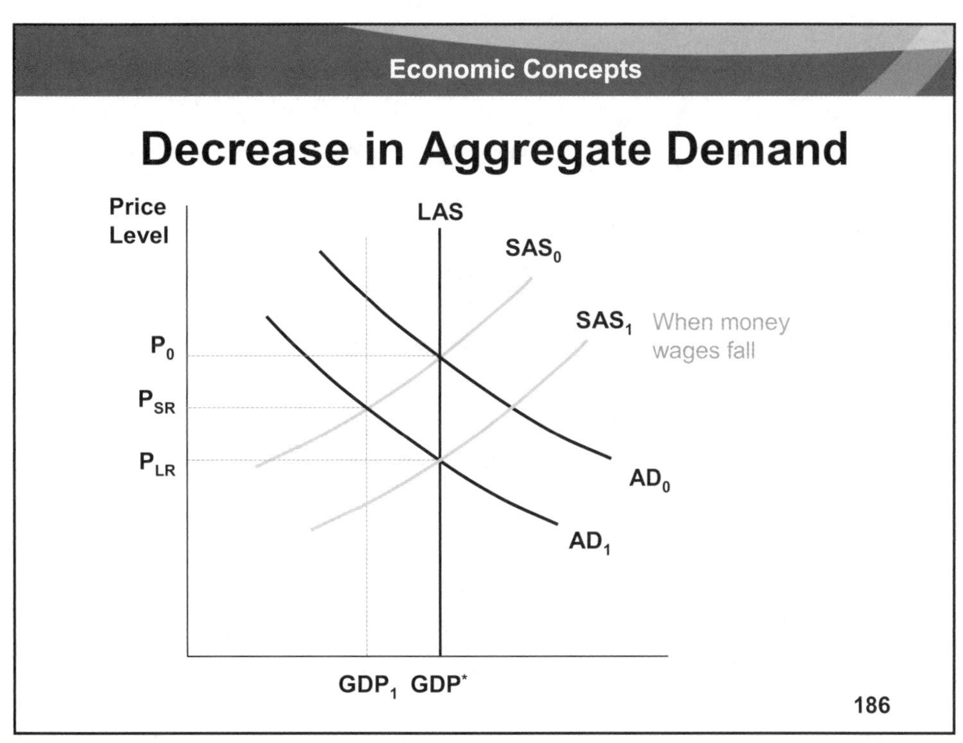
Economic Concepts
Decrease in Aggregate Demand
Price Level
LAS
SAS0
SAS1
When money wages fall
P0
PSR
PLR
AD0
AD1
GDP1 GDP*
186

Economic Concepts

Schools of Macroeconomic Thought

Classical economists believe:

- Shifts in AD and AS are driven by changes in technology over time
- Money wages change rapidly to restore LR equilibrium at full employment
- Taxes are the primary impediment to long-run equilibrium and efficient growth of real GDP

187

Economic Concepts

Schools of Macroeconomic Thought

Keynesian economists believe:

- Business cycles are caused by shifts in AD due to changes in expectations
- Wages are "downward sticky," SRAS does not shift up, recessions can be prolonged
- To restore full employment, increase AD directly through monetary or fiscal policy

New Keynesian economists believe:

- Prices of other productive inputs are also "downward sticky," another barrier to the restoration of full-employment equilibrium

188

Economic Concepts

Schools of Macroeconomic Thought

Monetarists believe:

- Monetary policy is the main factor leading to business cycles
- Recessions are caused by inappropriate decreases in the money supply
- Recessions can be persistent because money wage rates are downward sticky
- The central bank should follow a policy of steady and predictable money supply growth
- The best tax policy is to keep taxes low to minimize disruption and distortion

189

Economic Concepts

Measures of Money

- **M1** includes all currency not held at banks, travelers' checks, and checking account deposits of individuals and firms (but not government checking accounts)
- **M2** includes all the components of M1, plus time deposits, savings deposits, and money market mutual fund balances

190

Economic Concepts

How Banks Create Money

In a **fractional reserve banking** system, a bank is required to hold a fraction of its deposits in reserve, this fraction is the **required reserve ratio.**

Example: Bank 1 receives $1,000 in new reserves, can loan out $800 with RR of 20%...

$800 in loans deposited, $640 in new loans…

$640 deposited, 0.8 × 640 = $512 new loans…

- **Potential** increase in the money supply is 1 / 0.2 or 5 × $1,000 = $5,000
- **Deposit expansion multiplier** is 5

191

Economic Concepts

The Monetary Base

- The **monetary base** includes Federal Reserve notes, coins, and banks' reserve deposits at the Fed
- **Money multiplier** for a change in the monetary base: $\frac{1+c}{r+c}$

where: c = currency as a % of deposits
r = required reserve ratio

The higher the currency % (C), the lower the multiplier

192

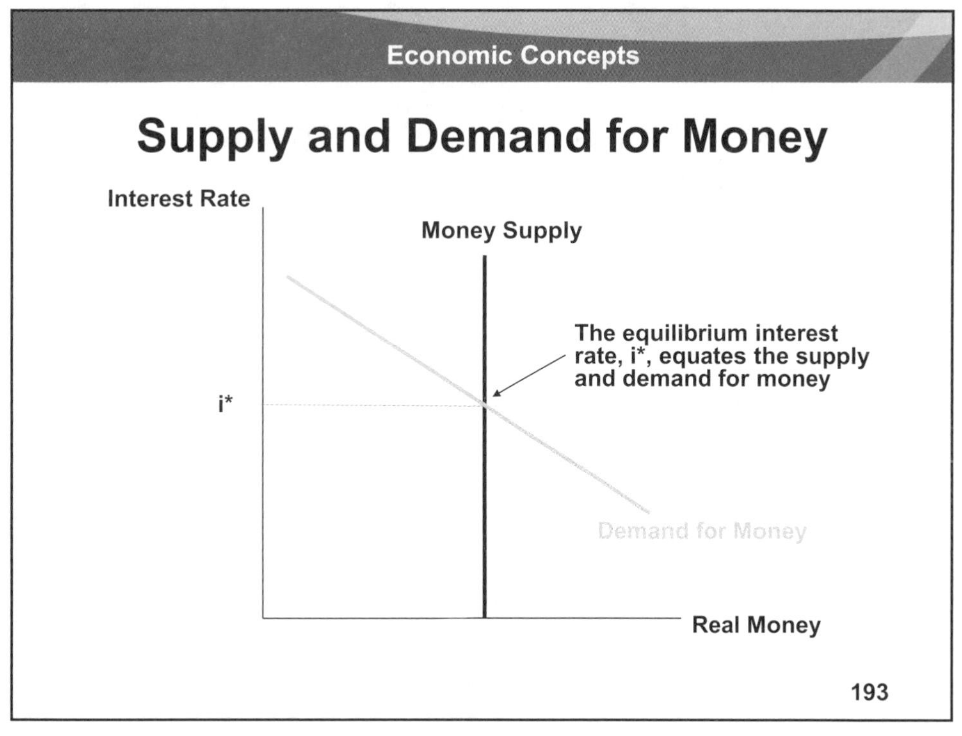

Economic Concepts

Demand for Money

- **Nominal** demand for money increases with price level
- The demand for **real money** increases with real GDP
- **Financial innovation** has decreased the demand for money on balance

194

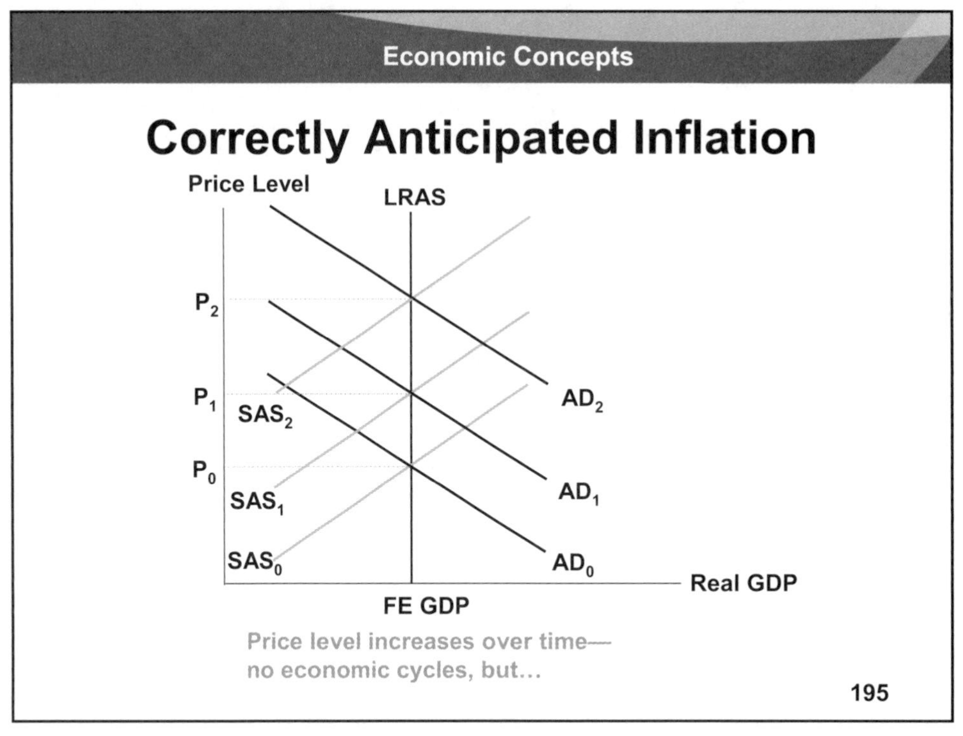
Economic Concepts
Correctly Anticipated Inflation
Price Level
LRAS
P2
P1
P0
SAS2
SAS1
SAS0
AD2
AD1
AD0
Real GDP
FE GDP
Price level increases over time—
no economic cycles, but...
195

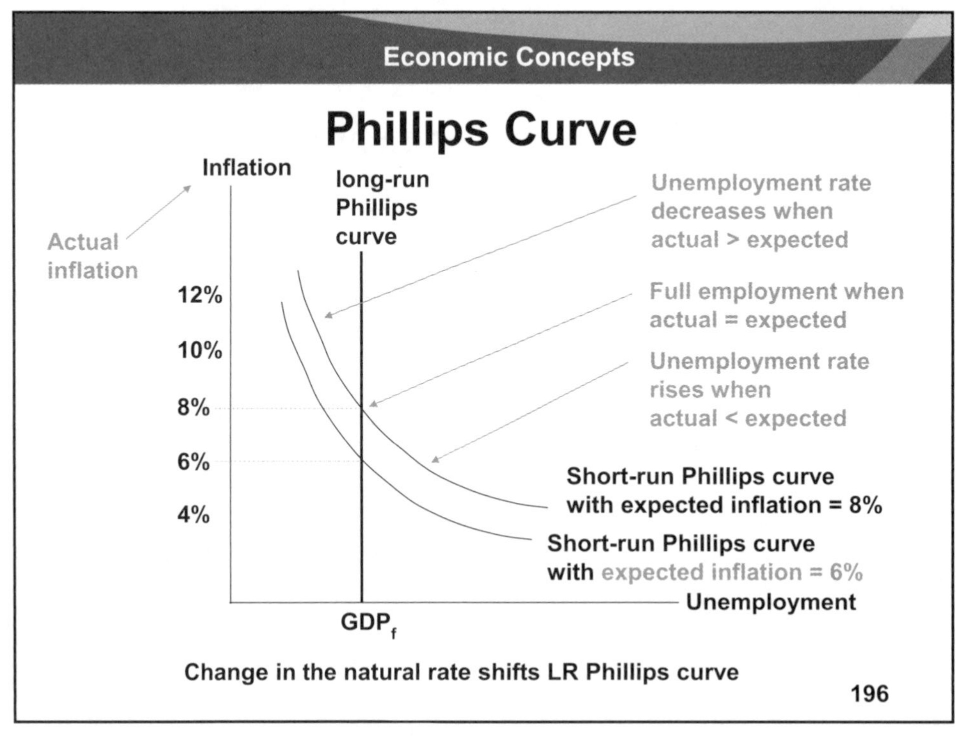
Economic Concepts
Phillips Curve
Inflation
Actual
inflation
long-run
Phillips
curve
Unemployment rate
decreases when
actual > expected
Full employment when
actual = expected
Unemployment rate
rises when
actual < expected
12%
10%
8%
6%
4%
Short-run Phillips curve
with expected inflation = 8%
Short-run Phillips curve
with expected inflation = 6%
Unemployment
GDPf
Change in the natural rate shifts LR Phillips curve
196

Fiscal Policy

Economics - Book 2

Economic Concepts

Discretionary Fiscal Policy

- **Discretionary fiscal policy**: Government spending and tax decisions **to stabilize the economy**
- During recessions, increase government spending or decrease taxes. Both increase AD, putting more money in the hands of corporations and consumers to invest and spend
- During inflationary booms, decrease government spending or increase taxes. Both decrease AD, taking money from corporations and consumers, causing investment and consumption spending to fall

198

Economic Concepts

Supply Side Effects

- Income taxes reduce the incentive to work, after-tax wage is lower (tax wedge)
- Expenditure (sales, value-added) taxes reduce purchasing power of wages, less incentive to work
- Either tax will reduce potential GDP

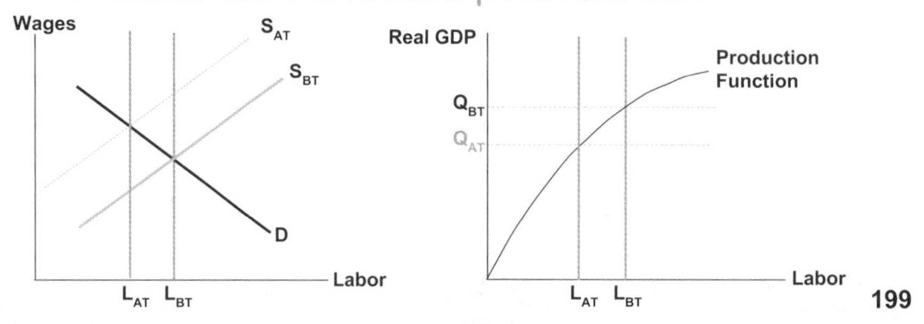

199

Economic Concepts

Laffer Curve

- Increase in tax rates will not always increase tax revenue
- Beyond some rate of taxation, increasing the tax rate reduces (taxable) economic output so much that total tax revenues actually decrease

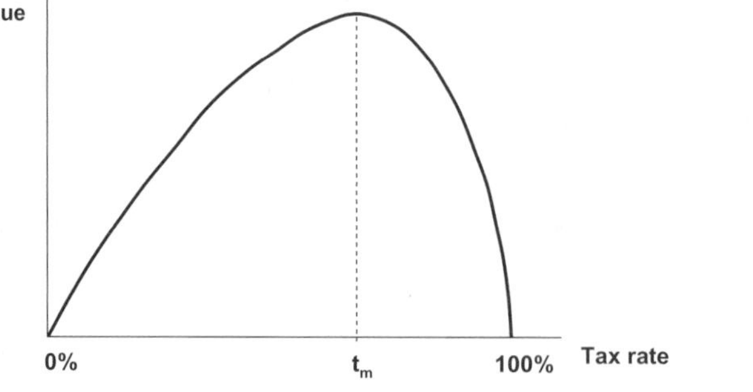

200

Economic Concepts

Fiscal Policy Multipliers

- Government purchases multiplier: An increase in government spending causes even greater increase in AD
- Tax multiplier: An increase in taxes causes a decrease in AD of more than the amount of the tax increase
- Balanced budget multiplier: Equal increases in taxes and spending have positive effect on AD because government purchases multiplier is stronger than tax multiplier

201

Economic Concepts

Limitations of Discretionary Policy

- **Recognition delay:** Time it takes to recognize a cyclical trend
- **Administrative delay:** Time it takes to pass new tax law
- **Impact delay:** Time it takes for the effects of the fiscal policy change to be felt

  These lags limit the ability of fiscal policy change to stabilize economic cycles

202

Economic Concepts

Automatic Stabilizers

- **Induced taxes:** Taxes rise during expansion and fall during recession
- **Needs-tested spending:** Government payments based on need, such as **unemployment compensation**, increase during recession and decrease during expansion

Automatic changes in fiscal policy: Taxes up and spending down during expansion; taxes down and spending up during recession

203

Monetary Policy

Economics - Book 2

Economic Concepts

U.S. Monetary Policy

Stated Objectives

- Maximum employment
- Stable prices → Inflation targeting only central bank goal in many countries
- Moderate long-term interest rates

Central Bank Tools

- Open market operations (most used)
- Discount rate
- Reserve requirement

205

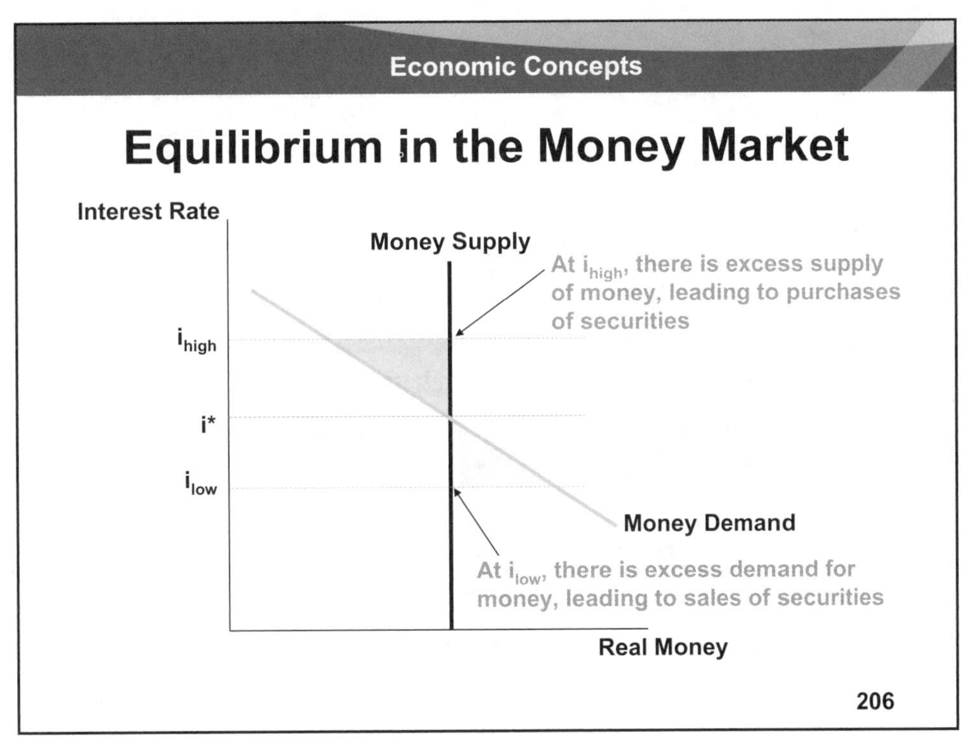

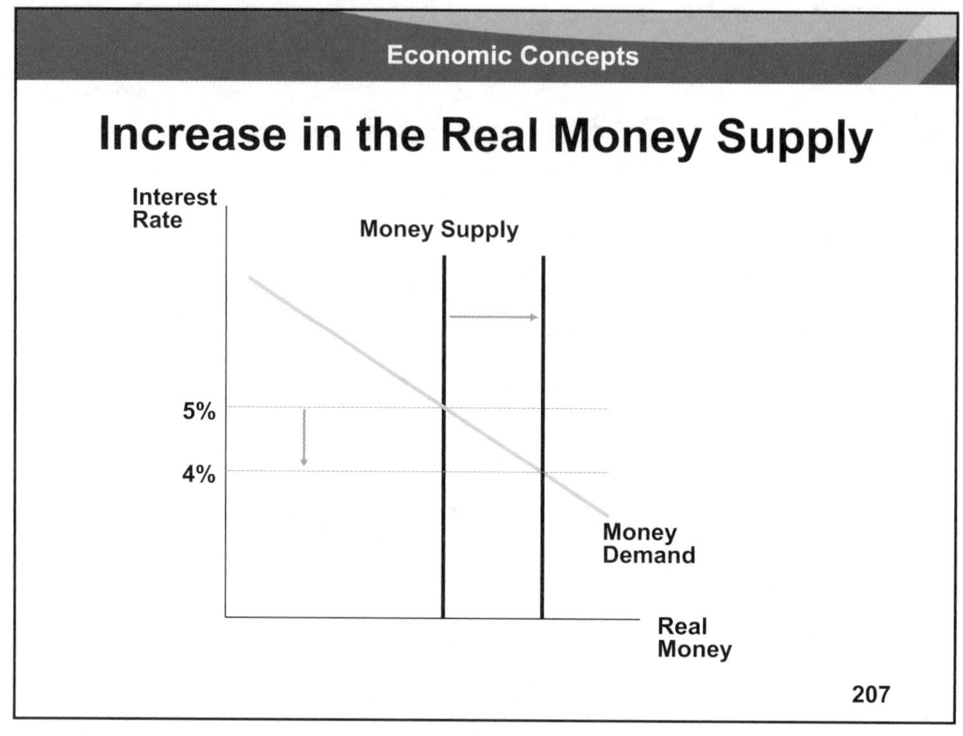

Economic Concepts

Effects of Money on Real GDP

1. Money supply increases
2. Nominal and real interest rates decrease
3. Businesses invest more, households increase purchases of durable goods
4. Foreigners invest less, exchange rate falls, imports down, exports up, net exports increase
5. Aggregate demand, real GDP, and price level increase in the short run
6. In long run, full-employment GDP

208

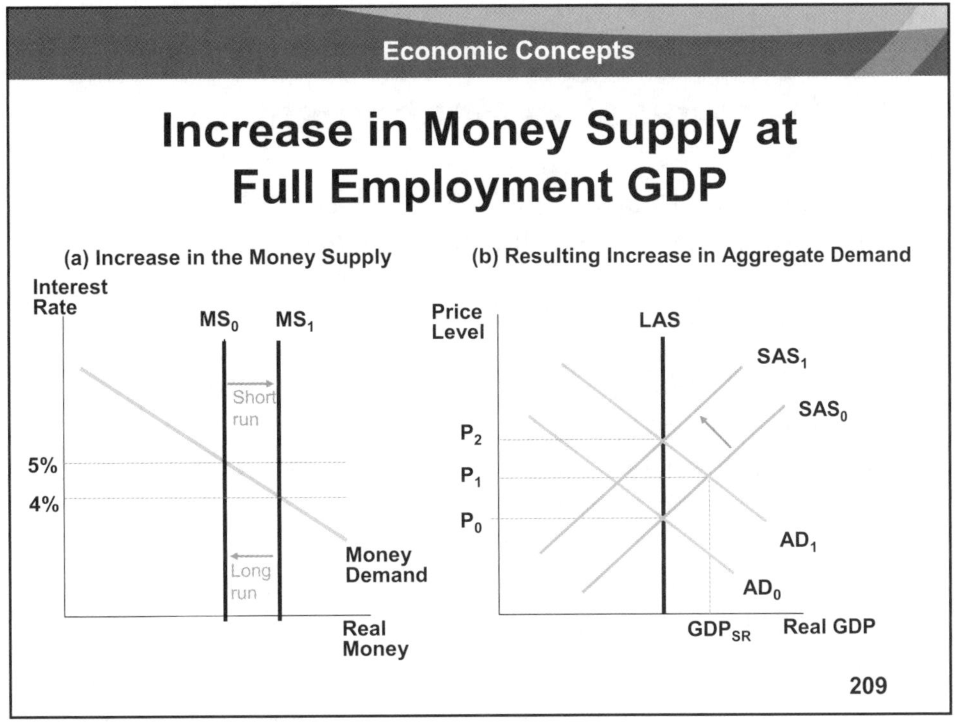

Economic Concepts

Transmission Mechanism (FFR decrease)

1. Fed buys Treasuries, excess reserves, FFR falls
2. Other short-term rates fall (e.g., T-bills)
3. Longer-term rates (= ST rates + expected inflation) fall as well
4. Businesses expand investment (AD up)
5. Less foreign investment, domestic currency value falls, imports down/exports up (AD up)
6. Consumers (financed) purchases increase (AD up)

210

Economic Concepts

Transmission Mechanism (cont.)

The increase in aggregate demand increases real GDP, employment and the price level

Opposite Effect for Open Market Sales

- Fed sells Treasury securities, decreases bank reserves, increases FFR, increases longer-term and other short-term rates, decreases business investment, consumer spending, and net exports
- Reduction in AD decreases real GDP and price level, increases unemployment

211

Economic Concepts

Quantity Theory of Money

Equation of exchange: MV = PY

money supply × velocity = price × real output

Since **velocity** and **real output** are relatively constant:

Increases in the money supply lead to **proportional increases in the price level**

212

Economic Concepts

Monetary Policy Strategies

Instrument Rule

The best known is the **Taylor Rule:**

$$FFR = 2\% + \text{inflation} + 0.5(\text{inflation} - 2\%) + 0.5(\text{output gap})$$

(Inflation) Targeting Rule

Set FFR so that the forecast of inflation is equal to the target inflation rate, typically 2%

Often, central banks use **core inflation:** without food and energy

213

Economic Concepts

Loose Links and Time Lags

- When money supply is increased to **decrease FFR**, increase in expected future inflation **can increase long-term rates**
- The lags between monetary policy changes and their effect on the economy may lead to expansionary or contractionary effects at the wrong times – can be **destabilizing**

214

CFA® LEVEL 1

3-Day Review Slide Workbook

FINANCIAL REPORTING AND ANALYSIS

Financial Statement Analysis: An Introduction

Financial Reporting and Analysis - Book 3

Financial Reporting and Analysis

Key Financial Statements

- **Income Statement** – summarizes events over a period
- **Balance Sheet** – at a point in time

  Assets = Liabilities + Owners' Equity
- **Cash Flow Statement** – reconciles beginning and ending cash balance
- **Statement of Changes in Owners' Equity** – amounts and sources of changes in investor's equity over the period

216

Financial Reporting and Analysis

Statement of Changes in Owners' (Shareholders') Equity

- Amounts and sources of changes in investor's equity over the period
- Sometimes called Statement of Retained Earnings
- Stock issuance and repurchase
- Certain adjustments to equity from events not recorded on the Income Statement
- Other Comprehensive Income

217

Financial Reporting and Analysis

Footnotes and Supplementary Schedules

Accounting Methods and Assumptions

Business Acquisitions/Disposals

Contingencies Legal Proceedings

Stock Options and Benefit Plans

Significant Customers Segment Data

Quarterly Data Related Party Transactions

218

Financial Reporting and Analysis

Management Discussion and Analysis

- Results from operations, business overview
- Trends in sales and expenses
- Capital resources and liquidity
- Cash flow trends
- Discussion of critical accounting choices
- Effects of inflation, price changes, and uncertainties on future results

219

Financial Reporting and Analysis

The Audit Report

- **Audit:** Independent review of company's financial statements
- **Reasonable assurance** that financial statements are free of material errors
- **Audit opinion:**

  Unqualified: "Clean" opinion

  Qualified: Exceptions to accounting principles

  Adverse: Statements not presented fairly
- Must provide opinion on company's **internal controls** under U.S. GAAP

220

Financial Reporting and Analysis

Audit Report

1. Responsibility of management to prepare accounts
2. Independence of auditors
3. Properly prepared in accordance with relevant GAAP
4. Free from material misstatement
5. Accounting principles and estimates chosen are reasonable
6. Opinion on internal control systems

221

Financial Reporting and Analysis

Sarbanes-Oxley

Management report on:

- Responsibility to establish and maintain adequate internal controls
- Management's framework for evaluating internal controls
- Assessment of the effectiveness of internal controls over the last operating period
- Statement of Auditor's attestment
- Certify that financial statements are fairly presented

222

Financial Reporting and Analysis

Supplementary Sources of Information

- **Quarterly, semiannual reports:** Updates of major financial statements and footnotes; SEC filings
- **Proxy statements:** Issued when shareholder vote is required; contain information on board elections, management compensation, stock options
- **Corporate reports, press releases** written by management
- **Economic, industry data** from trade journals, reporting services, government agencies

223

Financial Reporting and Analysis

Financial Statement Analysis Framework

1. Purpose and Context of Analysis
2. Collect Data
3. Process Data
4. Analyze/Interpret Data
5. Conclusions and Recommendations
6. Update analysis periodically

224

Financial Reporting and Analysis

Classification of Activity

Operating Activities

- Sale of goods and services
- Cost of providing goods and services
- Income tax expense
- Short-term assets and liabilities related to operating activities (working capital)

Classification often depends on nature of the firm rather than the nature of the transaction

225

Financial Reporting and Analysis

Classification of Activity

Investing Activities

- Purchase/sale of PP&E
- Purchase of debt and equity

Financing Activities

- Issue/repurchase of common/preferred equity
- Issue/repayment of debt
- Payment of distributions (interest/dividends)

226

Financial Reporting and Analysis

Common Asset Accounts

- Cash and Cash Equivalents
- Accounts Receivable, Trade Receivables
- Prepaid Expenses
- Inventory
- PP&E (Property, Plant and Equipment)
- Investment Property
- Intangibles
- Financial Assets (Investment Securities)
- Investments Under the Equity Method
- Deferred Tax Assets

227

Financial Reporting and Analysis

Common Liability Accounts

- Accounts Payable, Trade Payables
- Provisions/Accrued Liabilities
- Financial Liabilities
- Current and Deferred Tax
- Minority Interest (U.S. GAAP)
- Unearned Revenue
- Debt Payable
- Bonds

228

Financial Reporting and Analysis

Common Equity Accounts

- Capital at Par Value
- Additional Paid In Capital
- Retained Earnings
- Other Comprehensive Income
- Minority Interest (IFRS)

229

Financial Reporting and Analysis

Common Income Statement Items

- Revenue
  - Sales
  - Gains
  - Investment Income
- Expense
  - Cost of Goods Sold
  - SG&A (Selling, General, and Admin)
  - Depreciation/Amortization
  - Interest
  - Tax Expense
  - Losses

230

Financial Reporting and Analysis

Accounting Equations

Assets = Liabilities + Owners Equity

Assets – Liabilities = Owners Equity

Owners Equity = Contributed Capital + Retained Earnings

Revenue – Expenses = Net Income

231

Financial Reporting and Analysis

Accounting for Transactions

1. Pay a bill E = A – L

Asset 'cash' goes down

Liability 'trade payables' goes down

Equity is unchanged

2. Sell a bond (borrow money) E = A – L

Asset 'cash' goes up by proceeds

Liability 'bonds payable' goes up by proceeds

Equity is unchanged

232

Accounting for Transactions

3. Make a credit sale E = A – L

Asset 'inventory' goes down

Asset 'accounts receivable' goes up by more

Equity 'retained earnings' increases by difference

On the Income Statement

Revenues increase, expenses increase by less

Net income and retained earnings increase

Retained earnings is an equity account

233

Accounting for Transactions

4. Buy materials on credit E = A – L

Asset 'inventory' increases

Liability 'accounts payable' increases

Equity is unchanged

5. Issue stock E = A – L

Asset 'cash' goes up

Liabilities unchanged

Equity 'common stock' increases

234

Financial Reporting and Analysis

Accounting for Transactions

6. Incur an expense E = A – L

Liability increases

Assets unchanged

Equity 'retained earnings' decreases

7. Pay a liability E = A – L

Asset 'cash' goes down

Liability goes down

Equity unchanged

235

Financial Reporting and Analysis

Accounting for Transactions

8. Declare dividend E = A – L

Liability 'dividends payable' increases

Assets unchanged

Equity 'retained earnings' decreases

9. Pay dividend E = A – L

Asset 'cash' goes down

Liability 'dividends payable' goes down

Equity unchanged

236

Financial Reporting and Analysis

Accruals & Valuation Adjustments

- Bad/Doubtful Debts
- Prepaid Expenses
- Unbilled (Accrued) Revenue
- Impairments / Writedowns
- Mark to Market Investments
  - Available for Sale
  - Trading Securities

(Assets)

- Accrued Expenses
- Unearned (Deferred) Revenue
- Provisions

(Liabilities)

237

Financial Reporting and Analysis

Relationship Between Financial Statements

Balance Sheet	$m		$m
Current Assets		**Current Liabilities**	70
Cash	50	**Long Term Liabilities**	180
Others	100		250
	150	**Owners Equity**	
Long Life Assets		Contributed Capital	100
Investments	20	Retained Earnings	70
PP&E	200		170
Intangibles	50		
Total Assets	420	**Liabilities and Equity**	420

238

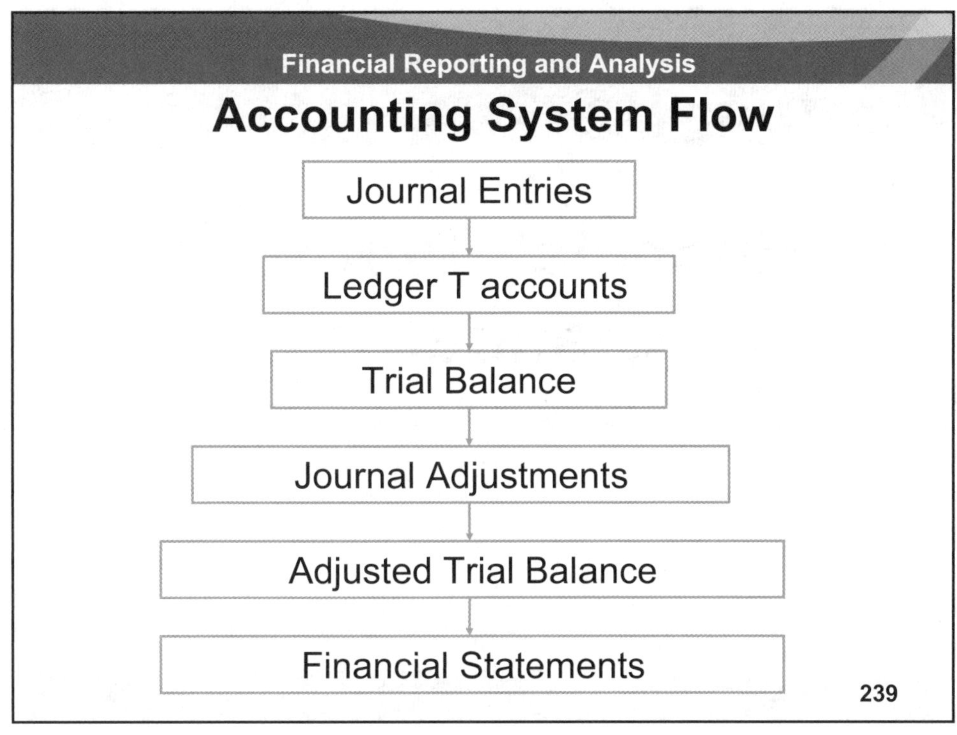

Financial Reporting and Analysis

Statements and Security Analysis

- Financial Statements contain:
  - Estimates
  - Judgements

  } Accruals and Valuations
- Analyst must review:
  - MDA
  - Footnotes

  } Critical accounting policies and estimates sections
- Misrepresentations:
  - Accounts may balance but still may not be correct!

Determine true picture of company performance and make appropriate adjustments for analysis

240

Financial Reporting Standards

Financial Reporting and Analysis - Book 3

Financial Reporting and Analysis

Objective of Financial Statements

"The objective of financial statements is to provide information about the financial position, performance and change in financial position of an entity; this information should be useful to a wide range of users for the purpose of making economic decisions"

IASB Framework for the Preparation and Presentation of Financial Statements

242

Financial Reporting and Analysis

Financial Accounting Standard Setting

American Institute of Certified Public Accountants (AICPA)

Securities and Exchange Commission (SEC)

(Recognize)

Financial Accounting Standards Board (FASB)

Statements of Financial Accounting Concepts (SFAC)

Statements of Financial Accounting Standards (SFAS)

243

Financial Reporting and Analysis

Accounting Standards

Financial Accounting Standards Board (FASB) United States

International Accounting Standards Board (IASB) most other countries

244

Financial Reporting and Analysis

Convergence between IASB and FASB

Convergence refers to reducing the differences in worldwide accounting standards.

1. Increase comparability
2. Decrease problems and expenses of raising capital in foreign market
3. Decrease problems and expenses of preparing consolidated financial statements for foreign subsidiaries

   U.S.'s SEC allows foreign companies to use IFRS but requires a statement reconciling those statements to U.S. GAAP.

245

Financial Reporting and Analysis

Financial Reporting Requirements and Regulation

Securities and Exchange Commission (SEC) – United States

Financial Services Authority – U.K.

International Organization of Securities Commissions (IOSCO) – many other countries

246

Financial Reporting and Analysis

International Organization of Securities Commissions (IOSCO)

- 181 members regulating 90% of the world's capital markets (SEC & FSA)
- 1998 Core Objectives of Securities Regulation:
  1. Protecting Investors
  2. Ensuring fair, transparent and efficient markets
  3. Reduction of systematic risk
- Goal = uniform regulation

247

Financial Reporting and Analysis

European Securities Regulation

2001 European Commission

European Securities Committee (ESC)

- Advises commission on policy issues

Committee of European Securities Regulators (CESR)

- Co-ordination and convergence of EU regulators
- Draft implementation measures
- Implementation of measures in member states

248

Financial Reporting and Analysis

Barriers to Convergence

- **Differences in view** between standard setting bodies
- **Pressure** from business and industry groups
- Many different countries involved

249

Financial Reporting and Analysis

IFRS Financial Reporting Standards Framework

Objective: Fair presentation of the company's:

- Financial position
- Financial performance
- Cash flows

Range of users:

- Investors, employees, lenders, suppliers, customers, creditors, government, public, analysts

250

Financial Reporting and Analysis

IFRS Financial Reporting Standards Framework

Qualitative Characteristics:

1. Understandability
2. Relevance
3. Reliability
4. Comparabilty

251

Financial Reporting and Analysis

Constraints

- Ideal to have all 4 characteristics
- In reality there are trade-offs:
  - Relevancy versus Reliability
  - Benefits versus Costs
  - Excludes non-quantifiable information

252

Financial Reporting and Analysis

IFRS Elements of Financial Statements

- Assets
  - Resources controlled by the entity resulting from past transactions
  - Probable future economic benefit flow to enterprise
- Liabilities
  - Obligations resulting from past events
  - Settlement results in probable resource outflow
- Equity
  - Shareholders' residual interest
  - Assets – Liabilities

253

Financial Reporting and Analysis

IFRS Elements of Financial Statements

- Income
  - Increases in economic benefits:
    - Enhancement of assets
    - Decrease of liabilities
    - Revenue and gains

    (Enhancement of assets and decrease of liabilities: That result in an increase in equity)
- Expenses
  - Decreases in economic benefits:
    - Outflows/depletion of assets
    - Increases in liabilities
    - Expenses and losses

    (Outflows/depletion of assets and increases in liabilities: That result in a decrease in equity)

254

Financial Reporting and Analysis

IFRS Measurement/Recognition

Measurement:
- Historical Cost
- Current Cost
- Realizable Value
- Present Value
- Fair Value

Recognition:
- Probable flows of benefit
- Measured with reliability

255

Financial Reporting and Analysis

IASB General Requirements IAS 1

Required Financial Statements
- Balance Sheet
- Income Statement
- Change in Equity
- Cash Flow Statement
- Accounting policies and notes

Fundamental Principles
- Fair Presentation
- Going Concern
- Accrual Basis
- Consistency
- Materiality

Presentation Requirements
- Aggregation where appropriate
- No offsetting
- Classified balance sheet
- Minimum information on face
- Minimum disclosure
- Comparative info

256

Financial Reporting and Analysis

IFRS vs. US GAAP Frameworks

- Joint IASB-FASB project – 2004
- Common conceptual framework
  - Objectives
  - Qualitative characteristics
  - Element recognition
  - Measurement

257

Financial Reporting and Analysis

Characteristics of an Effective Framework

- Transparency
  - Accounts reflect economic substance
  - Full disclosure and fair presentation
- Comprehensiveness
  - Full spectrum of financial transactions
  - Framework flexible enough to adapt to new transactions
- Consistency
  - Transactions measured and presented in a similar way (across companies and time)
  - Sufficient flexibility to show economic substance

258

Financial Reporting and Analysis

Barriers to a Single Framework

- Valuation
  - Historic cost = minimal judgement - reliable
  - Fair Value = considerable judgement – relevant
  - Both IASB and FASB recognize that some elements should be measured at fair value
- Standard Setting
  - Principles-based – few specific rules
  - Rules-based – prescriptive but not flexible
  - Objectives-based – combines principles and rules

259

Financial Reporting and Analysis

Barriers to a Single Framework

- Measurement
  - 2 potential approaches:
    - B/S Asset/Liability approach
    - I/S Revenue/Expense approach
  - Standards regarding one statement will have an effect on the other—conflict
  - Standard writers—focus asset/liability approach

260

The Income Statement

Financial Reporting and Analysis - Book 3

Financial Reporting and Analysis

Income Statement

Dynamic Statement *"The Bottom Line"*

Revenue – Expenses = Net Income

- **Revenues:** Inflows from a firm's primary operations
- **Expenses:** Cost of producing goods and services sold over the period
- **Gains/Losses:** Increases/decreases in equity or net assets from peripheral or incidental transactions

EPS/Diluted EPS

Analyst focus = profitability/growth

262

Financial Reporting and Analysis

Revenue Recognition Methods

Sales-basis method: Used when good or service is provided at time of sale, cash or credit with high payment probability (majority of transactions)

Exceptions

1) Percentage-of-completion method: Used for L-T projects under contract, with **reliable estimates** of revenues, costs and completion time

2) Completed-contract method: Used for L-T projects when there is no contract, or estimates of revenue or costs are unreliable
Revenue/expenses/profit are not recognized until **project is completed**

263

Financial Reporting and Analysis

Revenue Recognition Methods

3) Installment sales method: Used when you cannot estimate likelihood of collection, but cost of goods/services is known—Revenue and profit are based on percentage of cash collected

4) Cost recovery method **(most extreme):** Used when cost of goods/services is unknown and when you cannot estimate the likelihood of collection—Only recognize profit after all costs are recovered

264

Percentage-of-completion Problem

3-yr. contract for $1.8 million, estimated profit $600,000

Yr. 1: costs $400,000, invoiced $800,000, cash collected $500,000

What is Yr. 1 Revenue and profit?

Percentage-of-Completion (POC) vs. Completed Contract (CC) Method

- Net income is **higher** for POC because CC does not recognize any revenue until completion
- Income volatility is **greater** with CC method because POC recognizes some revenue and income each year instead of all at one time
- Cash flow is the **same** for both (CF is unaffected by the revenue recognition method used)

Financial Reporting and Analysis

Barter

- Exchange of goods or services between two parties (no exchange of cash)
- A agrees to exchange inventory in exchange for a service provided by B
- IASB: Revenue = fair value of similar non-barter transactions with unrelated parties
- FASB: Revenue = fair value only if the company has received cash payments for such services historically

267

Financial Reporting and Analysis

Gross vs. Net Reporting

- Internet-based merchandising companies
- Sell product but never hold in inventory
- Arrangement for supplier to ship directly to end customer

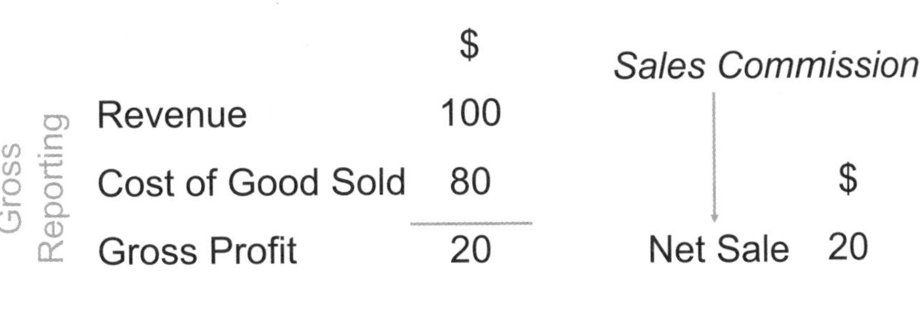

268

Financial Reporting and Analysis

Gross vs. Net Reporting

- U.S. GAAP Report Gross if:
  - Company is primary obligator
  - Bears inventory risk
  - Bears credit risk
  - Can choose supplier
  - Latitude to set price

If criteria is not met then company is acting as an agent = report net

269

Financial Reporting and Analysis

Implications for Analysis

- Review revenue recognition policies in footnotes
- Earlier revenue recognition = aggressive
- Later revenue recognition = conservative
- Consider estimates used in methods
- Assess how different policies affect financial ratios

270

Financial Reporting and Analysis

Expense Recognition

- Accrual basis – Matching Principle
  - Match costs against the recognized revenues
  - Examples
    - Inventory
    - Depreciation/Amortization
    - Warranty expense
    - Doubtful debt expense
- Period Expenses
  - Expenditures that less-directly match the timing of revenues, e.g., Admin costs

271

Financial Reporting and Analysis

Analysis Implications

- Revenue Recognition
- Warranty Expense
- Depreciation
- Amortization
- Doubtful Debt Provisions
- Inventory Valuation

All require significant estimates and assumptions affecting Net Income

- Review year-on-year consistency
- Review footnotes and MD&A

272

Financial Reporting and Analysis

Unusual or Infrequent Items

- "Or" is the key word that describes these items
- Reported pre-tax before net income from continuing operations (above the line)
- Items include:

  Gain (loss) from disposal of a *business segment or assets*

  Gain (loss) from sale of investment in subsidiary

  Provisions for environmental remediation

  Impairments, write-offs, write-downs, restructuring

  Integration expense for recently acquired business

273

Financial Reporting and Analysis

Discontinued Operations

- Operations that management has decided to dispose of but (1) has not done so yet or (2) did so in current year after operations generated profit or loss
- Reported net of taxes after net income from continuing operations (below the line)
- Assets, operations, and financing activities must be physically and operationally distinct from firm

274

Financial Reporting and Analysis

Extraordinary Items – U.S. GAAP

- Items that are both unusual and infrequent
- Reported net of taxes after net income from continuing operations (below the line)
- Items include:
  - Losses from expropriation of assets
  - Uninsured losses from natural disaster

Prohibited under IAS 1

275

Financial Reporting and Analysis

Accounting Changes

Two types of accounting changes:

1) Change in accounting principle

(e.g., LIFO to FIFO)

- Retrospective application: IFRS and U.S. GAAP require prior years' data shown in the financial statements to be adjusted

276

Financial Reporting and Analysis

Accounting Changes

2) Change in accounting estimate

(e.g., change in the estimated useful life of a depreciable asset)

Does not require restatement of prior period earnings

Disclosed in footnotes

Typically, changes do not affect cash flow

277

Financial Reporting and Analysis

Accounting Changes

Prior Period Adjustments

- Correcting errors or changing from an incorrect accounting method to one that is acceptable under GAAP
- Typically requires restatement of prior period financial statements
- Must **disclose** the nature of the error and its effect on net income

278

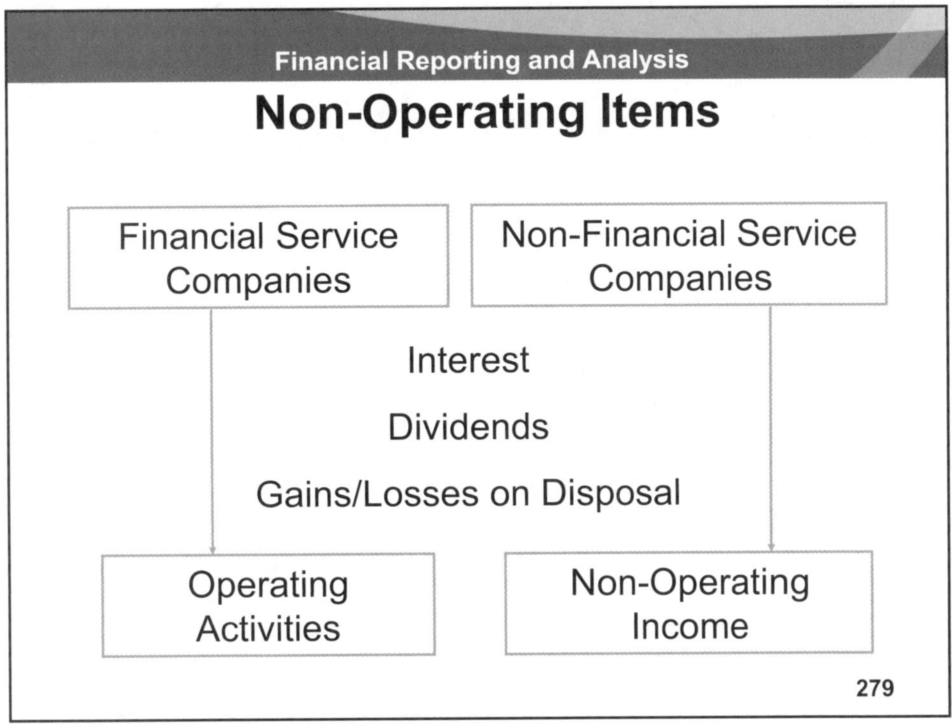

Financial Reporting and Analysis

Weighted Shares Outstanding – Problem

1/1/X3	Shares outstanding	10,000
5/1/X3	Shares issued	2,000
7/1/X3	3 for 2 stock split	
9/1/X3	Shares repurchased	3,000

What is weighted average number of shares outstanding?

280

Financial Reporting and Analysis

Simple vs. Complex Capital Structures

- A simple capital structure contains no *potentially* dilutive securities

  Firm reports only basic EPS

- A complex capital structure contains *potentially* dilutive securities

  Firm must report both basic and diluted EPS

281

Financial Reporting and Analysis

Dilutive vs. Antidilutive Securities

Potentially dilutive securities

- Stock options
- Warrants
- Convertible debt
- Convertible preferred stock

- **Dilutive securities** decrease EPS if exercised or converted to common stock
- **Antidilutive securities** increase EPS if exercised or converted to common stock

282

Financial Reporting and Analysis

Basic EPS

$$\text{Basic EPS} = \frac{\text{NI} - \text{Preferred Div}}{\text{Weight Ave N}^{\text{o}}\text{ Common Stock}}$$

- Net income minus preferred dividends equals earnings available to common stockholders (EAC)
- Note that common stock dividends are not subtracted from net income

283

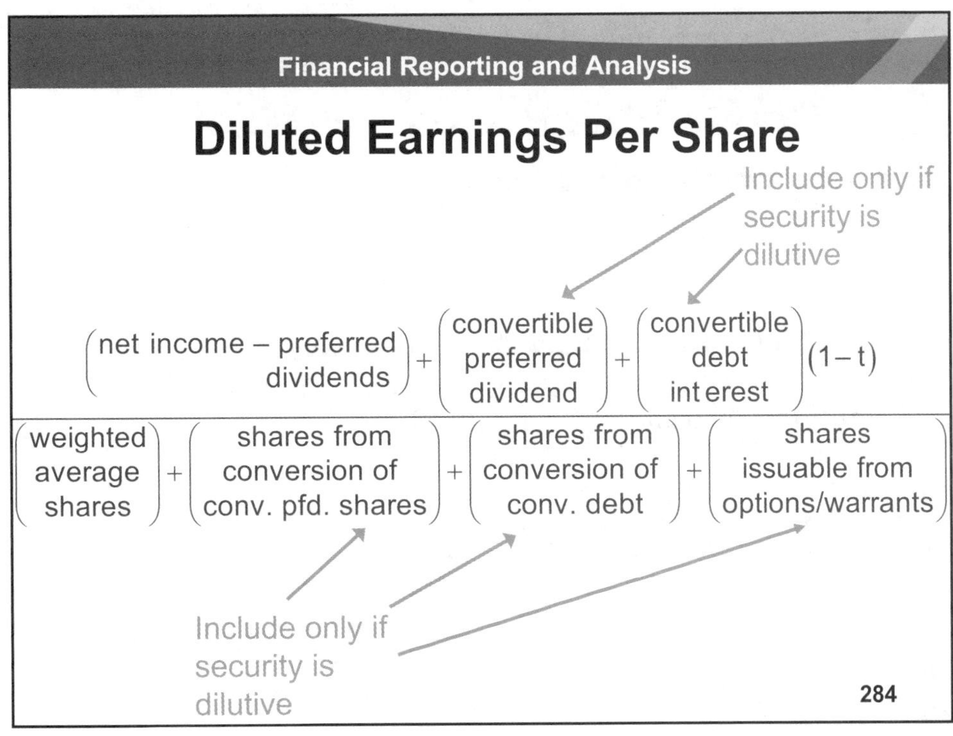

Financial Reporting and Analysis
Diluted Earnings Per Share
Include only if security is dilutive
(net income – preferred dividends) + (convertible preferred dividend) + (convertible debt interest)(1–t)
(weighted average shares) + (shares from conversion of conv. pfd. shares) + (shares from conversion of conv. debt) + (shares issuable from options/warrants)
Include only if security is dilutive
284

Financial Reporting and Analysis

Diluted EPS Problem

Earnings available to common, year 20X9	$4,000,000
Common stock	2,000,000 sh
Basic EPS	$2.00
Tax rate	35%

$5,000,000 par value of 7% convertible preferred stock
Each $10 par value of preferred can be converted to 1.1 sh.

Calculate fully diluted EPS for 20X9.

285

Financial Reporting and Analysis

Convertible Bonds – Problem

Earnings available to common, year 20X9	$1,500,000
Common stock	1,000,000 sh
Basic EPS	$1.50
Tax rate	30%

$2,000,000 par value of 8% convertible bonds.
Each $1,000 bond can be converted to 35 common shares.
Calculate fully diluted EPS for 20X9

286

Financial Reporting and Analysis

Employee Stock Options Example

Average price of common stock during year	$20
Exercise price	$16
Year-end common stock price	$13
Number of options outstanding in the year	100,000

Calculate the # shares to account for dilution

$20 > $16 so options are dilutive

Add (20 – 16)/20 × 100,000 = 20,000 shares to denominator

287

Financial Reporting and Analysis

Common-Size Income Statement

Example: Consider a common-size income statement that reveals the following (selected items only).

Income statement item	20X7	20X8	Industry Avg.
COGS	58%	62%	60%
SG&A	18%	22%	18%
Net Income	9%	8%	10%

288

Financial Reporting and Analysis

Measures of Operating Performance

Operating profitability ratios:

$$\text{gross profit margin} = \frac{\text{gross profit}}{\text{net sales}}$$

$$\text{net profit margin} = \frac{\text{net income}}{\text{net sales}}$$

Both can be seen on common-size income statement

289

Financial Reporting and Analysis

Comprehensive Income

Comprehensive Income = the change in equity from non-owner sources

Net Income

Other Comprehensive Income:

+Δ Foreign Currency Translation Adjustment

+Δ Minimum Pension Liability Adjustment

+Δ Unrealized gains or losses on derivatives contracts accounted for as hedges

+Δ Unrealized gains and losses on available for sale securities

Comprehensive Income

290

Understanding the Balance Sheet

Financial Reporting and Analysis - Book 3

Financial Reporting and Analysis

Balance Sheet

Static Statement

Assets = Liabilities + Owners Equity

Assets – Liabilities = Owners Equity

- **Assets:** Firm's economic resources
- **Liabilities:** Probable future economic costs
- **Owners' equity:** Residual interest in assets after deducting liabilities

Analyst's Focus: Liquidity
Solvency
Financial Position

292

Financial Reporting and Analysis

Components and Format of Balance Sheet

Balance Sheet	$m		$m
Current Assets		**Current Liabilities**	70
Cash	50	**Long Term Liabilities**	180
Others	100		250
	150	**Owners Equity**	
Long Life Assets		Contributed Capital	100
Investments	20	Retained Earnings	70
PP&E	200		170
Intangibles	50	**Liabilities and Equity**	420
Total Assets	420		

293

Financial Reporting and Analysis

Accruals

Revenue reported before cash is received:

- Accounts Receivable – asset
- Accrued Revenue – asset

Cash paid before and expense is reported:

- Prepaid Expense – asset

Cash Received before revenue is reported:

- Deferred Revenue – liability

Expense Recorded before cash is paid:

- Accrued Expense – liability
- Accounts Payable – liability

294

Financial Reporting and Analysis

Assets

Asset Recognition

- Probable future flow of future economic benefit to the entity
- Measurable with reliability

Assets Disclosed on the B/S

Cash and Equivalents	Property Plant and Equipment
Inventories	Investment Property
Trade and other Receivables	Intangible Assets
Prepaid Expenses	Equity a/c Investments
Financial Assets	Natural Resources
Deferred Tax Assets	Assets held for sale

295

Financial Reporting and Analysis

Liabilities

Liability Recognition

- Probable sacrifice of future economic benefit to the entity as a result of past transactions/events
- Amounts received but not reported as revenue in the income statement
- Amounts reported as expenses but which have not been paid

Liabilities Disclosed on the B/S

Bank Borrowings	Financial Liabilities
Notes Payable	Accrued Liabilities
Provisions	Deferred Tax Liabilities
Unearned Revenues	

296

Financial Reporting and Analysis

Equity

Assets – Liabilities = Equity

Net Assets

Capital Characteristics

- Permanent
- No mandatory charges against earnings
- Legal subordination to creditors

297

Financial Reporting and Analysis

Balance Sheet Format

- Report Format
  - Assets, Liabilities and Equity in a single column
- Account Format
  - Assets on the left
  - Liabilities and Equity on the right
- Classified Balance Sheet
  - Grouping of accounts into sub-categories
  - Current vs. non-current
  - Financial vs. non-financial
  - Liquidity based presentation

298

Financial Reporting and Analysis

Measurement of Assets/Liabilities

B/S contains assets/liabilities at both:

Fair Value

Amount at which:

An asset could be exchanged

A liability could be settled

Arm's-length transactions

Market Price = Fair Market value

Historic Cost

Cost or fair value at acquisition

Includes all costs of acquisition and preparation

Other basis

Current Cost (replacement)

Present Value

299

Financial Reporting and Analysis

Balance Sheet Disclosure

- Specific accounting policies used
  - Policy
  - Measurement basis
  - Judgements used
- Key assumptions about the future
- Terms of debt agreements
- Lease information
- Off-balance-sheet financing
- Segmental data
- Contingent assets and liabilities
- Pension plan disclosure

300

Financial Reporting and Analysis

Current Liabilities

- Trade and other payables (Accounts payable)
- Notes payable
- Current portion of non-current borrowings
- Current tax payable
- Accrued liabilities
- Unearned revenue

301

Financial Reporting and Analysis

Current Assets

- Cash or cash equivalents
- Marketable securities
- Trade receivables (net of bad debt provision): accounts receivable/customer related notes receivable
- Inventory:
  - Raw Materials
  - Finished Good
  - Work in Progress
- Others e.g., prepaid expenses

302

Financial Reporting and Analysis

Noncurrent Assets

Current assets

Cash and other assets that will likely be converted into cash or used up within one year or one operating cycle, whichever is greater

Noncurrent Assets

Held for continuing use within the business not resale not consumed or disposed in the current period

303

Financial Reporting and Analysis

Long-Term Assets

- **Tangible assets**: e.g., land, buildings, and equipment (depreciation)
- **Intangible assets**: e.g., copyrights, patents, trademarks, franchises, and goodwill (amortize or test for impairment)
- **Natural resources**: oil fields, mines, timberland (depletion)

Plant property and equipment recorded at purchase cost including shipping and installation, or construction cost including labor, materials, overhead, and interest

304

Financial Reporting and Analysis

Expensed Items

- Internally generated brands, mastheads, publishing titles, customer lists, etc.
- Start-up costs
- Training costs
- Admin and general overhead
- Advertising and promotion
- Relocation and reorganization costs
- Redundancy and termination costs
- R&D (Development may be capitalized IAS)

305

Financial Reporting and Analysis

Goodwill

Goodwill is:

Price of acquisition minus fair market value of the acquired net assets

Asset with indefinite life, not amortized, tested for impairment (value below balance sheet goodwill)

306

Financial Reporting and Analysis

Financial Assets/Liabilities

- Stocks
- Bonds
- Receivables
- Notes Receivable
- Notes Payable
- Loans
- Derivatives

307

Financial Reporting and Analysis

Marketable Securities

Classification of securities based upon company's intent with regard to eventual sale:

Held-to-maturity securities:

- Debt securities which the company intends to hold to maturity
- Securities are carried at cost
- Interest and realized gains/(losses) on sale to Income Statement

Available-for-sale securities:

- May be sold to satisfy company needs
- Debt or equity
- Current or non-current
- Carried in the balance sheet at market value
- Interest and realized gains/(losses) on sale to Income Statement

308

Marketable Securities

Trading securities:

- acquired for the purpose of selling in the near term
- carried in the balance sheet as current assets at market value
- income statement includes interest, dividends, realized & unrealized gains/losses

309

Components of Equity

- Capital Contributed by Owners
- Minority Interest (not owned by firm)
- Retained Earnings
- Treasury Stock (reduces equity)
- Accumulated Other Comprehensive Income

310

Financial Reporting and Analysis

Common Size Balance Sheet

$$\frac{\text{Balance sheet account}}{\text{Total assets}} \quad \textit{e.g.} \quad \frac{\textit{Inventory}}{\textit{Total Assets}}$$

Inventory as percentage of total assets

311

Financial Reporting and Analysis

Liquidity Ratios

Current ratio $$\frac{\text{Current assets}}{\text{Current liabilities}}$$

Quick ratio $$\frac{\text{Current assets} - \text{inventory}}{\text{Current liabilities}}$$

Cash ratio $$\frac{\text{Cash + marketable securities}}{\text{Current liabilities}}$$

312

Financial Reporting and Analysis

Solvency Ratios

Long-Term Debt to Equity	$\frac{\text{Total Long-Term Debt}}{\text{Total Equity}}$
Debt to Equity	$\frac{\text{Total Debt}}{\text{Total Equity}}$
Total Debt	$\frac{\text{Total Debt}}{\text{Total Assets}}$
Financial Leverage	$\frac{\text{Total Assets}}{\text{Total Equity}}$

313

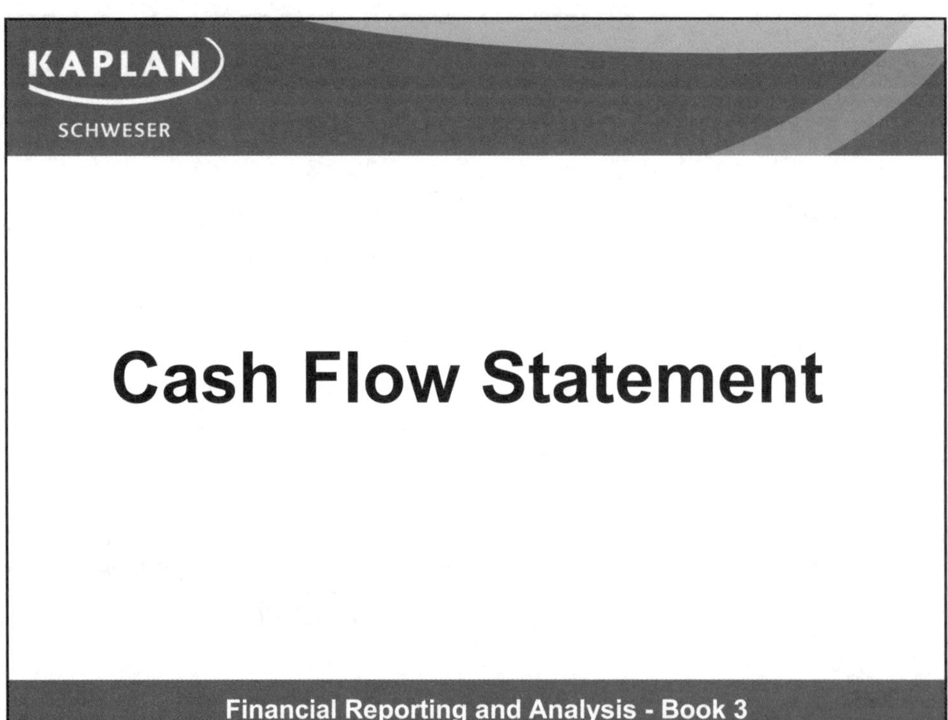

Financial Reporting and Analysis

Three Elements of Cash Flow

Cash flow from operations (CFO)
\+ Cash flow from investing (CFI)
\+ Cash flow from financing (CFF)
Change in the cash balance
\+ Beginning cash (last years B/S)
Ending cash balance (this years B/S)

315

Financial Reporting and Analysis

Statement of CFO: Direct vs. Indirect Method

Direct vs. indirect method refers only to the calculation of CFO, the value of CFO is the same for both methods; CFI and CFF are unaffected

- Direct method: begin at the top of the income statement and identify cash inflows and outflows
- Indirect method: begin at the bottom of the income statement with net income and make necessary adjustments

316

Financial Reporting and Analysis

Direct Method of Presenting CFO

Cash received from customers
+ Cash dividends received
+ Cash interest received
+ Other cash income
– Payments to suppliers
– Cash expenses (wages, etc.)
– Cash interest paid
– Cash taxes paid

CFO

317

Financial Reporting and Analysis

CFO – Indirect Method

1. Start with Net Income
2. Adjust for relevant Balance Sheet changes:

Asset: ↑increase uses cash, ↓decrease is a source of cash

Liability: ↑increase is a source of cash, ↓decrease uses cash

Inventory, Receivables, Accounts Payable, Deferred Taxes

3. Add back **depreciation and amortization**
4. Deduct gains/add back losses on asset disposal (these are CFI, not CFO)

318

Financial Reporting and Analysis

Investing Cash Flows (CFI)

- Purchase or sale of non-current assets or marketable securities (not cash equivalents)
- Investment in/purchase of company/joint ventures
- Gain on sale is inflow, loss on sale is outflow

  Change in fixed assets adjusted for change in accumulated depreciation

  Beginning assets = £10 mill

  Ending assets = £10.5 mill

  Depreciation for the year = £1 mill

  CFI = (10.5 + 1) – 10 = £1.5 mill

319

Financial Reporting and Analysis

Financing Cash Flows

Issue and redemption of:

- Common stock
- Preferred stock
- Treasury Stock repurchases
- Debt
- Dividend payments (divs rec'd = CFO) U.S. GAAP

320

Financial Reporting and Analysis

U.S. GAAP vs IFRS

	U.S. GAAP (SFAS 95)	IAS GAAP (IAS 7)
Interest received	CFO	CFO or CFI
Interest paid	CFO	CFO or CFF
Dividends received	CFO	CFO or CFI
Dividends paid	CFF	CFO or CFF
Taxes Paid	CFO	CFO or CFI & CFF
Bank Overdraft	CFF	*

* Considered part of cash and cash equivalents

321

Financial Reporting and Analysis

Non-Cash Investing and Financing Activities

- Converting debt or preferred into common
- Assets acquired under capital leases
- Purchase of assets by issuing debt/equity
- Exchanging one non-cash asset for another
- Stock dividends

322

Financial Reporting and Analysis

Putting the Cash Flow Statement Together

	$
Cash flow from operations	85,000
Cash flow from investments	(20,000)
Cash flow from financing	(17,000)
Net increase in cash	48,000
Cash balance 12/31/X2	18,000
Cash balance 12/31/X3	66,000

323

Financial Reporting and Analysis

Converting an Indirect Statement to a Direct Statement of Cash Flows

Most firms use the indirect method, but the analyst may want information on the cash flows by function; some examples of this technique are:

Net sales – Δ accounts receivable + Δ advances from customers = cash collections

Cost of goods sold – Δ inventory + Δ accounts payable = cash paid for inputs

Interest expense + Δ interest payable = cash interest

324

Financial Reporting and Analysis

Cash Flow Statement Analysis

Benefits for the analyst:

- Do regular operations generate enough cash to sustain the business?
- Is enough cash is generated to pay off maturing debt?
- Highlights the need for additional finance
- Ability to meet unexpected obligations
- Flexibility to take advantage of new business opportunities

325

Financial Reporting and Analysis

Analysis

1. Analyze the major sources and uses of cash flow (CFO, CFI, CFF)
   - Where are the major sources and uses?
   - Is CFO positive and sufficient to cover capex?
2. Analyze CFO
   - What are the major determinants of CFO?
   - Is CFO higher or lower than NI?
   - How consistent is CFO?

326

Financial Reporting and Analysis

Analysis

3. Analyze CFI
   - What is cash being spent on?
   - Is the company investing in PP&E?
   - What acquisitions have been made?

4. Analyze CFF
   - How is the company financing CFI and CFO?
   - Is the company raising or repaying capital?
   - What dividends are being returned to owners?

327

Financial Reporting and Analysis

Common Size Statements

2 Approaches

Show each item as a % on Net Revenue

Show each inflow as a % of total inflows

Show each outflow as a % of total outflows

Useful for:

Trend analysis (time series)

Forecasting future cash flows

328

Financial Reporting and Analysis

Free Cash Flow (FCF)

- FCF is cash available for discretionary uses
- Frequently used to value firms

$$FCFF = CFO + Int\,(1-T) - FCInv$$

$$FCFE = CFO - FCInv + Net\ Debt\ Increase$$

329

Financial Reporting and Analysis

Cash Flow Performance Ratios

Cash Flow to Revenue	$\frac{CFO}{Net\ Revenue}$
Cash Return on Assets	$\frac{CFO}{Ave\ Total\ Assets}$
Cash Return on Equity	$\frac{CFO}{Ave\ Equity}$
Cash to Income	$\frac{CFO}{Operating\ Income}$

330

Financial Reporting and Analysis

Cash Flow Performance Ratios

Cash Flow Per Share $= \dfrac{\text{CFO} - \text{Pref Div}}{\text{N}^{\text{o}}\ \text{Common Stock}}$

331

Financial Reporting and Analysis

Cash Flow Coverage Ratios

Debt Coverage $= \dfrac{\text{CFO}}{\text{Total Debt}}$

Interest Coverage $= \dfrac{\text{CFO} + \text{Interest} + \text{Tax}}{\text{Interest Paid}}$

Reinvestment $= \dfrac{\text{CFO}}{\text{Cash Paid for Long-term Assets}}$

332

Financial Reporting and Analysis

Cash Flow Coverage Ratios

Debt Payment: $\dfrac{\text{CFO}}{\text{Cash Paid for Long-term Debt Repayment}}$

Dividend Payment: $\dfrac{\text{CFO}}{\text{Dividends Paid}}$

Investing and Financing: $\dfrac{\text{CFO}}{\text{Cash Outflows for CFI \& CFF}}$

333

Financial Analysis Techniques

Financial Reporting and Analysis - Book 3

Financial Reporting and Analysis

Limitations of Financial Ratios

- **Not useful in isolation** – only valid when compared to other firms or the company's historical performance
- **Different accounting treatments** – particularly when analyzing non-U.S. firms
- **Finding comparable industry ratios** for companies that operate in multiple industries (homogeneity of operating activities)
- Determining the target or comparison value requires some **range of acceptable values**

335

Financial Reporting and Analysis

Interpreting Ratios

1. **Cross-sectional** analysis:

   Comparison to industry norm or average

2. **Time-series** analysis (trend analysis):

   Comparison to a company's past ratios

336

Financial Reporting and Analysis

Vertical Common-Size Statements

Income Statement

$$\frac{\text{Income Statement Account}}{\text{Sales}} \quad \text{e.g.,} \quad \frac{\textit{Marketing Expense}}{\textit{Sales}}$$

Balance Sheet

$$\frac{\text{Balance Sheet Account}}{\text{Total Assets}} \quad \text{e.g.,} \quad \frac{\textit{Inventory}}{\textit{Total Assets}}$$

337

Financial Reporting and Analysis

Horizontal Common-Size Statements

- Each line shown as a relative to some base year
- Facilitates trend analysis

Assets	Year 1	Year 2	Year 3
Cash	1.0	1.2	1.1
AR	1.0	1.3	1.0
Inventory	1.0	0.8	1.2
PP&E	1.0	1.5	2.0
Total	1.0	1.25	1.5

338

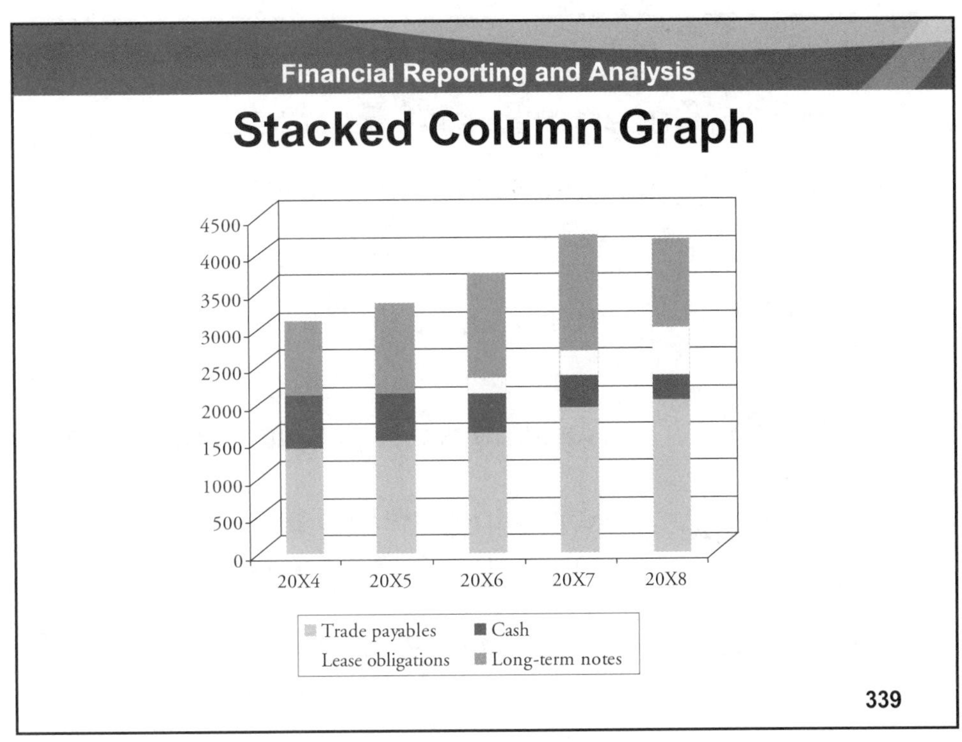
Financial Reporting and Analysis
Stacked Column Graph
4500
4000
3500
3000
2500
2000
1500
1000
500
0
20X4
20X5
20X6
20X7
20X8
Trade payables
Cash
Lease obligations
Long-term notes
339

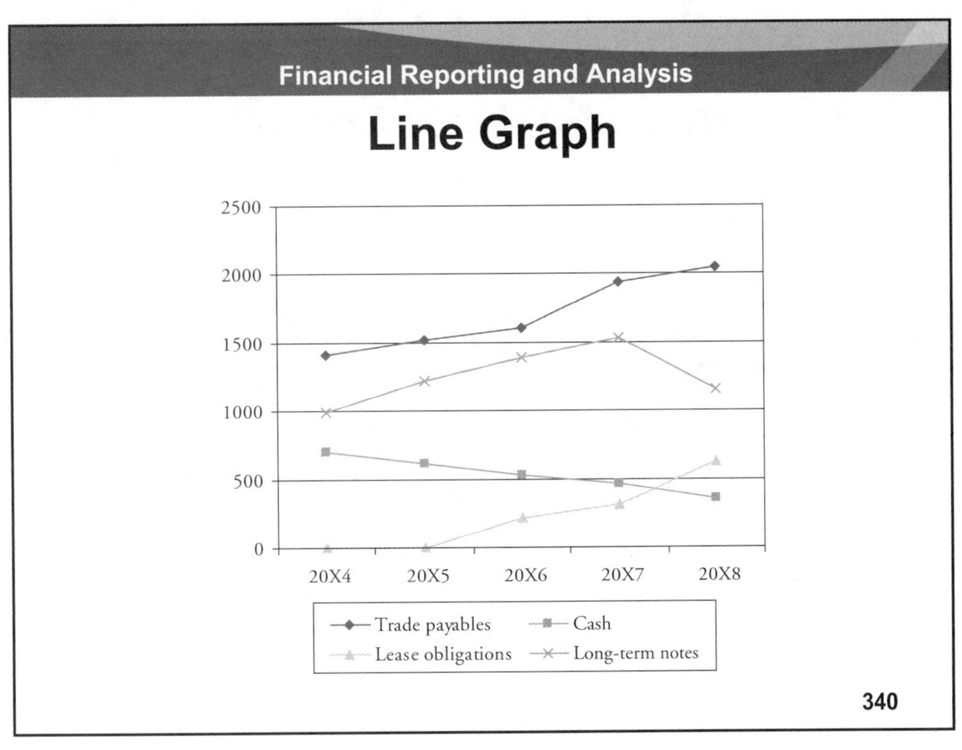
Financial Reporting and Analysis
Line Graph
2500
2000
1500
1000
500
0
20X4
20X5
20X6
20X7
20X8
Trade payables
Cash
Lease obligations
Long-term notes
340

Financial Reporting and Analysis

Categories of Ratios

- **Activity** → Efficiency of day-to-day tasks/operations
- **Liquidity** → Ability to meet short-term liabilities
- **Solvency** → Ability to meet long-term obligations
- **Profitability** → Ability to generate profitable sales from asset base
- **Valuation** → Quantity of asset or flow associated with an ownership claim

341

Financial Reporting and Analysis

Ratio Analysis Context

1. Company goals and strategy
2. Industry norms
   - Ratios may be **industry specific**
   - **Multiple lines** of business distort aggregate ratios
   - Differences in **accounting methods**
3. Economic conditions
   - Cyclical businesses and the **stage of the business cycle**

342

Financial Reporting and Analysis

Ratio Analysis

Some general rules:

- For ratios that use only **income statement items**, use the values from the current income statement
- For ratios using only **balance sheet items**, use the values from the current balance sheet
- For ratios using **both income statement and balance sheet items**, use the value from the current income statement and the **average value for the balance sheet item**

343

Financial Reporting and Analysis

Activity Ratios

$$\textbf{Inventory turnover} = \frac{\text{Cost of goods sold}}{\text{Average inventory}}$$

$$\textbf{Days of inventory on hand (DOH)} = \frac{365}{\text{Inventory turnover}}$$

$$\textbf{Receivables turnover} = \frac{\text{Revenue}}{\text{Average receivables}}$$

$$\textbf{Days of sales outstanding (DSO)} = \frac{365}{\text{Receivables turnover}}$$

344

Financial Reporting and Analysis

Activity Ratios

$$\textbf{Payables turnover} = \frac{\text{Purchases}}{\text{Average trade payables}}$$

$$\textbf{Number of days of payables} = \frac{365}{\text{Payables turnover}}$$

$$\textbf{Working capital turnover} = \frac{\text{Revenue}}{\text{Average working capital}}$$

$$\textbf{Working capital} = \text{Current assets} - \text{Current liabilities}$$

345

Financial Reporting and Analysis

Activity Ratios

$$\textbf{Fixed asset turnover} = \frac{\text{Revenue}}{\text{Average net fixed assets}}$$

↓

Net of accumulated depreciation

$$\textbf{Total asset turnover} = \frac{\text{Revenue}}{\text{Average total assets}}$$

346

Financial Reporting and Analysis

Liquidity Ratios

Current ratio $= \dfrac{\text{Current assets}}{\text{Current liabilities}}$

Quick ratio $= \dfrac{\text{Cash + short term marketable securities + receivables}}{\text{Current liabilities}}$

Cash ratio $= \dfrac{\text{Cash + short term marketable securities}}{\text{Current liabilities}}$

347

Financial Reporting and Analysis

Definitions: Liquidity Ratios

Defensive interval ratio $= \dfrac{\text{Cash + short term marketable investments + receivables}}{\text{Daily Cash Expenditure}}$

Cash conversion cycle =

	Days
DOH	X
DSO	X
No of days of payables	(X)
Cash conversion cycle	X

348

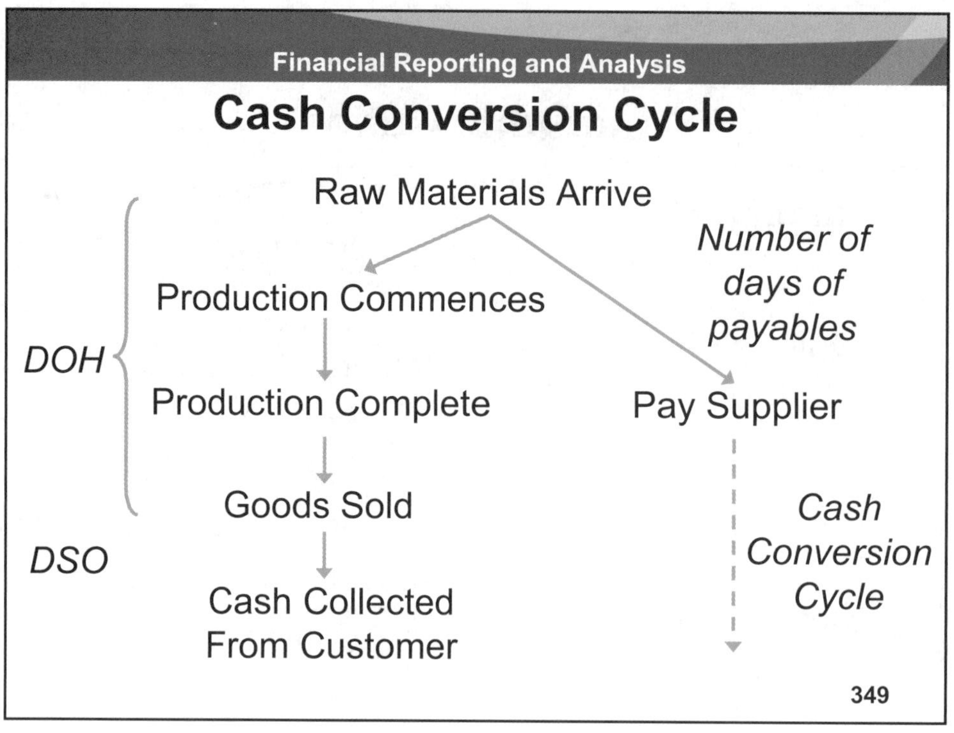
Financial Reporting and Analysis
Cash Conversion Cycle
Raw Materials Arrive
Number of days of payables
Production Commences
DOH
Production Complete
Pay Supplier
Goods Sold
Cash Conversion Cycle
DSO
Cash Collected From Customer
349

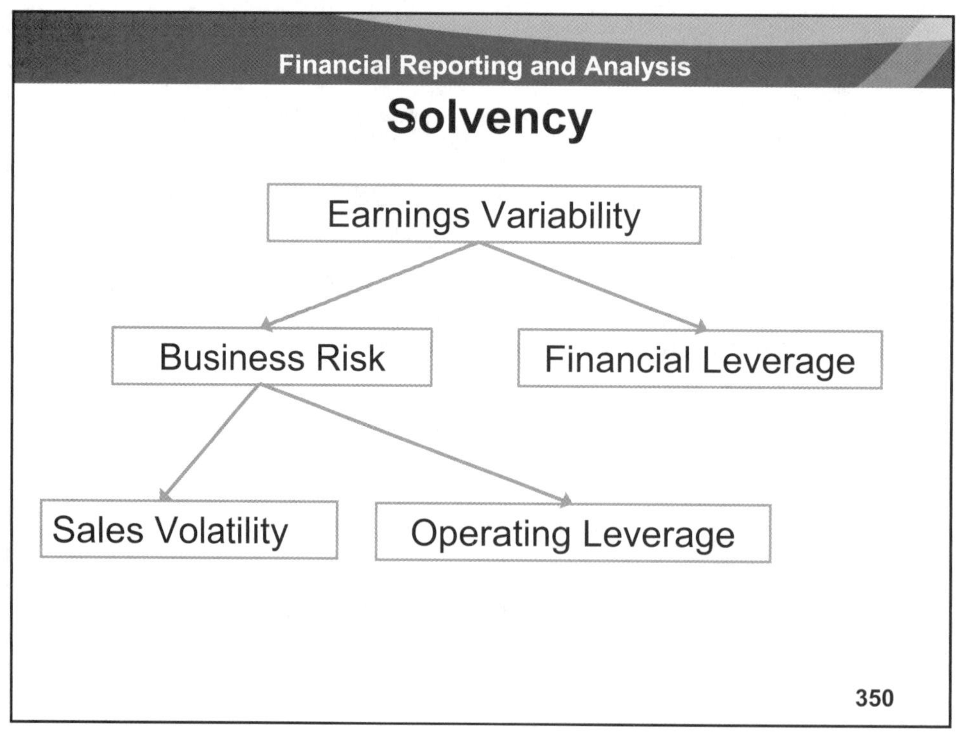
Financial Reporting and Analysis
Solvency
Earnings Variability
Business Risk
Financial Leverage
Sales Volatility
Operating Leverage
350

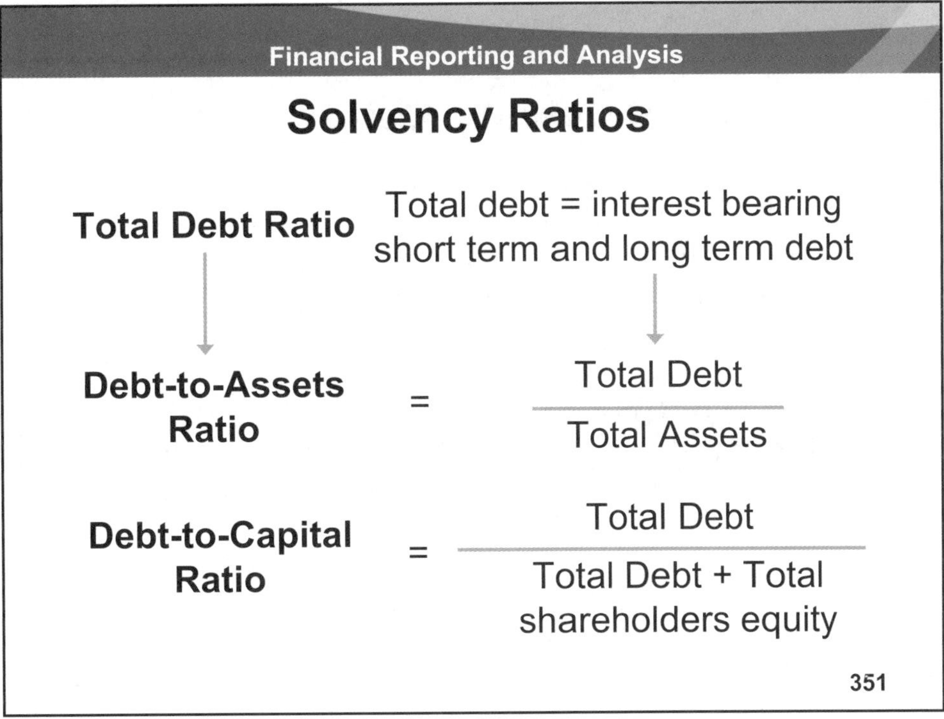

Financial Reporting and Analysis

Solvency Ratios

Debt-to-equity ratio = $\frac{\text{Total debt}}{\text{Total shareholders' equity}}$

Financial leverage ratio = $\frac{\text{Average total assets}}{\text{Average total equity}}$

352

Financial Reporting and Analysis

Solvency Ratios

$$\text{Interest coverage} = \frac{\text{EBIT}}{\text{Interest payments}}$$

$$\text{Fixed charge coverage} = \frac{\text{EBIT + lease payments}}{\text{Interest payments + lease payments}}$$

353

Financial Reporting and Analysis

Profitability Ratios

$$\text{Gross profit margin} = \frac{\text{Gross profit}}{\text{Revenue}}$$

$$\text{Operating profit margin} = \frac{\text{Operating income}}{\text{Revenue}}$$

<u>Operating income</u>

Gross profit – operating costs

Approximation = EBIT

EBIT contains non-operating items (dividends rec'd and gains and losses on investment securities)

354

Financial Reporting and Analysis

Profitability Ratios

$$\textbf{Pretax margin} = \frac{\text{Earnings before tax but after interest}}{\text{Revenue}}$$

$$\textbf{Net profit margin} = \frac{\text{Net income}}{\text{Revenue}}$$

Most of the return on sales profitability ratios are on the face of the common-size income statement

355

Financial Reporting and Analysis

Profitability Ratios

$$\textbf{Return on Assets ROA} = \frac{\text{Net Income}}{\text{Average Total Assets}}$$

Alternatively:

$$\textbf{Return on Assets ROA} = \frac{\text{Net Income + Interest Expense (1 – T)}}{\text{Average Total Assets}}$$

$$\textbf{Operating ROA} = \frac{\text{Operating Income}}{\text{Average Total Assets}}$$

356

Financial Reporting and Analysis

Profitability Ratios

$$\text{Return on Total Capital} = \frac{\text{EBIT}}{\text{Short + Long-Term Debt + Equity}}$$

$$\text{Return on Equity ROE} = \frac{\text{Net Income}}{\text{Average Total Equity}}$$

$$\text{Return on Common Equity} = \frac{\text{Net Income – Pref. Div.}}{\text{Average Common Equity}}$$

357

Financial Reporting and Analysis

Integrated Financial Ratio Approach

- Important to **analyze** all ratios **collectively**
- Use information from one ratio category to answer questions raised by another ratio
- Classic example = DuPont analysis

358

Financial Reporting and Analysis

Integrated Financial Ratios – Example

	20X8	20X7	20X6
Current Ratio	2.0	1.5	1.2
Quick Ratio	0.5	0.8	1

	20X8	20X7	20X6
DOH	60	50	30
DSO	20	30	40

What can you conclude about this firm's performance? (Note that years are presented right-to-left)

359

Financial Reporting and Analysis

Integrated Financial Ratios – Example

1. Current ratio up – Quick ratio down – Why?
2. DOH has increased – indicates rising inventory rather than low cash
3. DSO decreasing – collecting cash from customers sooner
4. Current and quick ratios indicate the collected cash is being spent on inventory accumulation
5. Appears collections have been accelerated to make up for poor inventory management

360

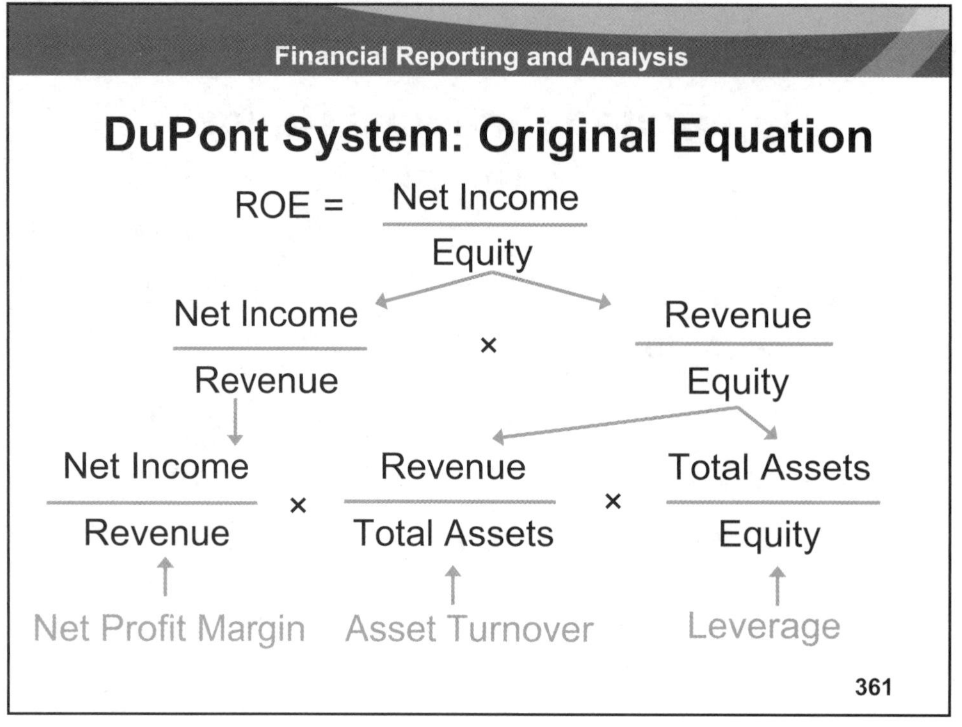
Financial Reporting and Analysis
DuPont System: Original Equation
ROE = Net Income / Equity
Net Income / Revenue × Revenue / Equity
Net Income / Revenue × Revenue / Total Assets × Total Assets / Equity
Net Profit Margin
Asset Turnover
Leverage
361

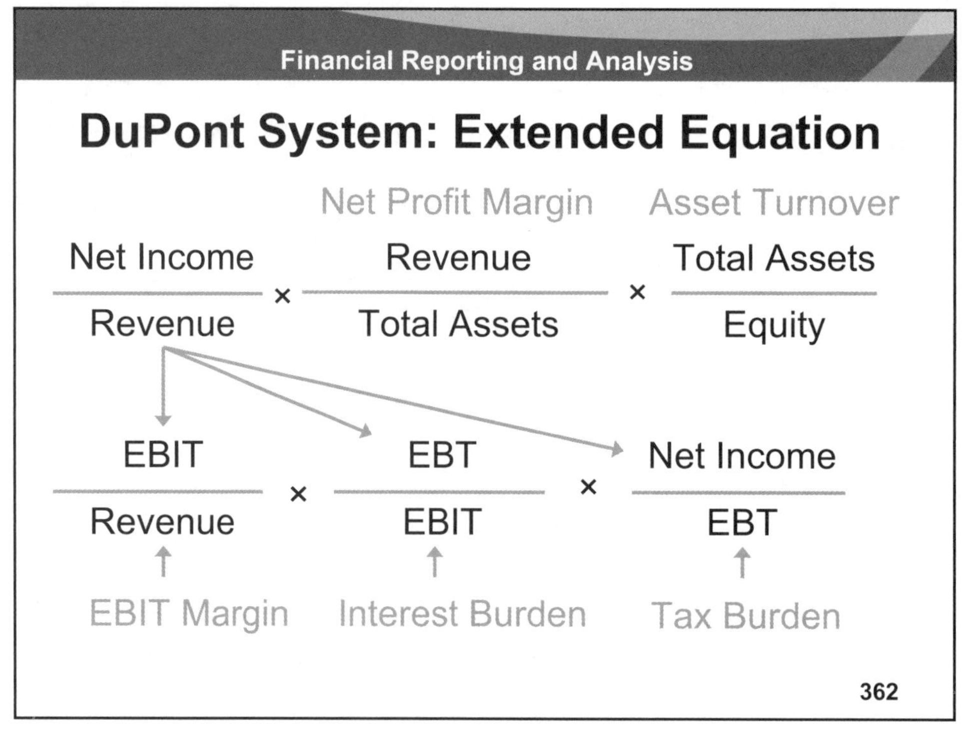
Financial Reporting and Analysis
DuPont System: Extended Equation
Net Profit Margin
Asset Turnover
Net Income / Revenue × Revenue / Total Assets × Total Assets / Equity
EBIT / Revenue × EBT / EBIT × Net Income / EBT
EBIT Margin
Interest Burden
Tax Burden
362

Financial Reporting and Analysis

DuPont System: Extended Equation

EBIT Margin × Interest Burden × Tax Burden × Asset Turnover × Leverage

EBIT Margin ↑ Operating Profit Margin

Tax Burden ↖ 1 – Effective Tax Rate

363

Financial Reporting and Analysis

Per Share Ratios – for Valuation

$$\frac{P}{E} = \frac{\text{Price Per Share}}{\text{Earnings Per Share}}$$

$$\frac{P}{CF} = \frac{\text{Price Per Share}}{\text{Cash Flow Per Share}}$$

$$\frac{P}{S} = \frac{\text{Price Per Share}}{\text{Sales Per Share}}$$

$$\frac{P}{BV} = \frac{\text{Price Per Share}}{\text{Book Value Per Share}}$$

364

Financial Reporting and Analysis

Per-Share Quantities

$$\textbf{Basic EPS} = \frac{\text{NI – Pref Div}}{\text{Weighted Ave \# Ordinary Shares}}$$

$$\textbf{Diluted EPS} = \frac{\text{Income Adjusted for Dilutive Securities}}{\text{Weighted Ave \# Shares Adjusted for Dilution}}$$

$$\textbf{Cash Flow per Share} = \frac{\text{CFO}}{\text{Weighted Ave \# Shares}}$$

365

Financial Reporting and Analysis

Per-Share Quantities

$$\textbf{EBITDA per Share} = \frac{\text{EBITDA}}{\text{Ave \# Ordinary Shares}}$$

$$\textbf{Dividends per Share} = \frac{\text{Common Dividend}}{\text{Weighted Ave \# Common Shares}}$$

366

Financial Reporting and Analysis

Dividend Related Quantities

$$\text{Dividend Payout Ratio} = \frac{\text{Common Dividend}}{\text{Net Income} - \text{Pref Div}}$$

Net Income – Pref Div: Net Income attributable to common shares

$$\text{Retention Rate } (b) = \frac{\text{Net income attributable to common shares} - \text{common dividend}}{\text{Net income attributable to common shares}}$$

367

Financial Reporting and Analysis

Dividend Related Quantities

$$\text{Sustainable Growth Rate} = \text{RR} \times \text{ROE}$$

<u>Retention Rate</u> (RR)

1 – Dividend Payout Ratio

<u>Return on Equity</u> (ROE)

368

Sustainable Growth Rate – Problem

A firm has a dividend payout ratio of 35%, a net profit margin of 10%, an asset turnover of 1.4, and an equity multiplier leverage measure of 1.2. Estimate the firm's sustainable growth rate.

369

Using Ratios for Equity Analysis

Research has found ratios (and changes in ratios) can be useful in forecasting earnings and stock returns (valuation)

Some items useful in forecasting:

% change in: current ratio • quick ratio • inventory • inventory turnover • inventory/total assets • sales • depreciation • capex/assets • asset turnover • depreciation/plant assets • total assets

ROE • Δ ROE • debt/equity • ROA • gross margin • working capital/assets • dividends/cash flow • Δ dividend • % debt repaid • operating ROA • pretax margin

370

Financial Reporting and Analysis

Standard and Poor's Credit Ratios

$$\text{Return on total capital} = \frac{\text{EBIT}}{\text{Total Capital}}$$

$$\text{Interest coverage} = \frac{\text{EBIT}}{\text{Gross Interest}}$$

$$\text{EBITDA coverage} = \frac{\text{EBITDA}}{\text{Gross Interest}}$$

$$\text{Debt to EBITDA} = \frac{\text{Total Debt}}{\text{EBITDA}}$$

371

Financial Reporting and Analysis

Standard and Poor's Credit Ratios

$$\text{Funds from operations to total debt} = \frac{\text{NI adj. for noncash items}}{\text{Total Debt}}$$

$$\text{Free operating cash flow to total debt} = \frac{\text{CFO} - \text{Capex}}{\text{Total Debt}}$$

$$\text{Total debt to debt + equity} = \frac{\text{Total Debt}}{\text{Total Debt} + \text{Equity}}$$

Note: Adjustments are made for off-balance-sheet debt

372

Financial Reporting and Analysis

Segment Reporting

Reportable business or geographic segment:

50% of its revenue from sales external to the firm, **and** at least 10% of a firm's revenue, earnings, or assets

For each segment, firm reports *limited* financial statement information

For primary segments, must report: Revenue (internal and external), Operating Profit, Assets, Liabilities (IFRS only), Capex, Depreciation and Amortization

373

Financial Reporting and Analysis

Definitions: Segment Ratios

$$\text{Segment Margin} = \frac{\text{Segment Profit}}{\text{Segment Revenue}}$$

$$\text{Segment Asset Turnover} = \frac{\text{Segment Revenue}}{\text{Segment Assets}}$$

$$\text{Segment ROA} = \frac{\text{Segment Profit}}{\text{Segment Assets}}$$

$$\text{Segment Debt Ratio (IFRS only)} = \frac{\text{Segment Liabilities}}{\text{Segment Assets}}$$

374

Financial Reporting and Analysis

Model Building

- Common-size statements and ratios can be used model/forecast results
  - Expected relationships among financial statement data
  - Earnings model
  - Revenue driven models
- Sensitivity analysis
- Scenario analysis
- Simulation

375

Inventories

Financial Reporting and Analysis - Book 3

Financial Reporting and Analysis

Inventory Equation

Beg. Inv + purchases – COGS = End Inv

or

Beg. Inv + purchases – End Inv = COGS

Beginning Inventory (BI)	X
Purchases (P)	X
Ending Inventory (EI)	(X)
Cost of Goods Sold (COGS)	X

377

Financial Reporting and Analysis

Inventory

Lower of cost and net realizable value

All costs of bringing the inventory to its current location and condition (based on normal production levels)

Excludes:

- Abnormal amounts
- Storage costs
- Admin overheads
- Selling costs

IAS 2

NRV

Estimated Selling Price	X
Estimated cost of completion	(X)
Selling costs	(X)
NRV	X

Reversal of writedowns allowed

378

Financial Reporting and Analysis

Inventory Valuation

- Valuation methods
  - U.S. GAAP: FIFO, LIFO, AVCO
  - IFRS: FIFO, AVCO
- Techniques
  - Standard Cost: normal levels of materials, labour and production overheads
  - Retail method: Sales price less standard gross margin

379

Financial Reporting and Analysis

Inventory

Lower of cost and market value

Same as IAS

Current replacement cost, subject to:

Upper Limit = NRV

Lower Limit = (NRV – normal profit margin)

Reversal of writedowns prohibited under US GAAP

380

Financial Reporting and Analysis

Inventory Management Ratios

$$\text{Inventory turnover} = \frac{\text{Cost of goods sold}}{\text{Average inventory}}$$

$$\text{Number of days of Inventory} = \frac{365}{\text{Inventory turnover}}$$

$$\text{Gross profit margin} = \frac{\text{Gross profit}}{\text{Revenue}}$$

381

Financial Reporting and Analysis

Inventory Valuation and Price Changes

- When prices are **rising** (as in the example):
    1. FIFO provides an artificially **low value of COGS** while LIFO is more useful (reflects current costs)
    2. LIFO provides an artificially **low value of ending inventory** while FIFO is more useful (reflects current costs)
- When prices are declining, the reverse is true
- With stable prices, all methods result in the same COGS and ending inventory

382

Financial Reporting and Analysis

LIFO vs. FIFO Inflationary Environment

		LIFO	FIFO
Income Statement	COGS	HIGHER	LOWER
	EBT	LOWER	HIGHER
	TAXES	LOWER	HIGHER
	NI	LOWER	HIGHER
Balance Sheet	INV	LOWER	HIGHER
	W/C	LOWER	HIGHER
	R/E	LOWER	HIGHER
Statement of Cash Flows	CFO	HIGHER	LOWER

383

Financial Reporting and Analysis

Profitability Ratios and Inventory Method

- Given rising prices, LIFO is a better measure of economic cost; LIFO produces:
  - Higher COGS
  - Lower income values
  - Lower gross margin
  - Lower net profit margin
- For firms using FIFO, analysts should re-calculate profitability ratios using estimates of LIFO COGS

384

Financial Reporting and Analysis

Liquidity Ratios and Inventory Method

- When prices are rising, FIFO produces inventory values that are higher and a better measure of current inventory value
- Given rising prices, FIFO produces higher liquidity ratios (like the current ratio)
- For firms using LIFO, analysts should recalculate liquidity ratios using estimates of FIFO inventory

385

Financial Reporting and Analysis

Activity Ratios and Inventory Method

Inventory turnover ratio (COGS/avg. inventory)

- With LIFO, numerator reflects current prices; denominator reflects historical prices: not useful
- With FIFO, numerator reflects historical prices; denominator reflects current prices: may be more useful than LIFO
- **Best method**: Use LIFO COGS and FIFO average inventory (called the current cost method)

386

Financial Reporting and Analysis

Solvency Ratios and Inventory Method

FIFO produces a higher value of equity because of the *higher inventory value* on the left side of the balance sheet; therefore:

- Under FIFO, the debt ratio and debt-to-equity ratio are lower (and more meaningful)
- Under LIFO, analysts should add the *LIFO reserve* to both inventory and equity to generate more meaningful solvency ratios

387

Financial Reporting and Analysis

Analyst Adjustments: LIFO to FIFO

Balance Sheet

Inventory $_{FIFO}$	= Inventory $_{LIFO}$ + LIFO reserve
Deferred Tax	= LIFO reserve × tax rate
Equity	= LIFO reserve × (1 – tax rate)

Income Statement

COGS $_{FIFO}$ = COGS $_{LIFO}$ – change in LIFO reserve

FIFO net profit = LIFO profit + Δ LIFO reserve (1 – t)

388

Financial Reporting and Analysis

Declines in the LIFO Reserve

The LIFO reserve will decline if:

1. **Inventory quantity is declining**
   - A LIFO liquidation relative overstatement of earnings
   - Analysts should adjust COGS (the amount is disclosed in footnotes)
2. **Prices are falling**
   - FIFO still gives more accurate value for inventory
   - LIFO still gives a more accurate value for COGS
   - No adjustments necessary

389

Long-Lived Assets

Financial Reporting and Analysis - Book 3

Financial Reporting and Analysis

Capitalizing vs. Expensing:

- **Capitalizing costs** involves putting the expense on the balance sheet and writing off the cost to the Income Statement over a number of years (like fixed asset depreciation)
- **Expensing costs** involves realizing the entire cost in the current year

391

Financial Reporting and Analysis

Capitalizing vs. Expensing: Financial Statement Effects

- **Profitability in the early years**: Firms expensing costs have **higher expenses/lower profitability** in the current year
- **Profitability in later years**: Firms that capitalize costs have **lower profitability in later years**
- **Income variability**: Firms that expense costs have **greater income variability**

392

Financial Reporting and Analysis

Capitalizing vs. Expensing: Financial Statement Effects

- **Assets**: Firms capitalizing costs have higher assets as the capitalized assets are on the balance sheet
- **Equity**: Firms capitalizing costs have higher equity as an offsetting entry to assets on the balance sheet (higher NI → higher retained earnings)
- **ROA and ROE** in later years: Capitalizing firms have lower profitability ratios because income is lower and assets/equity are higher

393

Financial Reporting and Analysis

Capitalizing vs. Expensing: Financial Statement Effects

- **CFO**: Lower for expensing firms, costs are CFO
- **CFI**: Less for capitalizing firms, costs are CFI
- **Total cash flow**: Equal for both (ignoring taxes)
- **D/E and D/A ratios**: Capitalizing firms have higher assets (equity) but same debt, resulting in lower D/E and D/A ratios than expensing firms

394

Financial Reporting and Analysis

Capitalizing Interest Costs

For constructed assets (e.g., a plant or a building) interest costs during construction must be capitalized as part of the asset cost (U.S. GAAP and IFRS)

Capitalizing interest costs results in higher net income and greater interest coverage ratios during the period of capitalization

395

Financial Reporting and Analysis

Capitalizing Intangible Assets

- Definition
  - Long-term assets with no physical substance
  - Contribute to higher future earnings
- Examples
  - Patents, copyrights, trademarks, franchises, goodwill
- General Rule
  - Internally developed intangible assets: usually expensed
  - Purchased intangibles: capitalized

396

Financial Reporting and Analysis

Capitalizing Intangible Assets

R&D costs

- Must be expensed when incurred according to U.S. GAAP
- IFRS expense research but may capitalize development

Computer software development costs

- Must be expensed until feasibility established
- Then **can** be capitalized as part of inventory

397

Financial Reporting and Analysis

Depreciation of Long-Lived Assets

		$
Purchase price + Installation costs + Transport costs →	Historic Cost	X
Cumulative total of depreciation expensed to I/S →	Accumulated Dep^n	(X)
	Net Book Value	X
		↑ B/S value, Carrying Value, Book value

Economic depreciation = decline in asset value

Analyst Issue: Accounting depreciation may not equal economic depreciation

398

Financial Reporting and Analysis

Depreciation Methods: Financial Reporting

Straight line (SL) Depreciation = each year

$$\text{depreciation expense} = \frac{\text{original cost} - \text{salvage value}}{\text{depreciable life}}$$

Accelerated Depreciation Methods

Allocation of cost is greatest in early years

DDB = (Cost – Acc Dep^n) × (2 / Useful Economic Life)

Do not depreciate below residual/salvage value

Units of production

Cost per unit × Units produced

399

Financial Reporting and Analysis

Impact of Depreciation Method on Financial Statements

	Straight Line	Accelerated
Depreciation expense	Lower	Higher
Net Income	Higher	Lower
Assets	Higher	Lower
Equity	Higher	Lower
Return on assets	Higher	Lower
Return on equity	Higher	Lower
Turnover ratios	Lower	Higher
Cash flow	Same	Same

400

Estimates in Depreciation Calculations

Changes in salvage value and depreciable life are changes in accounting estimates

- Firm does not restate past income, change disclosed in notes
- Given longer useful life or higher salvage value, depreciation is less, leading to increased EBIT, net income, and ROE
- Shorter life, or lower salvage value, has opposite effects

401

Using Balance Sheet Disclosures to Analyze Fixed Assets

$$\frac{\text{Historical cost}}{\text{Annual dep}^n} = \text{Estimated total useful life}$$

$$\frac{\text{Accumulated dep}^n}{\text{Annual dep}^n} = \text{Estimated age of equipment}$$

NBV

$$\frac{\text{Net PPE}}{\text{Annual dep}^n} = \text{Estimated remaining life}$$

402

Financial Reporting and Analysis

Using Balance Sheet Disclosures to Analyze Fixed Assets

Analysts can use financial statement items to estimate the average age of fixed assets and the average depreciable life of fixed assets

In order to:

- Identify firms with **older, inefficient assets**
- Identify need for **major capital investments**
- Identify firms with **inflated earnings** from the use of older assets that generate less depreciation

403

Financial Reporting and Analysis

Amortizing Intangible Asset Cost

Intangibles with finite lives

- Amortize over life
- Pattern should match consumption of benefits
- e.g., patents with specific expiration

Intangibles with infinite lives

- No amortization
- Periodic impairment review
- e.g., goodwill, renewable licenses, etc.

404

Financial Reporting and Analysis

Accounting for Asset Retirement Obligations (ARO)

1. Estimate liability for closure, removal, and environmental effects of a long-lived asset (ARO)
2. Add PV of ARO to assets and to LT **liabilities**
3. Over time, depreciate asset value, **accrete growing interest expense to liability**

Increases**:** assets, liabilities, depreciation, interest expense, liabilities/equity

Decreases**:** EBIT, net income, asset turnover, ROE, ROA, interest coverage ratio

405

Financial Reporting and Analysis

Disposal of Long-Lived Assets

	$m
Proceeds	X
Carrying Value	(X)
Gain/(Loss)	X/(X)

CFI

Cost and related accumulated depreciation removed from B/S

Accounting gain or loss taken to I/S

- Sales proceeds = zero for abandoned assets
- Sales proceeds = fair value if exchanged
- Discussed in MD&A and/or footnotes

406

Financial Reporting and Analysis

Impairment of Long-Lived Assets

Impaired assets are assets with book values (historical cost – accum. dep.) **>** the amount recoverable from future use of the asset

- Firm must realize the impairment as a **loss on the income statement** pretax (above the line) as soon as the impairment is known
- Under U.S. GAAP, asset values are marked down for impairment but never increased (assets held-for-use). Held-for-sale may be reversed
- IFRS: reversals allowed
- No immediate tax effect, disclosed in notes

407

Financial Reporting and Analysis

Impairment of Long-Lived Assets

Impairment = unanticipated decline in asset's fair value

- **Test for impairment:** Compare an asset's BV to the *undiscounted* expected future cash flows from the asset

408

Financial Reporting and Analysis

Impact of Impairment on Financial Statements

- **Balance sheet:** Reduces assets, liabilities (deferred taxes), and stockholders' equity
- **Income statement:** The loss **decreases current period income** from continuing operations; in future years, reduced depreciation results in higher net income (Potential for earnings management)
- **Cash flow:** Unaffected because the impairment is not deductible for tax purposes. Impairments are non-cash charges
- **Disclosure**: MD&A, footnotes

409

Financial Reporting and Analysis

Impact of Impairment on Ratios

- **Fixed asset and total asset turnover ratios** increase due to reduced assets
- **Debt-to-equity ratio** increases due to reduced equity
- **Current year ROA and ROE** decrease, reduction in net income > reduction in assets/equity
- **Future ROA and ROE** increase due to lower assets and equity, higher net income with lower depreciation

410

Financial Reporting and Analysis

Asset Revaluation

U.S. GAAP: Revaluation only to recover impairment for held-for-sale assets

IFRS: depreciated historic cost or fair value

Revaluation up to historic cost

- Subsequent reversals of value recognized in I/S up to historic cost

Revaluation above historic cost

- Gain taken directly to equity

411

Financial Reporting and Analysis

Revaluation Impacts

- Higher assets and higher stockholders' equity
- Lower leverage ratios
- Higher earnings in the period the revaluation occurs (if reversing a prior loss)
- Lower ROA and ROE in periods after revaluation (lower numerators and/or higher denominators)
- For depreciable assets, higher depreciation expense and, lower profitability in periods after revaluation

412

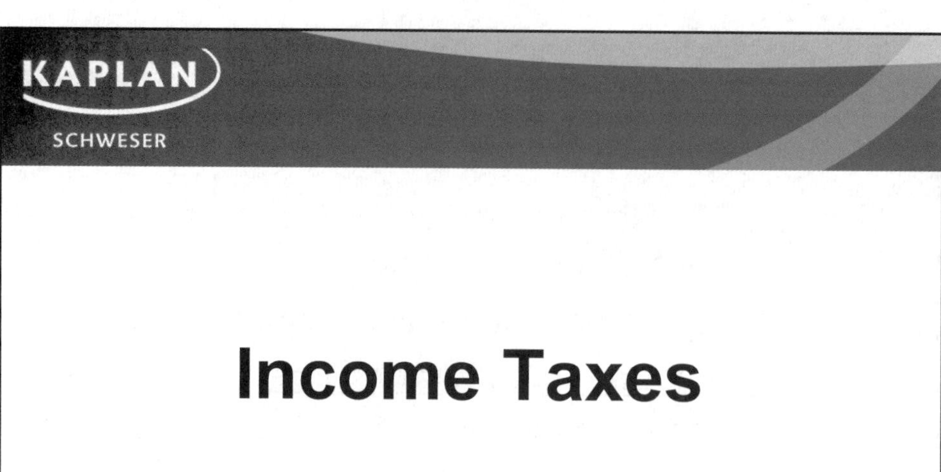

Tax Terms from the Tax Return

- Taxable income: Amount of income subject to taxes
- Taxes payable: Actual tax liability for the current period (based on taxable income, statutory rate)
- Income tax paid: Actual cash flow for taxes
- Tax loss carryforward: Current net taxable loss available to reduce taxes in future years. Can result in deferred tax assets
- Tax base: Value of asset or liability used for tax reporting purposes

414

Financial Reporting and Analysis

Tax Terms for Financial Reporting

Accounting Profit: Pre-tax financial income, earnings before tax

Income tax expense: Tax on the income statement (includes cash taxes and deferred taxes)

Valuation allowance: Reserve against deferred tax assets that may not reverse in the future

Carrying value: Balance sheet value of an asset or liability

415

Financial Reporting and Analysis

Tax Terms for Financial Reporting, cont.

Note that both DTLs and DTAs are presented on the balance sheet, not netted

IFRS: DTL and DTA always non-current

U.S. GAAP: DTL and DTA current and non-current depending on reversal

416

Financial Reporting and Analysis

Differences: Accounting vs. Taxable Profits

- Revenues and expenses recognised in different periods for accounts and tax, e.g. warranty expenses
- Carrying values of assets and liabilities may differ, e.g., depreciation
- Specific revenues and expenses not recognized for tax or accounting purposes
- Tax loss carryforwards
- Gains and losses from asset disposals calculated differently for tax and financial statements

417

Financial Reporting and Analysis

Temporary Differences Between Pretax Income and Taxable Income

Common examples of temporary differences that are expected to reverse in the future:

- Accelerated depreciation for tax
- Impairments
- Restructuring
- Warranty expense > actual costs
- Inventory Accounting
- Post-retirement benefit expense
- Gains and losses on marketable securities

418

Financial Reporting and Analysis

Deferred Taxes

Deferred Tax Liability

Taxable Income < Pre-tax Income

Due to temporary differences

Accelerated depreciation for tax

Gains/income not reportable as taxable

Deferred Tax Asset

Taxable Income > Pre-tax Income

Due to temporary differences

Expenses/losses not deductible for tax

e.g., Warranty expense, unrealized losses

419

Financial Reporting and Analysis

Deferred Tax Liabilities

Example of a deferred tax liability caused by using **different depreciation methods** for taxes and for financial reporting

Tax Reporting		**Financial Reporting**	
Tax rate = 40%	Yr 1		Yr 1
Revenue	150	Revenue	150
Depreciation	100	Depreciation	50
Taxable income	50	Pre-tax income	100
Taxes payable	20	Tax expense	40

Deferred Tax Liability 40 – 20 = 20

Difference in depreciation(50) × tax rate (40%) = 20

420

Financial Reporting and Analysis

Deferred Tax Assets

Example of a deferred tax asset caused by a **different treatment** of (accrued) expenses for taxes and for financial reporting

Tax Reporting		Financial Reporting	
Tax rate = 40%	Yr 1		Yr 1
Revenue	150	Revenue	150
Warranty Expense	0	Warranty Expense	100
Taxable income	150	Pre-tax income	50
Taxes payable	60	Tax expense	20

Deferred Tax Asset 60 – 20 = 40

Difference in warranty (100) × tax rate (40%) = 40

421

Financial Reporting and Analysis

Effect of a Change in Tax Rates

If tax rate decreases from 40% to 30%:

Deferred Tax Liability changes from

Difference in depreciation(50) × tax rate (40%) = **20**

to (50) × tax rate (30%) = 15, DTL down 5

Deferred Tax Asset changes from

Difference in warranty (100) × tax rate (40%) = 40

to (100) × tax rate (30%) = 30, DTA down 10

An **increase** in (expected) tax rate **increases** DTL and DTA

Net effect depends on relative sizes of DTL and DTA

422

Financial Reporting and Analysis

Effect of a Change in Tax Rates

tax expense = tax payable +ΔDTL – ΔDTA

(50) × tax rate (30%) = 15, DTL down 5

to (100) × tax rate (30%) = 30, DTA down 10

Assets down 10, Liabilities down 5

Tax payable + (– 5) + 10 = **tax expense, up by 5**

Increase in tax rate from 40% to 50% would reduce tax expense by 5

423

Financial Reporting and Analysis

Analyst Treatment of DTLs

- If capital expenditures are growing, DTL will not reverse in the foreseeable future—treat as equity
- If capital expenditures are slowing, DTL will reverse—treat as liability
- Analyst must decide on a case-by-case basis

424

Financial Reporting and Analysis

Permanent Differences (will not reverse)

Differences in tax and financial reporting that will not reverse in the future

Don't cause deferred tax

- Tax exempt income or non-deductible expenses
- Tax credits for some expenditures

Result: effective tax rate ≠ statutory rate

$$\frac{\text{Income tax expense}}{\text{Pretax income}}$$

425

Financial Reporting and Analysis

Valuation Allowance

- A valuation allowance reduces a deferred tax asset
- Is based on the likelihood that the asset will not be realized (e.g., no taxable income expected)
- Can be used to manipulate income: increasing the valuation allowance will decrease income, decreasing the allowance will increase income
- May affect analysts' assumptions regarding future earnings (earnings prospects)

426

Financial Reporting and Analysis

Required Deferred Tax Disclosures

- Deferred **tax liabilities/ assets**, any valuation allowance, and net change in valuation allowance
- Unrecognized deferred tax liability for **undistributed earnings of subsidiaries** and joint ventures
- **Current-year tax effect** of each type of temporary difference
- Components of income tax expense
- Tax loss **carryforwards and credits**
- **Reconciliation of difference between income tax expense as a % of pre-tax and statutory tax rate**

427

Financial Reporting and Analysis

Using Reconciliation Disclosures

Analysts most interested in predicting future tax rates

- If effective tax rate is lower than rate of comparable companies, could indicate aggressive accounting and poor quality earnings. One measure of effective tax rate is:

$$\frac{\text{Income tax expense}}{\text{Pretax income}}$$

- **Look for**: Permanent differences, changes in rates, deferred taxes of affiliates, different tax rates in foreign countries, tax holidays – when they end or requirements to pay accumulated taxes in future

428

Financial Reporting and Analysis

Disclosures About Deferred Tax Items

- Be aware of **differences** in tax reconciliation **between periods**
- Consider the firm's **growth rate and capital spending levels** when determining whether temporary differences due to accelerated depreciation will reverse
- Look for **cumulative differences due to** asset **impairments and post-retirement** benefits
- **Restructuring charges** can create a deferred tax asset

429

Financial Reporting and Analysis

Analyst Treatment of Deferred Tax Liabilities

- When differences are expected to reverse and result in future tax payments, **treat DTL as debt** in calculating leverage ratios
- When differences are not expected to reverse and result in future tax payments, **treat DTL as equity** in calculating leverage ratios
- When the amount and timing of future tax payments from reversal is uncertain, **exclude from both debt and equity**

430

Financial Reporting and Analysis

Key Differences IFRS & US GAAP

Deferred tax differences

- IFRS revaluation of PP&E and intangibles
- Undistributed profits from subsidiaries, associates, joint ventures
- Deferred tax assets
  - IFRS recognized if probable recovery
  - U.S. GAAP full recognition reduced by valuation allowance
- Tax rates used to measure deferred taxes
- Presentation
  - U.S. GAAP current and non-current
  - IFRS non-current

431

Long-Term Liabilities and Leases

Financial Reporting and Analysis - Book 3

Reporting Debt Issuance

- On **balance sheet**, create a liability equal to proceeds received
- On **income statement**, interest expense = beginning of period book value × market rate at the time of issuance
- On **cash flow statement**:
  - CFO is reduced by cash (coupon) interest
  - CFF is increased by proceeds at issuance
  - CFF is decreased by principal paid at maturity

433

Bonds Issued at Face Value

Bond trades at par if coupon rate = market rate

Each year **interest expense** = book value × market rate at the time of issuance

No premium or discount to amortize so,
interest expense = coupon interest paid

434

Financial Reporting and Analysis

Amortizing Bond Discount – Problem

Ledesma Corp issues a 3-year $1,000 par value bond with an annual coupon of 10% at $951.96. The YTM is 12%.

	Liability on Balance Sheet	12% Interest Expense	Coupon Int. Paid	Discount Amortization
Year 1			100	
Year 2			100	
Year 3			100	
Bond redemption				

435

Financial Reporting and Analysis

Amortizing Bond Premium – Example

Note interest expense is less than cash interest

Buswell Corporation issues a 3-year $1,000 par value bond with an annual coupon of 20% at $1,130.88. The YTM is 14.33%.

	Balance Sheet Liability	Interest Expense	Coupon Int. Paid	Premium Amortization
Year 1	1,130.88	162.05	200	-37.94
Year 2	1,092.93	156.62	200	-43.39
Year 3	1,049.55	150.40	200	-49.60
Bond redemption	1,000			

CFO is understated

436

Financial Reporting and Analysis

Debt Extinguishment

	$
B/S carrying value	X
Cash paid	(X)
Gain/(Loss)	X/(X)
Unamortized issuance costs	(X)
Gain/(Loss) on repurchase	X/(X)

US GAAP only (unamortized issuance costs)

I/S continuing operations

No gain/loss at maturity

Gain or loss if repurchased prior to maturity

Repurchase > carrying value = loss

Repurchase < carrying value = gain

Detail in MD&A, footnotes

437

Financial Reporting and Analysis

Disclosure of Long-Term Debt

- B/S split between:
  - Current liabilities
  - Long-term liabilities
- Footnotes
  - Nature of the liabilities
  - Maturity dates
  - Stated and effective interest rates
  - Call provisions and conversion privileges
  - Restrictions imposed by creditors
  - Assets pledged as security
  - Amount of debt maturing in each of the next five years

438

Financial Reporting and Analysis

Disclosure of Long-Term Debt

- MD&A
  - Financing trends (cost and mix)
  - Off-balance-sheet financing
- Analyst uses:
  - Timing and amount of future cash flows
  - Potential solvency issues
  - Liabilities not recorded on the B/S

439

Financial Reporting and Analysis

Effect of Changing Interest Rates

- Once debt is issued, firms report the Book Value (not market value) of debt; **changes in interest rates do not affect balance sheet or income statement**

  Δ interest rate: carrying value ≠ fair value

Exception: liabilities hedged with derivatives "fair value hedges"

440

Effect of Changing Interest Rates

Analysis: Market value of debt more relevant than book value

- Market value reflects the cost to buy back the debt and cancel the liability
- Lower market values reflect stronger solvency positions

Note: SFAS 107 & IAS 32 require disclosure of the fair value of outstanding debt and give option of fair value reporting

441

Accounting for Convertible Debt

U.S. GAAP

- Record full proceeds as debt
- On conversion reclassify the debt to equity

IFRS

Value of bond without conversion option is recorded as debt

Proceeds above option-free bond value recorded as equity

Debt ratios (D/A and D/E) lower with IFRS treatment

442

Financial Reporting and Analysis

Debt with Warrants

Warrants are like stock options

Give holders of bonds some upside equity participation

U.S. GAAP and IFRS

Value of debt without warrants is recorded as debt

Value of warrants recorded as equity

Debt ratios (D/A and D/E) lower than with U.S. GAAP convertible bonds

443

Financial Reporting and Analysis

Reasons to Lease

Alternative to borrowing and purchasing asset

Advantages:

1. Short period of use
2. Cheaper financing (potentially)
3. No down payments
4. Fixed rates
5. May have less covenants
6. Less risk of obsolescence
7. Potential financial reporting adv (op lease)
8. Tax advantages – synthetic leases

444

Financial Reporting and Analysis

Finance vs. Operating Leases

Finance (capital) lease: reported as if the firm borrowed money and purchased the asset

Asset and Liability added to balance sheet

Operating lease: no balance sheet entries

Lease payments reported as expense on income statement

Keeps liability off balance sheet

IAS 17 Finance Lease if it transfers substantially all the risks and rewards incident to ownership (No quantitative criteria)

445

Financial Reporting and Analysis

Accounting for Finance Lease

Treat as if **assets were purchased** with debt

- Value equal to PV of future lease payments is shown as a **balance sheet asset**
- Asset is **depreciated** over time
- A **liability** = PV of future lease payments shown on balance sheet
- Lease payments treated like amortizing debt — each payment is **part interest and part principal**

446

Financial Reporting and Analysis

Finance Lease Example

Firm leases asset for 3 years

Payments = $10,000 year

Straight line depreciation, no salvage value

Fair market value = $26,243

Lease discount rate = 7%

Balance Sheet Effects:

Asset = PV lease payments

Liability = PV lease payments

I/Y = 7
N = 3
PMT = $10,000

} $26,243

447

Financial Reporting and Analysis

Finance Lease Example cont.

Year	Beg. value	Interest expense @7%	Payment	Year-end value lease	Book value asset
1	26,243	1,837	10,000	18,080	17,495
2	18,080	1,266	10,000	9,346	8,747
3	9,346	654	10,000	0	0

Principal payment = $10,000 – interest

Depreciation = $26,243 ÷ 3 = $8,748/yr.

$18,080 long term, $8,163 current, Total $26,243

448

Financial Reporting and Analysis

Finance Lease Example cont.

	CFO (Interest)	*CFF (Principal)*
1	**1,837**	10,000 – 1,837 **= 8,163**
2	**1,266**	10,000 – 1,266 **= 8,734**
3	**654**	10,000 – 654 **= 9,346**

Operating lease CFO = $10,000 each year
Expense = lease payment = $10,000/year

Finance lease expense = interest + depreciation
Net income lower for capital lease in early years
Interest portion is CFO, principal portion is CFF

449

Financial Reporting and Analysis

Income Statement Effects

Year	Finance Lease: Interest	Finance Lease: Dep^n	Finance Lease: Total	Operating Lease: Rental Expense
1	$1,837	$8,748	$10,585	$10,000
2	$1,266	$8,748	$10,014	$10,000
3	$654	$8,747	$9,401	$10,000
Total	$3,757	$26,243	$30,000	$30,000

450

Financial Reporting and Analysis

Finance vs. Operating Lease

Financial Statement Totals	Finance	Operating
Assets	Higher	Lower
Liabilities	Higher	Lower
NI (in the early years)	Lower	Higher
NI (later years)	Higher	Lower
Total Net Income	Same	Same
Cash flow from operations	Higher	Lower
Cash flow from financing	Lower	Higher
Total cash flow	Same	Same

451

Financial Reporting and Analysis

Finance vs. Operating Lease

Ratios	Finance	Operating
Asset turnover (Sales/TA)	Lower	Higher
Return on assets (EAT/TA)	Lower	Higher
Return on equity (EAT/E)	Lower	Higher
Debt/assets	Higher	Lower
Debt/equity	Higher	Lower

452

Financial Reporting and Analysis

Lease Disclosure

- SFAS 13 US GAAP
  - **Finance Leases**
    - Gross amounts capitalized
    - Grouped by classes
    - MLPs for next 5 years
    - Aggregate MLPs > 5 years
  - **Operating Leases**
    - MLPs for next 5 years
    - Aggregate MLPs > 5 years
    - Minimum rental payment receivable under subleases

453

Financial Reporting and Analysis

Lessor Treatment Leases

Operating Lease

- Report leased item as (depreciable) asset
- Record lease payments as revenue

Finance (capital) Lease

- Asset carrying value is taken off BS
- Lease Receivable is added to BS
- Interest portion of lease payments recorded as revenue

454

Financial Reporting and Analysis

Sales-type and Direct Financing Leases

- Lessor records finance lease as either a **Sales-type Lease** or a **Direct Financing Lease**
- If carrying value < lease receivable then **sales-type lease**
- If carrying value = lease receivable then **direct financing lease**

For sales-type lease lessor records profit on sale, revenue = lease receivable, COGS, **and** interest revenue as with a direct financing lease

455

Financial Reporting and Analysis

Types of Off-Balance-Sheet Financing

Operating leases:

- The most prominent type, minimum lease payments shown in footnotes

Take-or-pay contract or throughput arrangement:

- A firm commits to buying a minimum amount of product (raw materials) from another firm
- No balance sheet liability, commitment disclosed in footnotes
- Analyst can add total liability to debt and to assets to recalculate leverage ratios

456

Financial Reporting and Analysis

Types of Off-Balance-Sheet Financing

Sale of receivables with recourse:

- Shown as a sale on the balance sheet, actually a collateralized loan
- An analyst can add back receivables, treat "sale" proceeds as loan (current liability) and as CFF rather than CFO, increase interest expense
- Analyst adjustment will: reduce receivables turnover, reduce CFO, increase CFF
- Adding proceeds to receivables and current liabilities will affect current ratio

457

Financial Reporting Quality

Financial Reporting and Analysis - Book 3

Financial Reporting and Analysis

Motivation: Over-report Earnings

- Meet analysts expectations, debt covenants, incentive compensation

Motivation: Under-report Earnings

- Obtain trade relief, negotiate lower payments or concessions from unions

459

Financial Reporting and Analysis

Motivation for Manipulation of B/S

- Overstate assets/understate liabilities to improve leverage and liquidity ratios
- **Understate assets** to improve ROA and turnover or decrease solvency to help negotiate concessions from creditors/employees

460

Financial Reporting and Analysis

Signs of Low Quality of Earnings

1. Selecting alternatives within GAAP that bias or distort reported results

   e.g., Inventory valuation, depreciation

2. Using loopholes or bright line criteria to report legal rather than economic substance

   e.g., Operating vs. finance leases

3. Using unrealistic or inappropriate accounting estimates and assumptions

   e.g., Economic lives and residual values of PP&E

461

Financial Reporting and Analysis

Signs of Low Quality of Earnings

4. Stretching an accounting rule to achieve a desired result rather than economic substance

   e.g., past non-consolidation of SPEs

5. Fraudulent financial accounting (Zero quality of earnings)

   e.g., capitalization of operating expenses

462

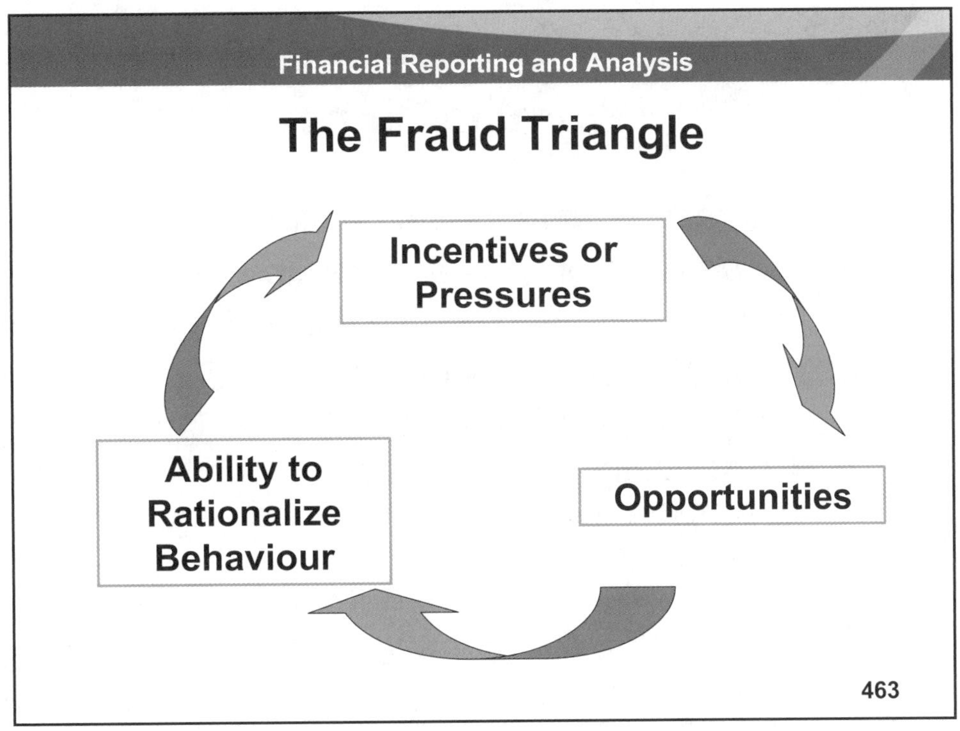

Financial Reporting and Analysis

SEC Improper Practice

- Identified 4 categories based on enforcement actions:

1. Improper revenue recognition
2. Improper expense recognition
3. Improper accounting of business combinations
4. Other accounting and reporting issues

464

Financial Reporting and Analysis

Warning Signs

1. Aggressive revenue recognition
2. Divergence of CFO and earnings
3. Growth of revenue out of line with peers
4. Growth in inventory out of line with peers/stock holding days increasing
5. Classification of non-recurring or non-operating items as revenue
6. Deferral of expenses
7. Excessive use of operating leases

465

Financial Reporting and Analysis

Warning Signs

8. Classification of losses and expenses as extraordinary or non-recurring
9. LIFO liquidations
10. Gross/Operating margins out of line with peers
11. Useful economic lives
12. Aggressive pension assumptions
13. 4th Quarter earnings surprises
14. Equity accounting/unconsolidated SPEs
15. Off-balance-sheet financing

466

Financial Reporting and Analysis

Enron: Warning Signs

Pressures

- Contracts that settled early if stock price declined
- Debt that matured if credit rating declined below investment grade

Warning signs

- Strange items in CFO
- CFI > CFO need for financing
- Unusual accounting treatments: mark-to-market of hedging derivatives (10% of revenues)

467

Financial Reporting and Analysis

Enron: Warning Signs

Warning signs

- Premature revenue recognition
- Disproportionate revenues in 3rd and 4th quarters
- Equity accounting of SPEs
- Mark-to-market treatment of affiliates
- Doubtful-debt provision decreasing as a percentage of trade receivables

468

Financial Reporting and Analysis

Enron: Warning Signs

Warning signs

- Related party transactions with senior management
- Confusing/non-industry standard use of SPEs
- Management compensation largely from bonus/stock awards (90%)
- Resignations of chairman and vice chairman

469

Financial Reporting and Analysis

Sunbeam: Warning Signs

Pressure

- New CEO charged with turning the company around

Warning Signs

- Cookie jar reserves – inventory writedowns followed by gross margin improvements
- Divergence of NI and CFO due to restructuring charges
- Change in revenue recognition policies
  - Bill-and-hold

470

Financial Reporting and Analysis

Sunbeam: Warning Signs

Warning signs

- Declining bad debt reserve %
- Revenue recorded from contingent sales
- Disproportionate 4th quarter revenues not explained by seasonality

471

Accounting Shenanigans on the Cash Flow Statement

Financial Reporting and Analysis - Book 3

Financial Reporting and Analysis

Cash Flow Shenanigans

- Increased focus on cash flow statements post accounting scandals
- Misconception: CFO cannot be manipulated
  - Difficult to manipulate change in total cash flow
  - Manipulation between classifications: CFO, CFI, CFF

473

Financial Reporting and Analysis

Manipulation of Payables

'Stretching Payables' – Delaying payment to suppliers – increases CFO, but

- Increase not sustainable
- Suppliers may reduce future credit terms

Using **borrowing to pay off accounts payable**

- Decreases CFO and increases CFF

474

Financial Reporting and Analysis

Sales of Receivables

Sales of accounts receivable to financing company or VIE treated like collection, increases CFO

- Unsustainable source of cash
- Borrowing against receivables is treated as CFF

475

Financial Reporting and Analysis

Tax Benefits From Stock Options

- Exercise of employee options results in tax deduction
- Lower tax → ↑ CFO
- Issue: The boost to CFO is unsustainable

476

Financial Reporting and Analysis

Buybacks to Offset Dilution

	$
Share repurchase	24,000
Less: proceeds from exercise	(20,000)
Net cash outflow	4,000

- U.S. GAAP treats the $4,000 as CFF
- An analyst should reclassify it as CFO (part of employee compensation)

477

Financial Statement Analysis: Applications

Financial Reporting and Analysis - Book 3

Financial Reporting and Analysis

Evaluating Past Financial Performance

- How have key ratios changed and why?
- How do key ratios and trends compare with competitors/industry?
- What aspects of performance are critical for a competitive advantage?
- How did the company perform in these areas?
- What is the company's business model and strategy – are they reflected in key measures?

479

Financial Reporting and Analysis

Projecting Performance

1. Forecast expected GDP growth
2. Forecast expected industry sales based on historical relationship with GDP
3. Consider expected change of firm's market share
4. Forecast expected firm sales
5. Use historical margins for stable firms (gross, operating, net) or individual forecast for each expense item
   - Remove nonrecurring items
   - Historical margins are not relevant to new, volatile, or high fixed cost industries

480

Forecasting Net Income and Cash Flow

1. Spreadsheet can be developed based on the estimated growth rate of sales
2. Make assumptions about working capital, fixed assets, COGS, and SG&A as proportions of sales
3. Estimate interest rates for saving/borrowing, tax rate, and dividends
4. Project net income and cash flow based on assumptions

481

Financial Forecasting Example

- Sales expected to be $100 mil in year 1 and increase 5% per year
- COGS = 20% of sales
- SG&A = 40% of sales
- Interest income = 5% of cash (beg. year)
- Tax rate = 30%
- No dividends
- Non-cash working capital = 70% of sales (beginning non-cash working capital = $67 mil)
- Fixed capital investment = 5% of sales

482

Financial Reporting and Analysis

Financial Forecast

($ mil.)	Year 1	Year 2	Year 3
Sales	**100**	**105**	**110**
– COGS	20	21	22
– SG&A	40	42	44
+ Interest	0	1	2
Pretax income	40	43	46
– Taxes	12	13	14
Net income	**28**	**30**	**32**

483

Financial Reporting and Analysis

Financial Forecast, cont.

($ mil.)	Beg.	Year 1	Year 2	Year 3
Working capital	67	70	73	77
Net income		**28**	**30**	**32**
– Inv. in working cap.		3	3	4
– Inv. in fixed capital		5	5	6
Change in cash		**20**	**22**	**22**
Beginning cash		0	20	42
Ending cash	**0**	**20**	**42**	**64**

484

Financial Reporting and Analysis

Credit Risk

- Ability of issuer to meet interest and principal repayment on schedule (capacity)
- Cash flow forecast focus
- Variability of cash flows

- **Character**
- **Capacity**
- **Collateral**
- **Covenants**

} 4 C's

485

Financial Reporting and Analysis

Credit Scoring

Credit rating agencies employ formulas that are weighted averages of several specific accounting ratios and business characteristics

1. Scale and diversification
2. Operational efficiency
3. Margin stability
4. Leverage

486

Financial Reporting and Analysis

Credit Scoring

Coverage ratios of operating earnings, EBITDA, or some measure of free cash flow to interest expense or total debt make up the most important part of the credit rating formula

487

Financial Reporting and Analysis

Equity Investment Screening

- Screening: Application of a set of criteria to reduce a set of investments to a smaller subset having desired characteristics
- Involves comparing ratios to min/max values

Growth investors:	Focus on earnings growth
Value investors:	Focus on low share price in relation to earnings or assets
Market oriented:	Neither value or growth focused

488

Financial Reporting and Analysis

Analyst Adjustments

- Adjust financial statements for **differences in accounting choices** (e.g., LIFO/FIFO, accelerated/straight line depreciation, revenue recognition criteria)
- Adjust financial statements for **differences in accounting standards** (e.g., IFRS vs. U.S. GAAP)

489

Financial Reporting and Analysis

Analyst Adjustments

- Inventory
  - FIFO/LIFO/AVCO
- Property, Plant and Equipment
  - Depreciation methods
  - Estimated lives
  - Salvage values
  - IFRS allows revaluation
- Goodwill
  - Internally generated – not capitalized
  - Purchased – capitalized

490

Financial Reporting and Analysis

Analyst Adjustments

- Off-balance-sheet finance
  - Capital leases vs. operating leases
  - Equity accounted SPEs vs. non-qualifying SPEs
  - Sale of AR

491

International Standards Convergence

Financial Reporting and Analysis - Book 3

Financial Reporting and Analysis

IAS 16 Property, Plant, and Equipment

- Reported at historic cost less accumulated depreciation – like U.S. GAAP
- May revalue upward to fair value – unlike U.S. GAAP
- Revaluations below historic cost flow through income statement – like U.S. GAAP
- Upward revaluations go to equity unless they reverse previous revaluations below historical cost (that reduced net income)

493

Financial Reporting and Analysis

IFRS 3 Goodwill

- Treatment consistent with U.S. GAAP
- **Only purchased goodwill** capitalized
- **Not amortized**
- Subject to **annual impairment reviews**
- No negative goodwill – reported as a gain
- Analysts should remove impacts before calculating ratios
  - Remove from assets
  - Remove impairments from I/S

494

Financial Reporting and Analysis

IAS 38 Intangibles

- Broadly consistent with U.S. GAAP
- Historical cost less accumulated amortization and impairment
- Differences under IFRS:
  - May revalue upward – to equity unless…
  - Development costs must be capitalized if certain criteria are met
- Internally generated intangibles not capitalized (goodwill, brands, etc.) may have real economic value

495

Financial Reporting and Analysis

IAS 11 Revenue

IAS 11 Construction Contracts

Outcome reliably estimated = percentage-of-completion method

Outcome cannot be reliably estimated = revenue recognized to the extent it is probable to recover costs

(U.S. GAAP – completed contract)

496

Financial Reporting and Analysis

Depreciation

- IFRS & U.S. GAAP require that an asset's cost is recognized via expensing to the income statement over its life
- IFRS depreciation method must match the pattern of expected consumption

497

Financial Reporting and Analysis

Nonrecurring Items

- Discontinued operations: IFRS changed to align with U.S. GAAP
- Accounting changes (both principal and estimates) U.S. GAAP changed to align with IFRS – retrospective treatment
- Extraordinary items – convergence not yet reached
  - U.S. GAAP – unusual **and** infrequent
  - IFRS – no items reported as extraordinary

498

Financial Reporting and Analysis

Differences

The analyst must adjust for differences to increase comparability

Major Differences

- LIFO inventory accounting (U.S. only)
- Cash flow classifications (IFRS options)
- Asset upward revaluations (IFRS only)
- Proportional consolidation (IFRS only)
- Subsequent recovery of written down assets (IFRS only)

499

Financial Reporting and Analysis

Percentage-of-completion – Solution

3-yr. contract for $1.8 million, estimated profit $600,000

Yr. 1: costs $400,000, invoiced $800,000, cash collected $500,000

What is Yr. 1 Revenue and profit?

Total cost estimate = 1.8 million – 600,000 = $1.2 million

400K/1.2 million × 1.8 million = $600,000 Revenue

400K/1.2 million × 600,000 = $200,000 profit, or

600K revenue – 400K cost = $200,000 profit

500

Financial Reporting and Analysis

Weighted Shares Outstanding – Solution

1/1/X3	Shares outstanding	10,000	×3/2 × 1 =15,000
5/1/X3	Shares issued	2,000	×3/2 ×2/3 = 2,000
7/1/X3	3 for 2 stock split		
9/1/X3	Shares repurchased	3,000	×1/3 = –1,000

What is weighted average number of shares outstanding? 16,000

Can also multiply by months outstanding and divide total by 12

501

Financial Reporting and Analysis

Diluted EPS – Solution

Earnings available to common, year 20X9	\$4,000,000
Common stock	2,000,000 sh
Basic EPS	\$2.00
Tax rate	35%

\$5,000,000 par value of 7% convertible preferred stock
Each \$10 par value of preferred can be converted to 1.1 sh.

Calculate fully diluted EPS for 20X9.

$$\frac{7\% \times 5{,}000{,}000}{5{,}000{,}000/10 \times 1.1} = \frac{\$350{,}000}{550{,}000 \text{ sh.}} = \$0.64/\text{sh.} < \$2/\text{sh., dilutive}$$

$$\frac{4{,}000{,}000 + 350{,}000}{2{,}550{,}000} = \$1.71/\text{sh. Diluted EPS}$$

502

Financial Reporting and Analysis

Convertible Bonds – Solution

Earnings available to common, year 20X9	$1,500,000
Common stock	1,000,000 sh
Basic EPS	$1.50
Tax rate	30%

$2,000,000 par value of 8% convertible bonds.
Each $1,000 bond can be converted to 35 common shares.
Calculate fully diluted EPS for 20X9

$$\frac{8\% \times 2{,}000{,}000 \times (1-0.3)}{2{,}000{,}000 / 1{,}000 \times 35} = \frac{\$112{,}000}{70{,}000 \text{ sh.}}$$

$$= \$1.60/\text{sh.} > \$1.50/\text{sh., antidilutive}$$

503

Financial Reporting and Analysis

Amortizing Bond Discount – Solution

Note interest expense is greater than cash interest

Ledesma Corp issues a 3-year $1,000 par value bond with an annual coupon of 10% at $951.96. The YTM is 12%.

	Liability on Balance Sheet	12% Interest Expense	Coupon Int. Paid	Discount Amortization
Year 1	951.96	114.24	100	14.24
Year 2	966.20	115.94	100	15.94
Year 3	982.14	117.86	100	17.86
Bond redemption	1,000			

CFO is overstated

504

Financial Reporting and Analysis

Sustainable Growth Rate – Solution

A firm has a dividend payout ratio of 35%, a net profit margin of 10%, an asset turnover of 1.4, and an equity multiplier leverage measure of 1.2. Estimate the firm's sustainable growth rate.

Growth rate = Retention Ratio × ROE

$$(1 - 0.35) \quad 0.1 \times 1.4 \times 1.2$$

$$= 0.1092$$

$$= 10.92\%$$

505

CFA® LEVEL 1

3-Day Review Slide Workbook

CORPORATE FINANCE

Corporate Finance

Corporate Finance - Book 4

Corporate Finance

Types of Capital Projects

- Replacement projects to maintain the business
- Replacement projects for cost reduction
- Expansion projects
- New products or markets
- Mandatory projects – safety and environment
- Other projects: pet projects, R&D

507

Corporate Finance

Steps in the Capital Budgeting Process

- Step 1: Idea generation
- Step 2: Analyze project proposals
- Step 3: Create the capital budget for the firm
- Step 4: Monitor decisions and conduct a post-audit

508

Corporate Finance

Principles of Capital Budgeting

- Decisions are made based on the changes in **after-tax cash flows**
- Do not consider **sunk costs**
- Do not consider any project-specific financing costs – financing costs are in discount rate
- Consider cash **opportunity costs**
- Consider **externalities** – cannibalization
- **Timing** of cash flows is important

509

Corporate Finance

Project Interactions

- Independent projects
- Mutually exclusive projects
- Project sequencing – opportunity for profitable future projects
- Unlimited funds vs. capital rationing

510

Corporate Finance

Net Present Value (NPV)

- Uses discounted CFs and considers all CFs

$$NPV = CF_0 + \frac{CF_1}{(1+k)^1} + \frac{CF_2}{(1+k)^2} + \ldots + \frac{CF_n}{(1+k)^n}$$

Example (cost of capital of 6%):

End of Year	Project X	Discounted Cash Flow
0	–$500	–$500.00
1	100	94.34
2	250	222.50
3	400	335.85

– 500.00
+ 94.34
+ 222.50
+ 335.85
NPV = $152.69

511

Corporate Finance

Net Present Value (NPV)

- NPV indicates the expected change in the value of the firm, in current (PV) dollars, if the project is accepted
- Accepting projects with NPV > 0 is expected to increase shareholder wealth

Decision rule independent projects:
Adopt all projects with NPV > 0

512

Corporate Finance

Internal Rate of Return (IRR)

IRR is the discount rate that equates the PV of the project's CFs to the initial outlay

$$\text{NPV} = 0 = CF_0 + \frac{CF_1}{(1+\text{IRR})^1} + \frac{CF_2}{(1+\text{IRR})^2} + \ldots + \frac{CF_n}{(1+\text{IRR})^n}$$

Accept all independent projects with an IRR > marginal cost of capital

If NPV > 0 then IRR greater than cost of capital

NPV and IRR give the same accept/reject decision

513

Corporate Finance

Internal Rate of Return (IRR)

Use the CF keys on your calculator

End of Year	Project X CFs	Discounted Cash Flow at 18.79%
0	–$500	–$500.00
1	100	84.18
2	250	177.17
3	400	238.63

Because NPV = 0
IRR = 18.79%

$\sum \approx 0.00$ = NPV

514

Corporate Finance

Payback Period

- Primarily a measure of liquidity
- Projects with payback periods longer than an arbitrary number of years are rejected

Limitations

- Not a measure of value
- Ignores time value of money
- Ignores CFs beyond the payback period

515

Corporate Finance

Payback Period

Example:

End of Year	Project X	Cumulative Cash Flow
0	–$500	–$500
1	100	–400
2	250	–150
3	400	50

Payback period = 2 + 150 / 400 = 2.38 years

Firm recovers its initial investment in 2.38 years

516

Corporate Finance

Discounted Payback Period (DPP)

Cost of Capital is 6%

End of Year	Project X	Discounted Cash Flow	Cumulative Discounted Cash Flow
0	–$500	–$500.00	–$500.00
1	100	94.34	–405.66
2	250	222.50	–183.16
3	400	335.85	152.69

DPP = 2 + 183.16 / 335.85 = 2.55 years

- Ignores CFs after payback
- Both payback methods focus on liquidity

517

Corporate Finance

Profitability Index (PI)

- Present value of future cash flows divided by initial cash outlay

$$PI = \frac{\text{PV Future CF}}{CF_0} = 1 + \frac{NPV}{CF_0}$$

- Independent projects: Accept all projects where PI > 1
- If NPV is > 0, then IRR > discount rate, and PI > 1

518

Corporate Finance

NPV Profile

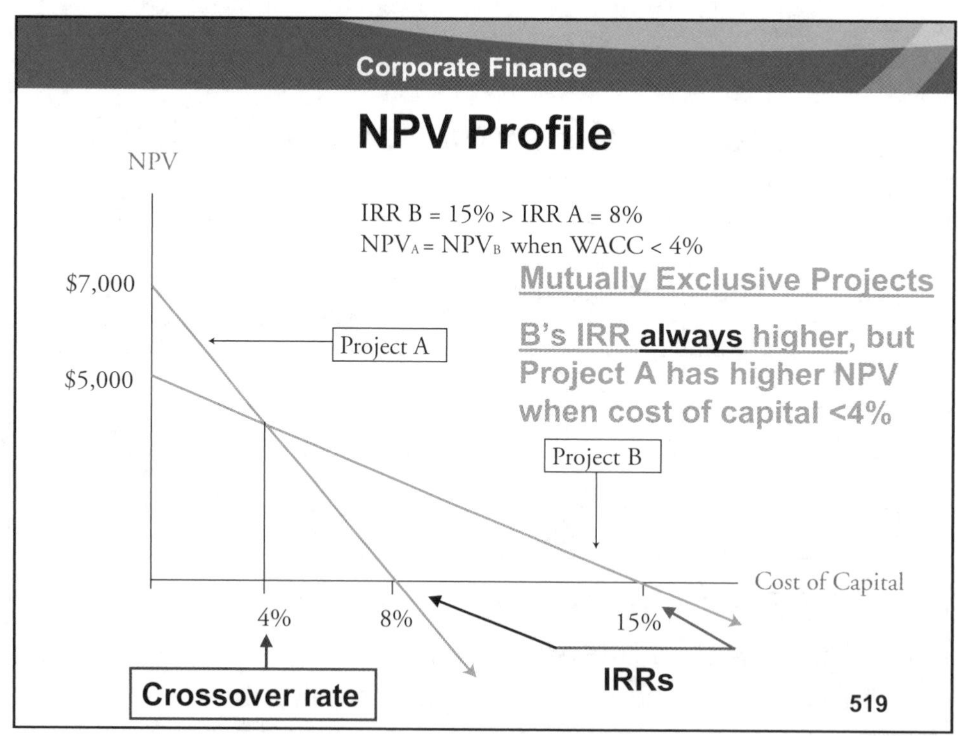

519

Corporate Finance

IRR vs. NPV Project Rankings

- For mutually exclusive projects, IRR and NPV project rankings may differ, when:
  - Projects have different timing of CFs
  - The projects (CF_0) are different sizes
- Different reinvestment rate assumptions:

  IRR assumes CF reinvestment at project's IRR
  NPV assumes CF reinvestment at the cost of capital (more conservative)

Use NPV to rank projects and for capital rationing

520

Corporate Finance

Problems with IRR

If project's cash flows change signs more than once, we may have:

Multiple IRRs – more than one IRR will make NPV = 0

No IRR – there is no IRR that will make NPV = 0

521

Corporate Finance

Relative Popularity of Capital Budgeting Methods

- **By location**: European companies more likely to use payback period
- **By size of company**: Larger companies more likely to use NPV
- **Public vs. private companies**: Private companies more likely to use payback
- **By management education**: Educated managers more likely to use NPV

522

Corporate Finance

Relationship Between NPV and Stock Price

- NPV is a direct measure of the expected change in shareholder wealth from a project
- Estimate increase in share value (if unexpected) as NPV divided by number of shares

523

Corporate Finance

Weighted Average Cost of Capital

- The overall opportunity cost of the firm's capital is a weighted average of the opportunity costs of capital from **debt, preferred equity, and common equity**

524

Corporate Finance

Weighted Average Cost of Capital (WACC)

$$WACC = (w_d)[k_d(1 - t)] + (w_{ps})(k_{ps}) + (w_{ce})(k_{ce})$$

- **Example:** Firm X target capital structure is 10% preferred, 45% debt, and 45% common equity

$k_d = 7.5\%$, $t = 40\%$, $k_{ps} = 9.0\%$, and $k_{ce} = 11.5\%$

$$WACC = 0.45 \times 7.5\% (1 - 0.4) + 0.1 \times 9\% + 0.45 \times 11.5\% = 8.1\%$$

525

Corporate Finance

Target (Optimal) Capital Structure

Target capital structure: The proportions (based on market values) of debt, preferred stock, and equity that the firm expects to achieve over time

How do analysts determine target weights?

- Can use existing capital structure weights
- Can adjust existing weights for firm trends
- Can use industry average weights

526

Corporate Finance

Adjust for Project Risk

- For project that has the same level of risk as the firm's (average) existing projects, use WACC
- For project with greater than average risk, use a discount rate greater than the firm's WACC
- For projects with below-average risk, use a discount rate less than the firm's WACC

527

Corporate Finance

The Cost of Debt

k_d = pretax cost of debt = current market YTM

After-tax cost of debt = k_d (1 – marginal tax rate)

- When available, use **market rate of interest (YTM)** on firm's current debt for k_d
- If firm debt is not publicly traded, estimate YTM using **debt rating and maturity of existing debt**
- For firms that primarily use floating-rate debt, estimate longer-term cost of firm's debt using **current yield curve** and firm's debt rating

528

Corporate Finance

The Cost of Preferred Stock

$$k_{ps} = \frac{\text{preferred dividend}}{\text{market price of preferred}}$$

The Cost of Common Stock

Method 1: CAPM $k_{ce} = RFR + \beta[E(R_{mkt}) - RFR]$

Method 2: Dividend Discount Approach $k_{ce} = \frac{D_1}{P_0} + g$

Method 3: k_{ce} = bond market yield + risk premium

3% to 5%

529

Corporate Finance

Cost of Common Equity – Problem

Stock sells for $35, expected dividend = $1.20, firm's ROE is 13.3% and its retention rate is 60%. What is firm's cost of common equity?

530

Corporate Finance

Equity Beta for a Project

- **Pure play method:**
  1. Calculate beta of a **comparable company** (or companies) that is a pure play in the industry
  2. Unlever it to adjust for differences in debt/equity ratio —this is the **Asset beta**
  3. Relever it to reflect debt/equity ratio of subject company to get the **Project beta**
  4. Use Project beta to **calculate the cost of equity for the project**
  5. Use that cost of equity to **calculate project WACC**

531

Corporate Finance

Country Risk Premium

- CAPM problematic for estimating project cost of equity in developing markets
- **Solution:** Add country risk premium (CRP) to market risk premium when using CAPM

$$k = R_F + \beta\left[E(R_{MKT}) - R_F + CRP\right]$$

532

Corporate Finance

Marginal Cost of Capital

- **MCC**: Opportunity cost of using an additional dollar of capital; WACC of raising an additional dollar
- Cost of each source of capital increases as the firm raises more new capital
- The result is an **upward sloping MCC schedule**

533

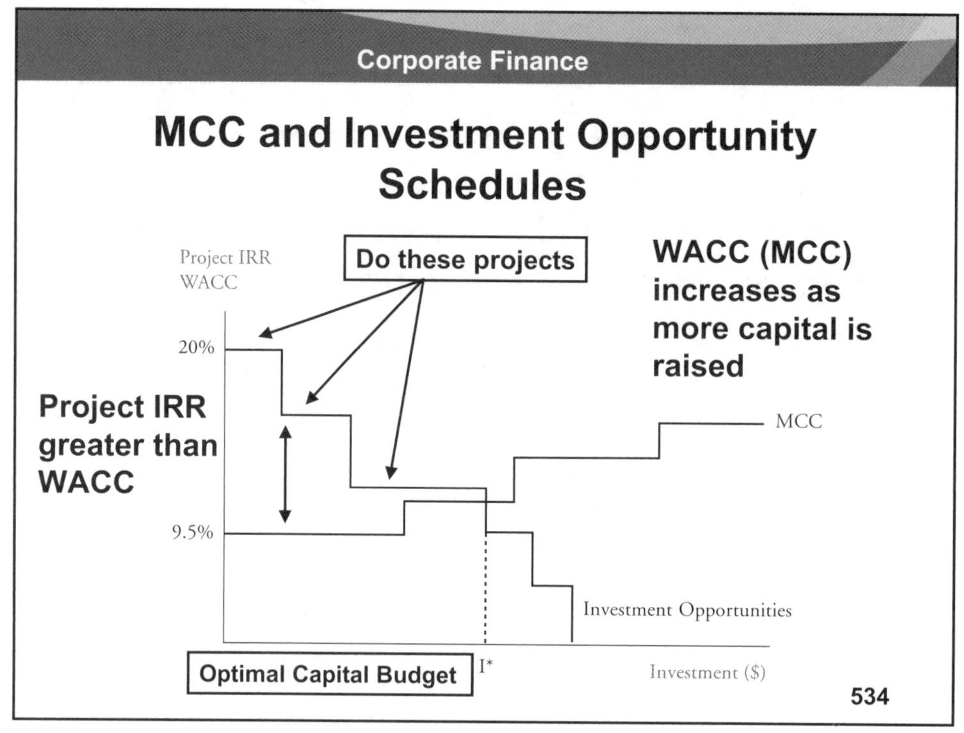

Corporate Finance

Calculating Breakpoints – Problem

Target Capital Structure:
30% preferred, 40% equity, 30% debt

Borrowing cost:
8% up to $1.2 mil, 9% up to $2.1 mil, then 10%

Where are breakpoints from increases in debt cost?

535

Corporate Finance

Treatment of Flotation Costs

What? Fees charged by investment bankers when a company raises external equity capital

Range: 2% to 7%

Adjust initial cash outflow to include flotation costs when computing NPV

536

Corporate Finance

Operating and Cash Conversion Cycles

Operating cycle = days of inventory + days of receivables

Cash conversion cycle = days of inventory + days of receivables – days of payables

Covered in Accounting

- Cash conversion cycle is also called ***net*** *operating cycle*

537

Corporate Finance

Cash Management

- Set firm **minimum cash balances** over time
- When cash flow shortfall is forecast, must look to **sources of cash** or credit to maintain minimum levels
- When excess cash is generated, firm should invest in **short-term securities**

538

Corporate Finance

Managing Net Daily Cash

Invest excess cash in **short-term securities**:

- U.S. Treasury bills
- Short-term federal agency securities
- Bank certificates of deposit
- Banker's acceptances
- Time deposits
- Repurchase agreements
- Commercial paper
- Money market mutual funds
- Adjustable-rate preferred stock

539

Corporate Finance

Comparing Short-term Yields

Same as in Quant Methods

$$\% \text{ discount} = \frac{\text{face value} - \text{price}}{\text{face value}}$$

$$\text{discount basis (bank discount) yield} = \% \text{ discount} \times \frac{360}{\text{days}}$$

$$\text{money market yield} = \left(\frac{\text{face value} - \text{price}}{\text{price}}\right)\left(\frac{360}{\text{days}}\right) = \text{HPY} \times \frac{360}{\text{days}}$$

$$\textbf{bond equivalent yield} = \left(\frac{\text{face value} - \text{price}}{\text{price}}\right)\left(\frac{365}{\text{days}}\right) = \text{HPY} \times \frac{365}{\text{days}}$$

Different from Quant Methods and Fixed Income definition

540

Corporate Finance

Cash Management IPS

- Purpose and objective of investment portfolio
- Strategy guidelines
- Types of securities
- Individuals responsible for the portfolio
- Corrective steps
- Limitations

541

Corporate Finance

Accounts Receivable Aging Schedule $ 000's

Days Outstanding	*Mar*	*Apr*	*May*
< 31 days	200	212	195
31–60 days	150	165	140
61–90 days	100	90	92
> 90 days	50	70	66

Can also be presented as percentages of total receivables

542

Corporate Finance

Weighted Average Collection Period

Days Outstanding	*Average Collection Days*	*% Weight*	*Days × Weight*
< 31 days	22	40%	8.8
31–60 days	44	30%	13.2
61–90 days	74	20%	14.8
> 90 days	135	10%	13.5
Weighted average collection period			**50.3 Days**

543

Corporate Finance

Evaluating Performance

- **Receivables:** Trade-off between credit terms and sales
- **Inventories:** Too low can lead to stock-outs, too high increases carrying costs
- **Payables:** Early payment can take advantage of discounts but gives up potential interest on cash; late payment increases interest costs, can damage supplier relationships

544

Corporate Finance

Sources of Short-term Funding

- Lines of credit
  - Committed – requires fee
  - Revolving – fee, larger, strongest (U.S.)
  - Uncomitted – less reliable, no fee (U.S.)
- Bankers' acceptances – import/export
- Factoring – smaller users, higher fees
- Commercial paper – large, strong credit
- Nonbank finance companies – weak credit

545

Corporate Finance

Pro Forma Financial Statements

1. Estimate relation between changes in sales and changes in sales-driven income statement and balance sheet items
2. Estimate future tax rate, interest rates on debt, lease payments, etc.
3. Forecast sales
4. Estimate fixed operating and financial costs
5. Integrate these estimates into pro forma financial statements

546

Corporate Finance

Methods of Estimating Sales

- Average compound historical growth
- Regression analysis
- Specific events (e.g., new products)
- Segment forecasts sum to total revenue

547

Corporate Finance

Pro Forma Income Statement

	Actual 20X1	*20X2E*	*% Sales*
Sales	30,000	33,000	100%
COGS	12,000	13,200	40%
SG&A	9,000	9,900	30%
EBIT	9,000	9,900	
Interest	5,000	5,000	(stable)
EBT	4,000	4,900	
Tax (40%)	1,600	1,960	
NI	2,400	2,940	

548

Corporate Finance

Pro Forma Balance Sheet

	Actual 20X1	*20X2E*	*% Sales*
Current Assets	10,000	11,000	33%
Net PPE	48,000	52,800	160%
Total Assets	58,000	63,800	
Current Liab	3,000	3,300	10%(stable)
LT Liab	45,000	45,000	
Equity	10,000	12,400	
Liab + Equity	58,000	60,700	

Doesn't balance 3,100 dif

549

Corporate Finance

Reconciliation

- More Assets than Funding by $3,100
- Must issue debt or issue equity
- If debt, interest cost goes up, net income and retained earnings go down
- If equity, any dividend reduces retained earnings
- Either, reduces equity, requires more funding
- Repeat to reconcile income statement and balance sheet

550

Corporate Finance

What is Corporate Governance?

- Corporate governance refers to the firm's **internal controls** and the procedures by which the firm is managed
- Defines **rights and responsibilities** of management, the board, and shareholders
- Good corporate governance ensures that **shareholder interests are protected**

551

Corporate Finance

Factors Affecting Corporate Governance

- **Board of directors –** independent directors should be majority and sometimes meet without management
- **Management** – Code of Ethics, board oversight, compensation, alignment of interests
- **Shareholder rights** – voting rights (e.g., cumulative), proxy voting, actions requiring shareholder approval

552

Corporate Finance

Independent Board Members

- Board members that do not have material relationships with management or significant shareholders
- No compensation from firm for other than board service (e.g., no consulting or finders fees)
- Works to protect shareholders' long-term interest

553

Corporate Finance

Provisions of a Code of Ethics

- Congruent with local laws
- Prohibit advantages to firm insiders
- Conditions for waivers (and frequency of use)
- Require timely information to board
- Periodic audits/reviews of Code

Weak code allows related-party transactions and personal use of company assets

554

Corporate Finance

Board Committees

- **Audit**: Ensures quality of financial reporting
- **Compensation**: Sets executive compensation
- **Nominations**: Nominates/recruits new members

555

Corporate Finance

Proxy Voting Rules and Takeover Defenses

Easy proxy voting = better shareholder rights

Takeover defenses reduce shareholder value

- Golden parachutes
- Poison pills
- Greenmail

556

Corporate Finance

Shareholder Sponsored Action

Greater ability to influence board = greater shareholder protection

- Board nominations
  - Can board member be removed?
- Resolutions/proposals, issues:
  - When can proposals be made?
  - Simple majority vs. supermajority?

557

Corporate Finance

Different Classes of Stock

- Classes separate voting rights and economic value
- Potential acquirers may only deal with one class of stockholders
- Generally, separation of voting rights works to the impairment of at least one set of shareholders
- Different classes can lead to trouble raising equity capital

558

Corporate Finance

Cost of Common Equity – Solution

Stock sells for $35, expected dividend = $1.20, firm's ROE is 13.3% and its retention rate is 60%. What is firm's cost of common equity?

$g = (13.3\%)(0.6) = 8.0\%$

$k_s = D_1 / P_0 + g$

$k_s = \$1.20 / \$35 + 8\% = 11.4\%$

559

Corporate Finance

Calculating Breakpoints – Solution

Target Capital Structure:
30% preferred, 40% equity, 30% debt

Borrowing cost:
8% up to $1.2 mil, 9% up to $2.1 mil, then 10%

Where are breakpoints from increases in debt cost?

1.2/0.30 = $4 mill and 2.1/0.3 = $7 mill

560

CFA® LEVEL 1

3-Day Review Slide Workbook

SECURITIES MARKETS AND EQUITY INVESTMENTS

Securities Markets

Analysis of Equity Investments - Book 4

Securities Markets

Primary vs. Secondary Capital Markets

Primary capital markets: Sales of new issues of stocks and bonds (IPOs and seasoned offerings), proceeds less underwriting fees to issuer

Secondary capital markets: Where securities trade after their initial offerings (e.g., NYSE, NASDAQ, other OTC)

Secondary markets are important because they **provide liquidity and information about value** to investors.

562

Securities Markets

- In call markets, stocks trade at specific times
- In continuous markets, trades occur at any time the market is open

- Exchanges are physical locations (e.g., NYSE)
  - Auction markets: Buyer and seller orders are matched
  - Specialists, floor brokers, floor traders
- Over the counter (OTC) markets are negotiated markets – a network of dealers who trade stocks from their own inventories

563

Securities Markets

Types of Orders

- Market order: Immediate execution, best price
- Limit order
  - To buy: Buy if price goes **down** to limit
  - To sell: Sell if stock goes **up** to limit
- Stop (loss) order
  - To sell: Market **sell** order if stock goes **down** to stop price; limits loss on long position
  - To buy: Market **buy** order if stock goes **up** to stop price; limits loss on short position

564

Securities Markets

Selling Short

1. Investor **borrows stock** and sells it
2. Later, **repurchases the stock** and returns it to the lender (covers the short position)
3. Short-seller's **profit (loss)** is the original selling price minus the repurchase price

Rules of short-selling:

- Short sellers **pay all dividends** to the lender
- Short seller **deposits margin/collateral**

Idea is to **sell high and buy low** to cover short sale

565

Securities Markets

Buying Stock on Margin

- **Margin transactions** involve borrowing part of the money needed to buy stock
- **Brokers lend** the money and hold the stock as collateral
- **Margin requirement** (required equity percentage) is set by the Federal Reserve Board (currently 50% for short or long)
- **Maintenance** (minimum) margin
- **Equity percentage** is stock value – loan value as a percentage of the stock value

566

Securities Markets

Buying Stock on Margin – Problem

Investor buys $10,000 worth of stock on 50% margin. Value of stock rises to $12,500 (a 25% rise).

What is the percentage gain to the investor (ignoring transactions costs and interest)?

567

Securities Markets

Margin Call – Problem

Buy 300 sh. of stock for $42 — 50% initial margin — 30% maintenance margin. At what price will he get a margin call?

What is equity % at price of 35?

What is amount of margin call at $25?

568

Securities Markets

Price-Weighted Index (PWI)

$$PWI = \frac{\text{sum of stock prices}}{\text{\# stocks in index, adjusted for splits}}$$

Price-weighted index bias: High-priced stocks have greater influence; stock splits reduce the price (and influence) of growing firms, giving the index an **overall downward bias**

569

Securities Markets

Market-Value Weighted Index

$$MVWI = \frac{\Sigma\ (\text{price}_{\text{today}})(\text{\# shares})}{\Sigma\ (\text{price}_{\text{base year}})(\text{\# shares})} \times \text{beg. index value}$$

$$= \frac{\text{Ending value of all stock}}{\text{Base year value of all stock}} \times \text{beg. index value}$$

Value-weighted index bias: Large capitalization firms influence the index more than small firms

570

Securities Markets

Unweighted Index

There are **two different methods** of calculating the average return on index stocks

$$\frac{\Sigma HPR}{n} = \text{arithmetic mean return}$$

$$[(1+HPR_1)(1+HPR_2)......(1+HPR_n)]^{\frac{1}{n}} - 1 = \text{geom. mean return}$$

<u>Unweighted index bias</u>: Geometric mean method causes a downward bias (geometric mean is always ≤ the arithmetic mean)

571

Securities Markets

Calculating a Price-Weighted Index

	Nov. 30			Dec. 31		
Stock	Share Price	# of Shares	Market Value	Share Price	# of Shares	Market Value
A	\$20	300	\$6,000	\$22	300	\$6,600
B	\$30	200	\$6,000	\$27	200	\$5,400
C	\$40	100	\$4,000	\$44	100	\$4,400
Total	\$90		\$16,000	\$93		\$16,400

Price-weighted index:

\$90 / 3 = 30.0

\$93 / 3 = 31.0

572

Securities Markets

Calculating a Value-Weighted Index

Nov. 30				Dec. 31		
Stock	Share Price	# of Shares	Market Value	Share Price	# of Shares	Market Value
A	\$20	300	\$6,000	\$22	300	\$6,600
B	\$30	200	\$6,000	\$27	200	\$5,400
C	\$40	100	\$4,000	\$44	100	\$4,400
Total	\$90		\$16,000	\$93		\$16,400

Beginning index value Nov 30 = 100

New value Dec 31 = (16,400 / 16,000) × 100 = **102.5**

The total market value of all index stocks is up 2.5%

573

Securities Markets

Calculating an Unweighted Index

Stock	Initial Cost	Current Price	HPR
X	\$3.00	\$2.70	2.7/3 – 1 = –10%
Y	\$1.00	\$1.50	1.5/1 – 1 = 50%
Z	\$2.00	\$2.20	2.2/2 – 1 = 10%

$$\text{Arithmetic mean} = \frac{-0.1 + 0.5 + 0.1}{3} = 16.7\%$$

$$\text{Geometric mean} = \sqrt[3]{0.9 \times 1.5 \times 1.1} - 1 = 14\%$$

Biased downward

574

Securities Markets

Correlations in Global Markets

Diversification benefits from combining securities from different countries

- Correlations between returns on U.S. stocks and Japanese, UK, German, emerging market stocks are significantly less than 1
- Correlation between returns on U.S. and global bonds is significantly less than 1
- Correlations between U.S. investment grade bond indexes are close to 1

575

Securities Markets

Assumptions of Capital Market Efficiency

- Large number of profit maximizing participants
- New information comes to the market randomly
- Investors adjust their estimates of security values rapidly to reflect new information
- Security prices implicitly reflect risk

576

Securities Markets

Efficient Market Hypothesis (EMH)

1. Weak form: Current stock prices fully reflect **all past price and volume information**

2. Semi-strong form: Security prices adjust rapidly to reflect **all publicly available information**

3. Strong form: Security prices fully reflect **all information** both public and private

577

Securities Markets

Tests of the Three Forms of the EMH

Weak form tests: Trading rules, runs tests, autocorrelation tests

Semi-strong form tests: Tests for predictable abnormal returns based on firm characteristics (e.g., low P/E) and event studies (e.g., accounting changes, earnings announcements, dividend changes)

Strong form tests: Abnormal returns to private information, insider trading, specialists' trades, security analysts' recommendations

578

Securities Markets

Six Market Anomalies

Anomalies that suggest some market inefficiency:

1. Quarterly earnings surprises (persist)
2. Calendar studies; January and weekend effects
3. P/E ratios (lower is better)
4. Small-firm effect (smaller is better)
5. Neglected stocks (low analyst coverage)
6. Book-to-market values (higher is better)

579

Securities Markets

Implications of EMH

- **Weak form efficiency → technical analysis has no value**
  Supported by the evidence
- **Semi-strong form efficiency → neither technical analysis nor fundamental analysis have value**
  Evidence is mixed
- **Strong form efficiency → not even non-public information has value**
  Not supported—insiders and specialists

580

Securities Markets

Portfolio Management with Efficient Prices

- Asset mix based on risk tolerance, returns requirement, and capital markets expectations
- Measure performance against benchmark
- Index funds attempt to match index returns while minimizing costs

581

Securities Markets

Behavioral Finance

Prospect theory – new alternative view

- Rank relative to some reference point
- Often starting point/initial wealth
- Explains irrational "loss aversion" behavior

582

Securities Markets

Bias

- **Overconfidence bias:** Analysts overemphasize supporting evidence, underemphasize contrary evidence
- Also known as **Confirmation bias:** Investors seek out information that supports their decisions and ignore information that does not
- **Escalation bias:** Investors commit more funds to losing positions they feel responsible for – averaging down, but not when they don't feel responsible

583

Securities Markets

Limitations to Fully Efficient Markets

1. Must be a **return to fundamental analysis** – but only for those who act rapidly
2. **Transactions costs** prevent arbitrage from bringing about precisely efficient prices
3. **Risk** limits the ability of arbitrage to make prices efficient

584

Securities Markets

Limitations of Arbitrage

1. Arbitrage is frequently not riskless
2. Even in **pairs trading** (where an arbitrageur buys the underpriced and shorts the overpriced security) significant risk from stock-specific factors remains
3. There is **no guarantee** that even correctly identified **mispricings will be corrected** in the near term
4. When there are many apparent mispricings, money will be used only to pursue the most attractive trades

585

Securities Markets

Reasons Anomalies May Be Justified

- **Model for estimating** abnormal (risk-adjusted) returns may be flawed
- **Strategy risk**: Anomaly may not persist, or may be reduced by investors pursuing the same strategy
- **Data mining**: Relationships in the data might result purely from chance; won't hold out of sample
- **Survivorship and sample selection biases**
- **Nonsynchronous trading**: Closing securities prices used in model may not be at the same time of day

586

Securities Markets

Why Valid Anomalies May Not Be Profitable

- Lack of theoretical explanation
- Transactions costs
- Small size of profit opportunity
- Trading restrictions
- Irrational behavior
- Other limits on arbitrage activity

587

Industry and Company Analysis

Analysis of Equity Investments - Book 4

Securities Markets

Top Down (Three-Step) Approach to Security Valuation

1. **Economic analysis**: Forecast economic growth, interest rate scenario, inflation, etc.
2. **Industry analysis**: Given the expected economic environment, identify industries that will perform well
3. **Firm analysis**: Within the industries expected to perform well, identify the firms that have the best prospects

589

Securities Markets

Valuing Preferred Stock

Preferred stock pays a constant dividend with no maturity date (perpetual preferred)

Value like a perpetuity:

$$P_0 = \frac{\text{preferred dividend}}{k_P}$$

590

Securities Markets

Valuing Common Stock: Multiple-Year Holding Period

For an n-year holding period:

$$\text{Value} = \frac{D_1}{(1+k_e)^1} + \text{........} + \frac{D_n}{(1+k_e)^n} + \frac{P_n}{(1+k_e)^n}$$

This equation tells us to find the PV of each dividend and the PV of the expected selling price just after D_n is paid. Summing these values gives us the value of the stock today.

591

Securities Markets

Valuing Common Stock – Example

A stock paid a \$1.50 dividend last year that will grow at 8% every year. You require a 12% return on the stock and you expect the stock price to be \$51.00 at the end of Year 3. What is the stock's value today?

$$\frac{1.50(1.08)}{1.12} + \frac{1.50(1.08)^2}{1.12^2} + \frac{1.50(1.08)^3}{1.12^3} + \frac{51.00}{1.12^3} = \$40.49$$

592

Securities Markets

Infinite Period Model

Model assumptions:

- Dividends grow at a constant rate forever
- $k_{ce} > g_c$

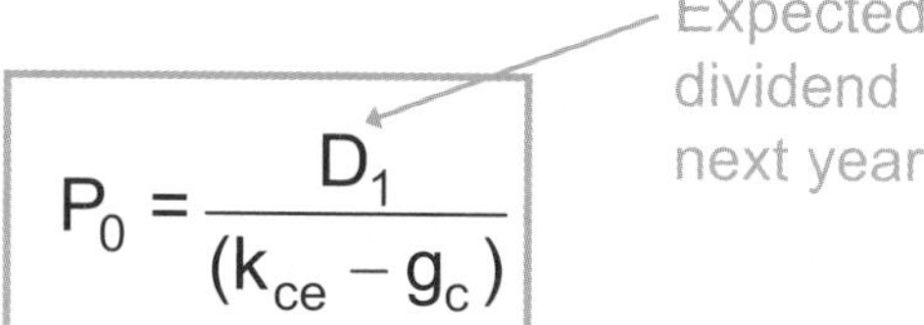

$$P_0 = \frac{D_1}{(k_{ce} - g_c)}$$

where g_c = constant dividend growth rate

593

Securities Markets

Infinite Period Model

Example: A stock paid a dividend of $1.50 a share last year which is expected to grow at a rate of 8.0% forever. If an investor requires a 12% return, what is the value of the stock today?

$$P_0 = \frac{D_1}{(k_{ce} - g_c)}$$

This is D_0

$$= \frac{1.50\ (1 + 0.08)}{(0.12 - 0.08)} = \$40.50$$

594

Securities Markets

Supernormal Growth Model – Example

Example:

- Last year's dividend (D_0) was $1.00
- Growth rate of dividend is 15% for the next two years
- Will grow at a constant rate of 5% beginning in Year 3
- You require an 11% return on the stock

595

Securities Markets

Supernormal Growth Model cont.

Step 1: Forecast the dividend for each year of non-constant growth and for the first year of constant growth

$$D_1 = \$1.00(1.15)^1 = \$1.15$$
$$D_2 = \$1.00(1.15)^2 = \$1.32$$
$$D_3 = \$1.00(1.15)^2\,(1.05) = \$1.39$$

Identify the first dividend that will grow at a constant growth rate.

596

Securities Markets

Supernormal Growth Model cont.

Find the PV of expected dividends and of the expected future stock price

$$P_0 = \frac{D_1}{1+k} + \frac{P_1}{1+k}, \text{ where } P_1 = \frac{D_2}{k-g}$$

$$P_0 = \frac{1.15}{1.11} + \frac{22.00}{1.11} = \$20.86 \qquad 22.00 = \frac{1.32}{0.11-0.05}$$

D_1 P_1 D_2

597

Securities Markets

Earnings Multiplier Model

We begin with the constant growth model:

$$P_0 = \frac{D_1}{k-g}$$

Dividing both sides of the equation by next year's projected earnings (E_1) results in:

$$\frac{P_0}{E_1} = \frac{D_1/E_1}{k-g} = \text{(leading) price to earnings ratio}$$

D_1/E_1 = expected dividend payout ratio

598

Securities Markets

Earnings Multiplier Model

$$\frac{P_0}{E_1} = \frac{D_1/E_1}{k - g}$$

- The primary determinants of a P/E ratio are the required rate of return (*k*) and the growth rate (*g*)
- The same factors that affect a stock's price affect the stock's P/E ratio

599

Securities Markets

Earnings Multiplier – Problem

You expect a firm to pay out 30% of its earnings as dividends. Earnings and dividends are expected to grow at a constant rate of 6%. If you require a 13% return on the stock, what is the stock's expected P/E ratio?

600

Securities Markets

Earnings Multiplier Valuation – Example

Recall that we estimated the P/E ratio of the stock described in the prior problem to be 4.3. If you forecast firm earnings **next year** of $2.75, what is the value of the stock today?

$$P_0 = \frac{P_0}{E_1} \times \hat{E}_1 = 4.3 \times \$2.75 = \$11.83$$

601

Securities Markets

Estimating the Value of *g*

***g* represents the earnings and dividend growth rate in the constant growth model**

g = (RR)(ROE)

where:

RR = earnings retention rate

ROE = return on equity

RR = (1 – dividend payout ratio)

602

Securities Markets

Estimating Growth – Problem

Use the following information about a firm to **estimate the firm's growth rate** (*g*).

Dividend payout ratio = 25%; Profit margin = 3%; Equity multiplier = 2.2; Total asset turnover = 1.8

603

Securities Markets

Inputs for the DDM

DDM requires **three inputs**:

1. Estimate of the stock's **future cash flows**
   - Dividends
   - Future price or constant growth value
2. Dividend **growth rate**, *g*
3. **Required return** on equity, *k*
   - Use CAPM
   - Use bond yield plus premium

604

Securities Markets

Structural Economic Factors Affecting Industries

- Demographics (e.g., aging population and health care/retirement housing)
- Lifestyles (e.g., two-working-parent households and meals outside the home)
- Technology (e.g., mobile telephones, long-distance call business)
- Regulation [e.g., free trade (NAFTA), steel tariffs, environmental regulation]

605

Securities Markets

Growth Company vs. Growth Stock

- A **growth company** is one where management consistently selects investments (projects) that earn higher returns than required by their risk
- A **growth stock** is one that earns higher returns than other stocks of equivalent risk

Note: This is not common usage for "growth stock"

MAIN POINT: Rapid growth of revenues and earnings do not necessarily mean rapidly increasing stock price

606

Securities Markets

Growth Stock vs. Value Stock

- The term **growth stock** is customarily used to refer to the stock of a firm with a high earnings growth rate (i.e., high P/E, high MKT/BOOK)
- The term **value stock** is customarily used to describe stocks that are priced low in relation to their **current** earnings or in relation to the value of their fixed assets, real estate, or cash (i.e., low P/E, low P/CF, low MKT/BOOK)

607

Securities Markets

Expected EPS for a Company

Sales forecast:

- Economic trends
- Industry and company specific factors

Expected profit margin:

- Competitive strategy
- Internal performance trends
- Company's relationship to its industry

$$\text{Exp. EPS} = \frac{\text{forecast sales} \times \text{expected profit margin}}{\text{number of shares outstanding}}$$

608

Securities Markets

Expected P/E for a Company

Method #1 – **Macroanalysis**: Involves estimating the company P/E by comparing it to forecasts of the market and/or industry P/E

Method #2 – **Microanalysis**: Calculate a point estimate of the firm's expected P/E :

- Estimate the firm's D_1 / E_1
- Estimate *k* using the CAPM (market risk) and measures of business risk, financial risk, liquidity risk, exchange rate risk, and credit risk
- Estimate *g,* where g = RR × ROE
- Put them together: $\mathbf{P_0 / E_1 = (D_1 / E_1) / (k - g)}$ 609

Securities Markets

Estimating Stock Value

Use the estimates of EPS and P/E to estimate the value of the firm's stock

P = EPS × P / EPS

610

Securities Markets

Price-to-Earnings Ratios in Valuation

Reasons for using P/Es in valuation:

- Earnings are the primary driver of stock value
- P/Es are widely used and accepted by investors
- Low P/E stocks may outperform in the long run on a relative basis

Drawbacks:

- Make no sense when EPS is negative
- There is a volatile transitory component of EPS
- Accounting choices affect P/Es

611

Securities Markets

Adjustments When Using P/Es

- **Remove non-recurring items**
- **Normalize earnings for cyclical firms:**
  - Average earnings over a cycle
  - Average ROE times shareholders' equity
    - Accounts for changes in firm size
- **Adjust for differences in accounting methods and in basic/diluted EPS when comparing P/Es**
- **Different definitions of P/E: Leading, lagging, or combination of both**

612

Securities Markets

Price-to-Book Value Ratio in Valuation

Price-to-book ratios are:

- **Generally positive** even when EPS is not
- **More stable** than EPS
- A good gauge of **net asset value** for firms holding mostly liquid assets (e.g., banks)
- Useful for firms **about to go out of business**

Studies show that P/BV ratios are negatively related to long-run average returns

613

Securities Markets

Price-to-Book Value Ratio in Valuation

Drawbacks of P/BV ratios:

- Do not recognize the **value of non-physical assets** like human capital and brand names
- Can be misleading when comparing firms with significantly **different use of fixed assets**
- **Differences in accounting** conventions can obscure true book values
- Can be misleading because **market values** may differ significantly from book values

614

Securities Markets

Price-to-Sales Ratio in Valuation

Price-to-sales ratios are:

- Useful even for **distressed firms** as sales will be positive
- More **difficult to manipulate** than EPS and BV
- **Less volatile** than P/Es
- Very **useful for start-ups** (no earnings) and firms in **mature or cyclical industries**

Studies find P/S ratios (like P/E and P/BV) are negatively related to long-run average stock returns

615

Securities Markets

Price-to-Sales Ratio in Valuation

Drawbacks of P/S ratios:

- High sales growth does **not guarantee high operating profit**
- P/S ratios do not reflect **different cost structures** across firms
- While less subject to accounting distortions than EPS and BV, **revenue recognition methods can still distort sales**

616

Securities Markets

Price-to-Cash-Flow Ratio in Valuation

Advantages of Price-to-Cash-Flow ratios:

- Cash flow is **more difficult for managers to manipulate** than earnings
- **Widely used** by institutional investors
- P/CF is **more stable** than P/E
- With CF, there is **no problem with earnings quality**
- Studies suggest that P/CF is negatively related to long-run average stock returns

617

Securities Markets

Price-to-Cash-Flow Ratio in Valuation

Drawbacks of P/CF:

- Using (EPS + non-cash charges) for CF ignores non-cash revenue and changes in working capital
- Using free cash flow to equity (FCFE) is theoretically preferable to CFO, but FCFE is more volatile than CFO
- Many definitions of “cash flow” are used, analyst must ensure consistency

618

Securities Markets

Buying Stock on Margin – Solution

Investor buys $10,000 worth of stock on 50% margin. Value of stock rises to $12,500 (a 25% rise).

What is the percentage gain to the investor (ignoring transactions costs and interest):

$$\frac{(\$12{,}500 - \$10{,}000)}{\$5{,}000} = 50\%$$

Gain on stock = $2,500

Required initial margin

619

Securities Markets

Margin Call – Solution

Buy 300 sh. of stock for $42 — 50% initial margin — 30% maintenance margin. At what price will he get a margin call?

$$\$42\left(\frac{1-0.50}{1-0.30}\right) = \$30$$

What is equity % at price of 35?

$$\frac{35-21}{35} = 40\%$$

What is amount of margin call at $25?

Equity = 25 – 21 = 4 0.3 × 25 = 7.50
need 3.50 / sh 300 × 3.50 = $1,050

620

Securities Markets

Earnings Multiplier – Solution

You expect a firm to pay out 30% of its earnings as dividends. Earnings and dividends are expected to grow at a constant rate of 6%. If you require a 13% return on the stock, what is the stock's expected P/E ratio?

$$\frac{P_0}{E_1} = \frac{D_1/E_1}{k-g} = \frac{0.30}{0.13-0.06} = 4.3$$

621

Securities Markets

Estimating Growth – Solution

Use the following information about a firm to **estimate the firm's growth rate** (*g*).

Dividend payout ratio = 25%; Profit margin = 3%; Equity multiplier = 2.2; Total asset turnover = 1.8

RR = (1 – 0.25) = 0.75
ROE = profit margin × total asset turnover × equity multiplier
ROE = 0.03 × 1.8 × 2.2 = 11.9%
g = RR × ROE = 0.75 × 0.119 = 8.9%

622

CFA® LEVEL 1

3-Day Review Slide Workbook

DERIVATIVES

Derivatives

Derivative Investments - Book 5

Derivatives

Role of Arbitrage

- Arbitrage is possible when two securities or portfolios have **identical future payoffs** but **different market prices**
- Trading by arbitrageurs will continue until they affect supply and demand enough to bring asset prices to efficient (no-arbitrage) levels

Arbitrage relations are used to value derivatives

624

Derivatives

Forwards vs. Futures

Forwards

- Private contracts
- Custom contracts
- Default risk present
- No margin
- Little regulation

Futures

- Exchange-traded
- Standardized
- Guaranteed by clearinghouse
- Margin required
- Regulated

625

Derivatives

Forward Contracts

- Customized: No active secondary market
- Long obligated to buy; short obligated to sell
- Specified asset (currency, stock, index, bond)
- Specified date in the future
- Long gains if asset price above forward price
- Short gains if asset price below forward price

626

Derivatives

Forward Contract Positions

Long position (promise to buy)

Asset – gains when price increases

FRA – gains when rates increase

Short position (promise to sell)

Asset – gains when price decreases

FRA – gains when rates decrease

Can require delivery or cash settlement

Neither party pays at contract initiation

627

Derivatives

Early Termination of Forward

1. One party pays the other cash (buys their way out)
2. Enter into an offsetting contract

628

Derivatives

Equity Index Forward – Problem

- 90-day S&P 100 forward contract
- Forward contract price = 400
- Notional amount = $10 million
- In 90 days index is at 384

What is the payment at settlement and which party receives it?

629

Derivatives

Forward on Zero-Coupon Bond

Example: 100 day, T-bill forward
Underlying: $10 million T-bill
Forward Price: $9,945,560 (1.96% discount)

- If interest rates rise, P↓, long loses/short gains
- If interest rates fall, P↑, long gains/short loses

Coupon bonds: Priced at YTM; same principle
Risky bonds: Must provide for default possibility

630

Derivatives

Forward Rate Agreement (FRA)

Exchange fixed-rate for floating-rate payment

- Notional amount
- Fixed rate = forward (contract) rate
- Floating rate (LIBOR) is underlying rate
- Long gains when LIBOR > contract rate

Long position can be viewed as a promise to borrow at the contract rate—gains when rates rise

631

Derivatives

FRA Example

Term = 30 days

Notional amount = $1 million

Underlying rate = 90-day LIBOR

Forward rate = 5%

- At t = 30 days, 90-day LIBOR = 6%
- Underlying floating rate > fixed rate
- Long position receives payment

632

Derivatives

FRA Example: Net Payment

Net payment due to the long
90 days after contract settlement:

$$(0.06-0.05)\times\left(\frac{90}{360}\right)\times 1{,}000{,}000=\$2{,}500$$

Interest savings

Payment at settlement:

$$\frac{\$2{,}500}{1+\left(0.06\times\frac{90}{360}\right)}=\$2{,}463.05$$

PV of interest savings

633

Derivatives

Currency Forward Contracts

- Long a 3-month forward contract on 1 million euros at $1.33
- At settlement, euro spot rate is $1.37

Long gains, receives either

- 1 million euros for $1.33 million or
- Cash of (1.37 – 1.33) × 1 million = $40,000

634

Derivatives

Futures Characteristics

- **Contract specifies**: Quality and quantity of good, delivery time, manner of delivery
- **Exchange specifies**: Minimum price fluctuation (tick), daily price limit
- Clearinghouse holds other side of each trade—no default (counterparty) risk
- Long 'buys' and short 'sells' the future

635

Derivatives

Futures

- Standardized so can close with offsetting trade
- Must deposit initial margin based on contract volatility
- Marked to market daily—add gains or subtract losses from margin deposit
- If margin falls below minimum, must be brought back up to initial

636

Derivatives

A Futures Trade

- July wheat futures call for delivery of 5,000 bu. of wheat in July, futures price is $5.00 per bushel Contract value is 5,000 × $5 = $25,000
- Initial margin $3,500/contract, maintenance margin $2,700/contract
- Long will get margin call if price falls by $0.16, –$0.16 × 5,000 = –$800
- If July wheat rises to $5.05, $0.05 × 5,000 = $250 is added to margin balance
- Could sell July wheat contract @$5.05 to close out position, realize gain of $250

637

Derivatives

Margin Calculation Example

Day	Required Deposit	Price/bu.	Daily Δ	Gain (+) Loss (–)	Balance
0	$3,500	$5.00		0	$3,500
1	0	$4.90	–$0.10	–$500	$3,000
2	0	$4.80	–$0.10	–$500	$2,500
3	$1,000	$4.85	+$0.05	+$250	$3,750

Loss if position closed out at $4.85?

$0.15 × 5,000 = $750

638

Derivatives

Methods to Terminate a Futures Position at Expiration

- **Reversal** (offsetting trade): Common
- **Delivery of asset**: < 1% of trades
- **Cash settlement**: May be required

639

Derivatives

Eurodollar Futures

- Based on 90-day LIBOR
- Price quotes are calculated as (100 – annualized LIBOR), e.g., 98.46
- Each 0.01 change is $25
- Contracts settle in cash
- LIBOR up, long loses
- Initial margin = $1,485
- Maintenance margin = $750
- Long gets margin call if price goes to 98.16

640

Derivatives

Treasury Bond Futures

- Traded for Treasury bonds with maturities greater than 15 years
- Deliverable
- Face value of $100,000
- Quoted as a percent and fractions of 1% (measured in 1/32nds) of face value
- Short has option of what bond to deliver and when in exp. month to deliver

641

Derivatives

Index Futures

- Long one contract at 840
- Contract value is 250 times the futures price
- Each index point in the futures price represents a gain or loss of $250 per contract
- At settlement date index is 852
- Long receives 12 × $250 = $3,000

642

Derivatives

Currency Futures – Euros in $

- Euro futures contracts on 125,000 euros
- Price = $1.2830/euro
- Every change of $0.0001 is $12.50
- Long gains if euro appreciates, price up

643

Derivatives

Characteristics of Swap Contracts

- Custom instruments
- Not traded in any organized secondary market
- Largely unregulated
- Default risk is a concern
- Most participants are large institutions
- Private agreements
- Difficult to alter or terminate

644

Derivatives

Swap Contract Terminology

- **Notional principal**: Amount used to calculate periodic payments
- **Floating rate**: Usually U.S. LIBOR
- **Tenor**: Time period covered by swap
- **Settlement dates**: Payment due dates

645

Derivatives

Terminating a Swap

Swap can be terminated by:

- Mutual agreement/payment with counterparty
- Enter offsetting swap
- Exercise swaption (to enter offsetting swap)
- Sell position to another institution with permission of counterparty

646

Derivatives

Plain Vanilla Interest Rate Swap Fixed for Floating

- Fixed interest rate payments are exchanged for floating-rate payments
- Notional amount is not exchanged at the beginning or end of the swap
- Net payment made to one party at settlement dates

647

Derivatives

Fixed-for-Floating Swap Example

Example: 2-year, semiannual-pay, LIBOR, plain vanilla interest rate swap for \$10 million with a fixed rate of 6. Semiannual fixed payments are: (0.06 / 2) × \$10 million = \$300,000

LIBOR t_0 = 5%, t_1 = 5.8%, t_2 = 6.2%, t_3 = 6.6%

1st payment: **Fixed-rate payer** pays \$50,000 net

(0.06 – **0.05**)(180/360)(10 million) = \$50,000

First net payment is known at swap initiation!

648

Derivatives

LIBOR t_0 = 5%, t_1 = 5.8%, t_2 = 6.2%, t_3 = 6.6%

****

2nd payment: **Fixed rate payer** pays $10,000 net

(0.06 – **0.058**)(180/360)(10 million) = $10,000

3rd payment: **Floating rate payer** pays $10,000 net

(0.06 – **0.062**)(180/360)(10 million) = –$10,000

4th payment: **Floating rate payer** pays $30,000 net

(0.06 – **0.066**)(180/360)(10 million) = –$30,000

649

Derivatives

Currency Swap Example

- Assume current exchange rate is $1.20/euro
- Company A lends $1.2 million to Company B at 5%/year (USD interest rate)
- Company B lends 1 million euros to Company A at 4%/year (euro interest rate)
- Loans are for two years and interest is paid semiannually

650

Derivatives

Currency Swap Cash Flows

At time 0:

Company A lends \$1.2 million to Company B

Company B lends €1 million to Company A

At each semi-annual settlement date (t = 1,2,3,4):

A pays 0.04 / 2 × €1 million = €20,000 to B

B pays 0.05 / 2 × \$1.2 million = \$30,000 to A

651

Derivatives

Currency Swap Cash Flows

At t = 4 settlement date, in addition to the interest payments:

- Company B repays \$1.2 million to Company A
- Company A repays €1 million to Company B

- This is a **fixed-for-fixed** currency swap because both loans carried a fixed rate of interest
- Could be **fixed-for-floating or floating-for-floating**

652

Derivatives

Equity (Stock, Index, Portfolio) Swaps

- **Equity return payer**:
  - Receives interest payment
  - Pays any positive equity return
  - Receives any negative equity return

- **Interest payer**:
  - Pays interest payment
  - Receives positive equity return
  - Pays any negative equity return

653

Derivatives

Equity Swap Example

- 2-year $10 million quarterly-pay equity swap
- Equity return = S&P 500 Index
- Fixed rate = 8% Current index level = 986
- Fixed rate payer pays 2%/qtr
- Equity payer pays return on index

Q1, S&P 500 = 1030
Return = 1030/986 – 1 = 4.46%
4.46% – 2.00% = 2.46%
$246,000 net payment by equity payer

Q2, S&P 500 falls from 1030 to 965
Return = 965/1030 – 1 = –6.31%
–6.31% – 2.00% = –8.31%
$831,000 net payment **to** equity payer

Q3, S&P 500 rises from 965 to 989
Return = 989/965 – 1 = +2.49%
2.49% – 2.00% = 0.49%
$49,000 net payment by equity payer

654

Derivatives

Options Basics

- **Call option**: Long has the right to purchase at the exercise (strike) price; short has the obligation to sell/deliver at the exercise price
- **Put option**: Long has the right to sell at the exercise (strike) price; short has the obligation to purchase at the exercise price

655

Derivatives

Call Intrinsic Value/Payoff at Expiration

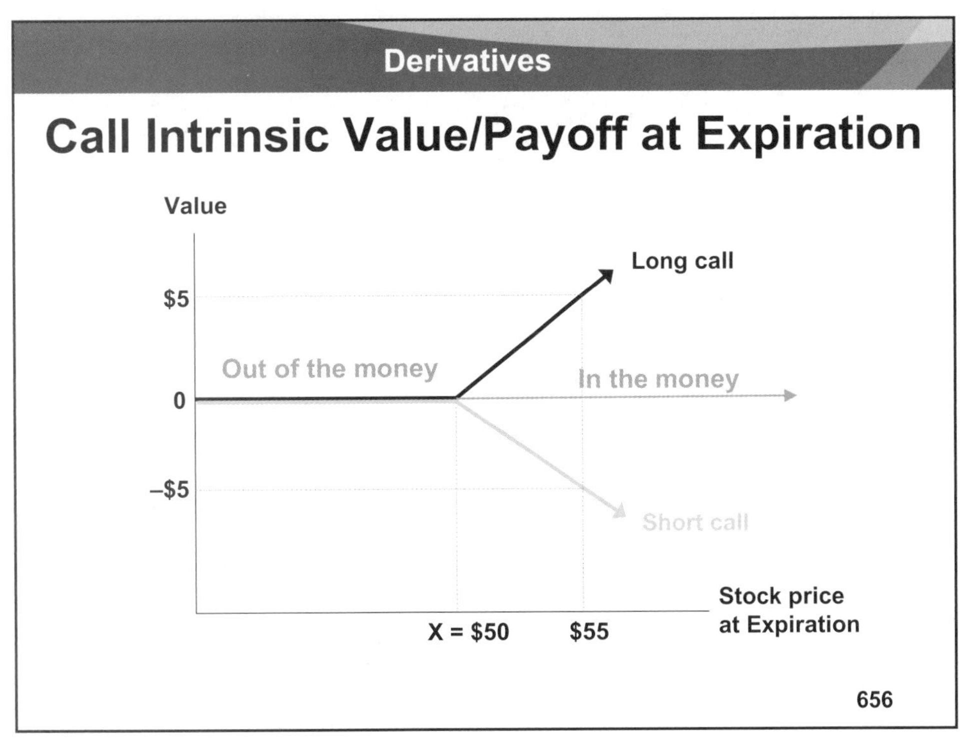

656

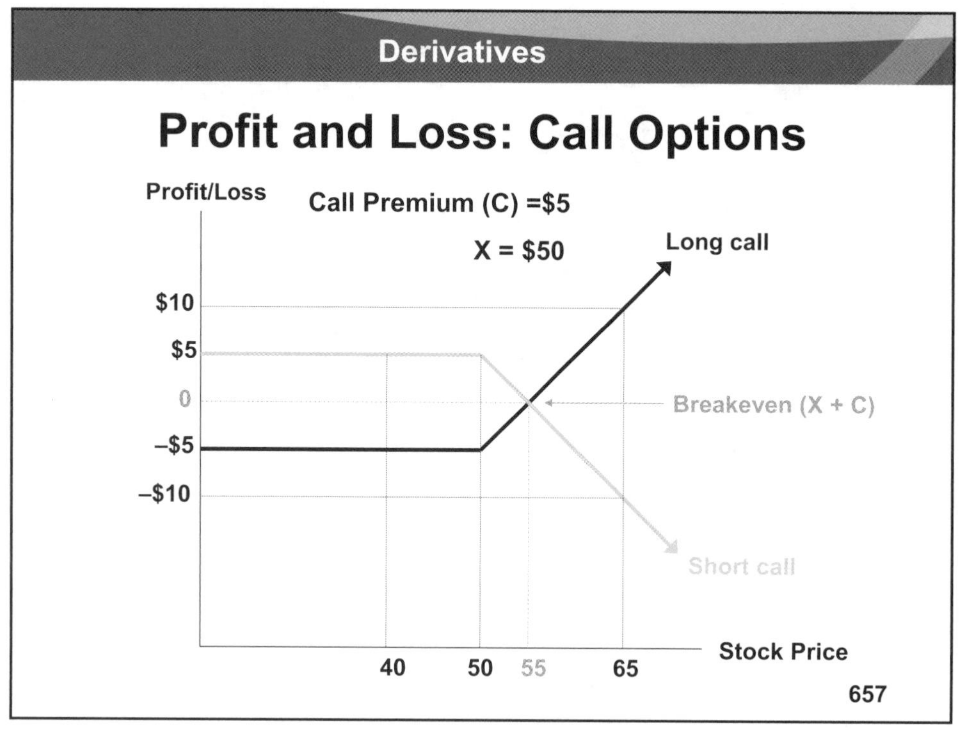
Derivatives
Profit and Loss: Call Options
Profit/Loss
Call Premium (C) =$5
X = $50
Long call
$10
$5
0
–$5
–$10
Breakeven (X + C)
Short call
40
50
55
65
Stock Price
657

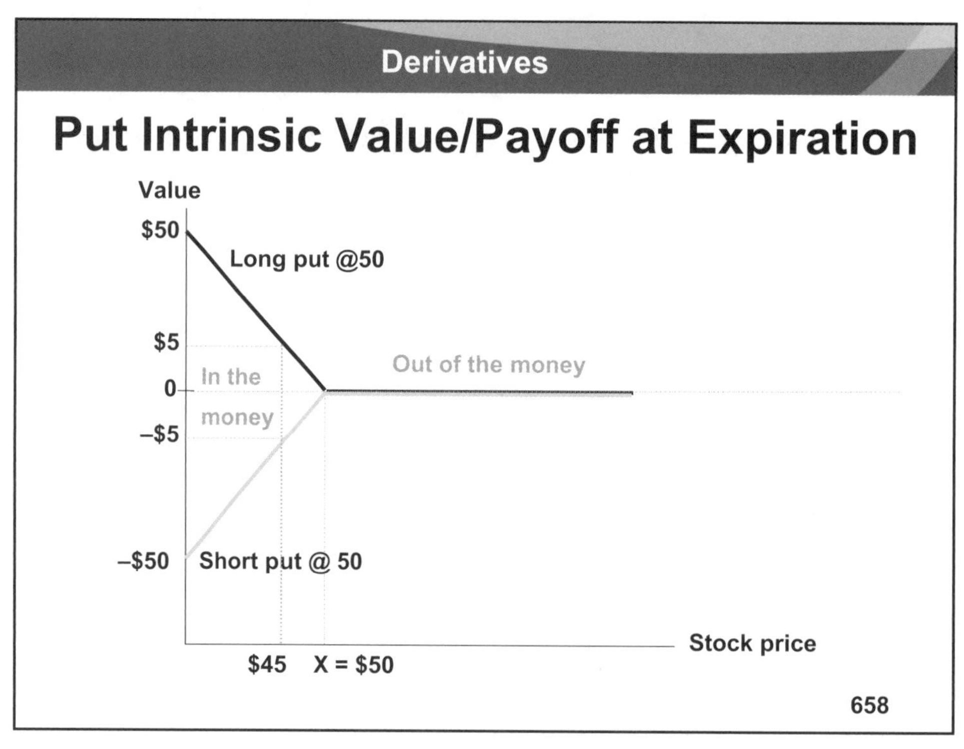
Derivatives
Put Intrinsic Value/Payoff at Expiration
Value
$50
Long put @50
$5
0
–$5
In the
money
Out of the money
–$50
Short put @ 50
$45
X = $50
Stock price
658

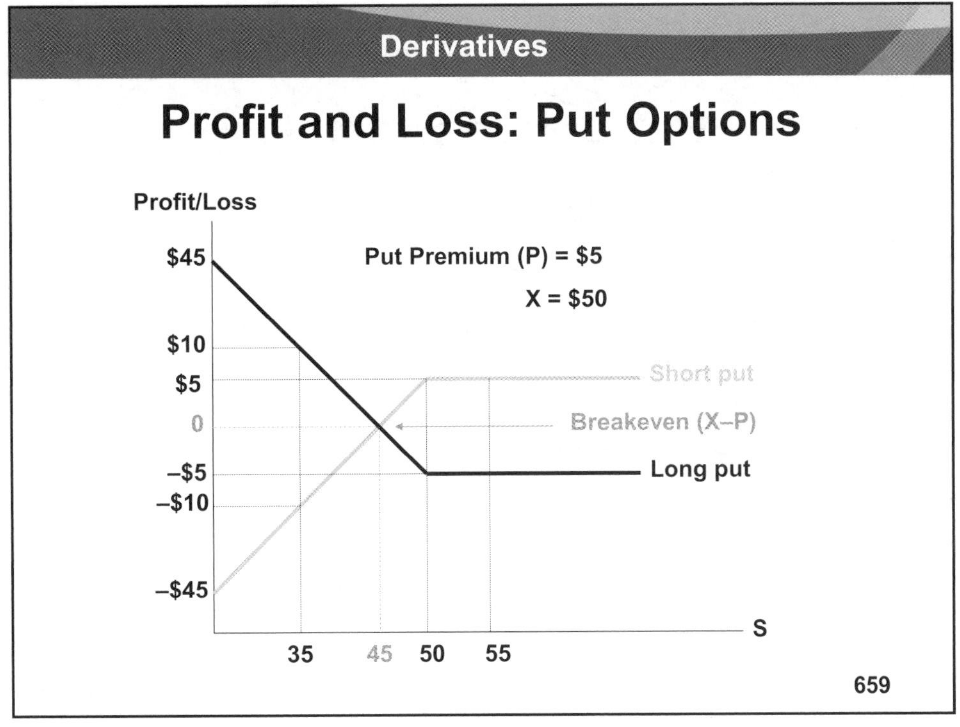

Derivatives

Call Option Example

Stock price is $27

- Call with exercise price of $30 is trading at $1.50
  - **Out of the money**: Intrinsic value is zero
  - Time value is $1.50 – 0 = $1.50

- Call with exercise price of $25 is trading at $3.00
  - **In-the-money**: Intrinsic value is $27 – $25 = $2
  - Time value is $3.00 – $2.00 = $1.00

660

Derivatives

Put Option Example

Stock price is $47

- Put with exercise price of $45 is trading at $1.50
  - Out-of-the-money: Intrinsic value is zero
  - Time value is $1.50 – 0 = $1.50
- Put with exercise price of $50 is trading at $4.00
  - In-the-money: Intrinsic value is $50 – $47 = $3
  - Time value is $4.00 – $3.00 = $1.00

661

Derivatives

Types of Options: Underlying Assets

- Commodity options: (e.g., call option on 100 ounce of gold at $820 per ounce)
- Stock options: Each contract for 100 shares
- Bond options: Like stock options, payoff based on bond price and exercise price
- Index options: Have a multiplier (e.g., payoff is $250 in cash for every index point the option is in the money at expiration)

662

Derivatives

Types of Options: Underlying Assets

Options on futures:

- **Calls** give the option to enter into a futures contract as the **long** at a specific futures price
- **Puts** give the option to enter into a futures contract as the **short** at the indicated futures price

At exercise, futures position is marked to market

663

Derivatives

Interest Rate Options

- Interest rate options: Payoff based on the difference between a floating rate, such as LIBOR, and the strike rate
- Long interest rate call gains when rates rise
- Long interest rate put gains when rates fall

Payoffs made at the **end of the interest rate term** (after option expiration) not at settlement like FRA

664

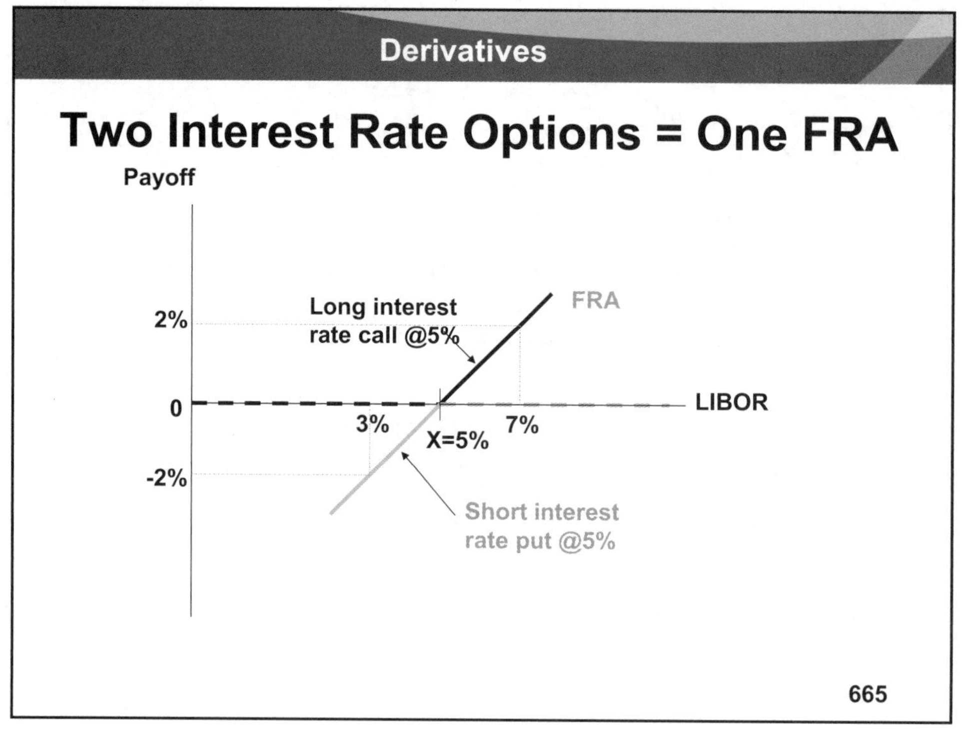
Derivatives
Two Interest Rate Options = One FRA
Payoff
2%
0
-2%
Long interest
rate call @5%
FRA
LIBOR
3%
X=5%
7%
Short interest
rate put @5%
665

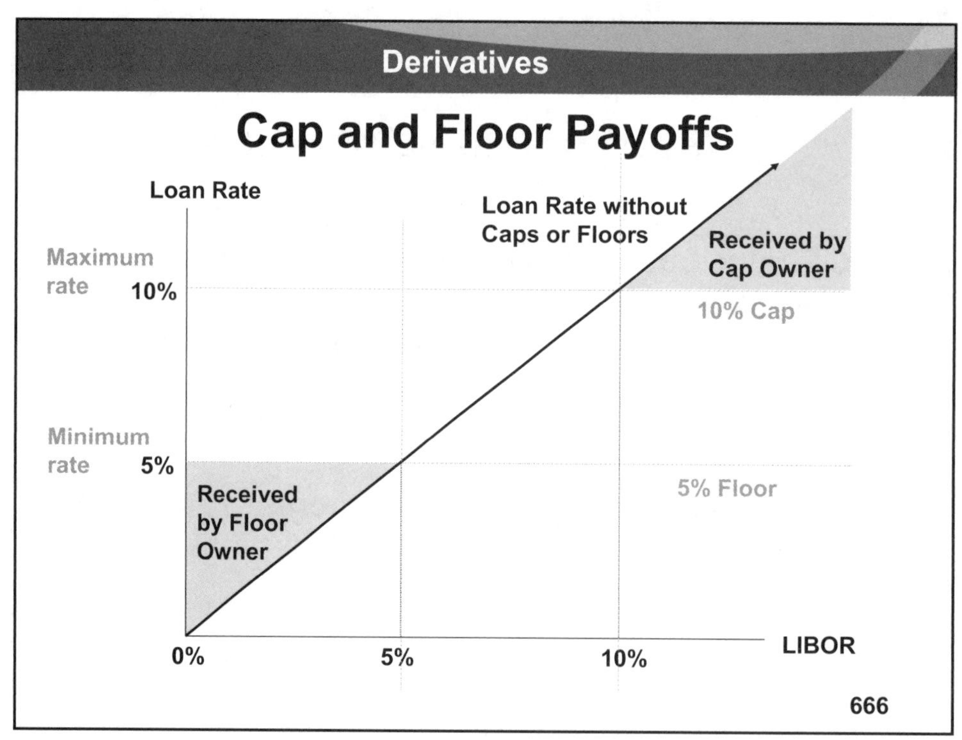
Derivatives
Cap and Floor Payoffs
Loan Rate
Loan Rate without
Caps or Floors
Received by
Cap Owner
Maximum
rate
10%
10% Cap
Minimum
rate
5%
Received
by Floor
Owner
5% Floor
0%
5%
10%
LIBOR
666

Derivatives

Interest Rate Option – Problem

- Long 30-day call on 180-day LIBOR
- Notional amount = $1 million
- Strike rate = 4%
- 90-day LIBOR at expiration (in 30 days) = 5%

What is payoff to long? When is it paid?

667

Derivatives

Five Variables for Option Value

Increase in	Call Option	Put Option
Asset Price	↑	↓
Time to Exp.	↑	↑
Strike Price	↓	↑
Volatility	↑	↑
Risk-free rate	↑	↓

668

Derivatives

Deriving Put-Call Parity

Fiduciary Call = Protective Put

call at X + bond pays X = stock + put at X

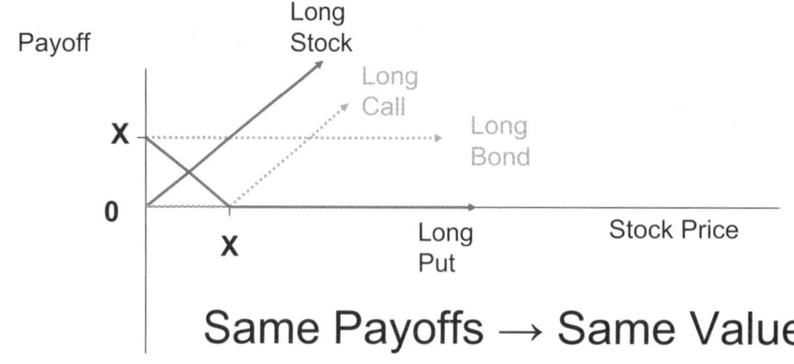

Same Payoffs → Same Value

669

Derivatives

Parity Conditions and Synthetic European Style Options

$$C + \frac{X}{(1+RFR)^T} = S + P \text{ can be rearranged}$$

$$\text{to get } P = C - S + \frac{X}{(1+RFR)^T}$$

$$\text{and } C = P + S - \frac{X}{(1+RFR)^T}$$

Borrow PV of X, buy put, buy stock.

Same payoff as a call at any stock price

670

Derivatives

Put-Call Parity – Problem

- Stock XYZ trades at $75
- Call premium = $4.50
- Expiration = 4 months (T = 0.3333)
- X = $75
- RFR = 5%

What's the price of the 4-month put on XYZ?

671

Derivatives

Cash Flows on the Underlying Asset

For assets with positive cash flows over the term of the option, we can **substitute, S – PVCF,** for **S** in all the parity relations.

672

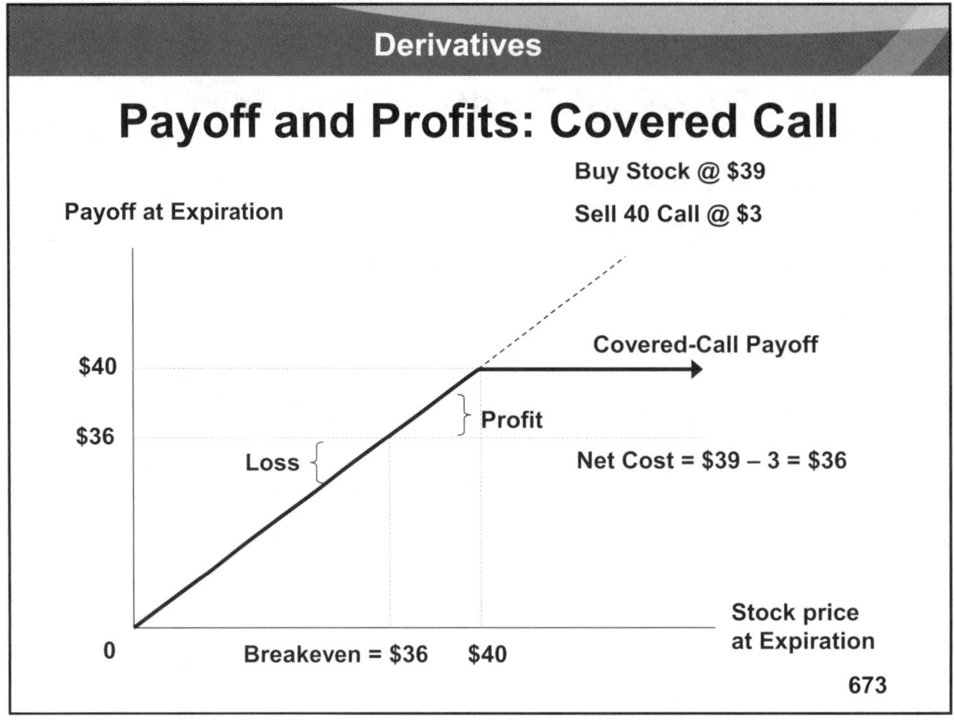

Derivatives

Covered Call – Problem

- Buy stock at $39
- Sell a 40 Call at $3
  - **<u>Net cost of *position*</u>**:
  - **<u>Breakeven stock price at expiration</u>**:
  - **<u>Maximum gain</u>**:
  - **<u>Maximum loss</u>**:
  - **<u>Profit/loss at stock price of 39</u>**:
  - **<u>Profit/loss at stock price of 32</u>**:

674

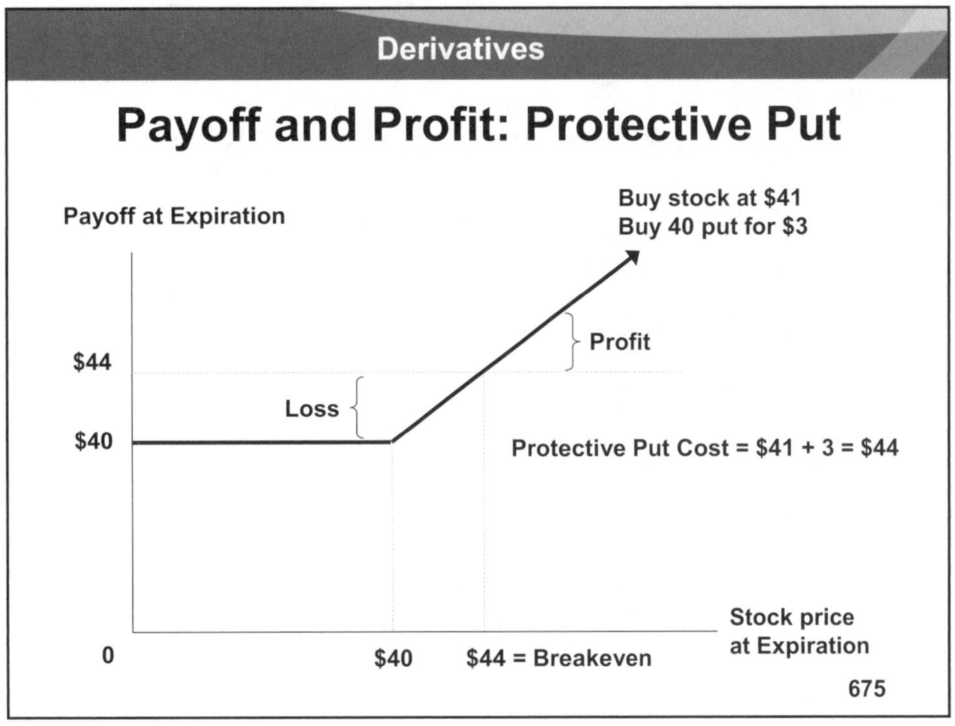

Derivatives

Example: Protective Put

- Buy stock at $41
- Buy a 40 put for $3
- Cost of protective put strategy = 41 + 3 = $44
  - **Breakeven** stock price at expiration = $44
  - **Maximum gain**: Unlimited
  - **Maximum loss**: $4 (if stock price ≤ 40)
    - At stock price of 47 → profit = $3
    - At stock price of 38 → loss = $4

676

Derivatives

Equity Index Forward – Solution

- 90-day S&P 100 forward contract
- Forward contract price = 400
- Notional amount = $10 million
- In 90 days index is at 384

What is the payment at settlement and which party receives it?

Short receives (400 – 384) / 400 × $10 million = $400,000 at settlement, paid by the long

677

Derivatives

Interest Rate Option – Solution

- Long 30-day call on 180-day LIBOR
- Notional amount = $1 million
- Strike rate = 4%
- 90-day LIBOR at expiration (in 30 days) = 5%

What is payoff to long? When is it paid?

$1,000,000 × (0.05 – 0.04) × (180/360) = $5,000

Paid by call writer **90 days after expiration**

678

Derivatives

Put-Call Parity – Solution

- Stock XYZ trades at $75
- Call premium = $4.50
- Expiration = 4 months (T = 0.3333)
- X = $75
- RFR = 5%

What's the price of the 4-month put on XYZ?

$$\text{put} = \text{call} - \text{stock} + \frac{X}{(1+\text{RFR})^T}$$

$$= 4.50 - 75 + \frac{75}{(1.05)^{.3333}} = \$3.29$$

679

Derivatives

Covered Call – Solution

- Buy stock at $39
- Sell a 40 Call at $3
  - **Net cost of *position***: 39 – 3 = $36
  - **Breakeven stock price at expiration**: $36
  - **Maximum gain**: 40 – 36 = $4
  - **Maximum loss**: $36 (if stock goes to zero)
  - **Profit/loss at stock price of 39**: $3
  - **Profit/loss at stock price of 32**: –$4

680

CFA® LEVEL 1

3-Day Review Slide Workbook

ALTERNATIVE INVESTMENTS

Alternative Investments

Alternative Investments - Book 5

Alternative Investments

Open-End Fund

- Continuous offering – by prospectus
- Shares created or redeemed at NAV
- Possible ongoing **distribution fees** (12b-1 fees)
- Typically priced at closing NAV
- No short sales
- May have **sales or redemption fees**
- **Ongoing management fees**

682

Alternative Investments

Net Asset Value (NAV)

$$NAV = \frac{\text{value of fund assets} - \text{fund liabilities}}{\text{number of shares outstanding}}$$

683

Alternative Investments

Closed-End Fund

- Fixed number of shares, IPO
- Shares trade like stocks: Short sales, margin
- Share price at premium or discount to NAV
- Bid-ask spread
- Management fees

684

Alternative Investments

Equity Fund Strategies

- Style (value, growth, large-cap, small-cap)
- Sector (energy, financials)
- Index
- Global
- Stable value (short-term debt)

685

Alternative Investments

Exchange-Traded Funds (ETFs)

- **Traded** like closed-end fund shares
- **Fixed portfolio**; usually mimics an index
- **Low fees**, low turnover, low tax liability
- **Cash redemption** by shareholders discouraged

Key Point

- **In-kind creation and redemptions** by exchange specialists keeps price close to NAV

686

Alternative Investments

ETFs

- **Efficient** method of **diversification**
- **Trade like traditional equity investments**; can be shorted or margined
- Patterned after **indexes with active futures and option markets**
- Published **list of underlying assets**
- Typically **very efficient** operating expense ratios
- **"In-kind" creation and redemption** of shares
- **Decreased** capital gains **tax liability**
- For some, **dividends may be reinvested** immediately

687

Alternative Investments

- Some ETFs have with low trading volume, high bid-ask spreads, **low liquidity**
- Some ETFs are **hard to borrow** to sell short
- ETF trading **prices can differ from NAV**, depending on depth and liquidity
- Some ETFs use derivatives and have **leverage and credit risk**

688

Alternative Investments

Real Estate Valuation Approaches

- (Replacement) Cost method
- Sales comparison method
- Income method
- Discounted after-tax cash flow value

689

Alternative Investments

Net Operating Income (NOI) – Problem

Apartment has 25 units, average rental $1,000/mo., Taxes are $70,000/yr., maintenance is $25,000/yr. Average vacancy is 5%, collection losses are 2% Calculate NOI.

Required return is 10%,what is income approach value?

690

Alternative Investments

Sales Comparison Approach

- Use recent prices of **comparable properties** and **adjust for differences/unique features**
- **Use a benchmark** (mean or median) in area, and adjust for differences/unique features
- Use **estimated regression coefficients** (Hedonic price estimation) from a large number of recent transactions

691

Alternative Investments

Real Estate Cash Flow Evaluation

- Cf_0 is down payment of –$370,000
- Cf_1 = $39,243
- Cf_2 = $38,991
- Cf_3 = $538,714

- Assume required after-tax return of 10%
  NPV = $102,643.22, so accept
  IRR = 20.18% > 10%, so accept

692

Alternative Investments

Stages in Venture Capital Investing

Formative Stage

1. Seed stage (business idea)
2. Early stage (prior to commercial sales)
   - **Start-up** (development, early marketing)
   - **First stage** (initiate manufacturing & sales)

Expansion Stage

3. Later stage
   - **Second stage** (expand to profitability)
   - **Third stage** (major expansion or marketing)
   - **Mezzanine** (preparing to go public)

693

Alternative Investments

Venture Capital Characteristics

- Illiquid
- Difficult to value
- Limited data
- Entrepreneurs can be poor managers
- Need proper incentives for fund managers
- Timing of exit strategy important to returns
- Requires extensive operations management

694

Alternative Investments

Venture Capital NPV – Problem

Initial investment = \$2 million, **req. return** = 20%

Estimated payoff after 3 years = \$9 million

Conditional Failure Rates – given survival

Yr. 1 → 8%, Yr. 2 → 15%, Yr. 3 → 10%

695

Alternative Investments

Hedge Funds

- Hedge funds typically **seek absolute return**
- Pursue **various investment strategies**
- Do **not necessarily involve hedging**
- Typically structured as **limited partnerships**
- Exempt from SEC regulation
- Flat percent fee plus **performance-based fee** (often based on returns above a target or benchmark return)

696

Alternative Investments

Fund of Funds Investing

Benefits

- Portfolio of hedge funds: ***diversification***, reduced risk
- **Professionally selected** funds
- Possible **access to closed funds**

Drawbacks

- **Additional management *fees*** → lower returns
- Manager **can select funds poorly**

697

Alternative Investments

Unique Risks of Hedge Funds

- Illiquidity
- Potential for mispricing
- Counterparty credit risk
- Settlement errors
- Short covering
- Margin calls
- Bernie Madoff

698

Alternative Investments

Hedge Fund Performance

Hedge funds as an asset class have had:

- Better returns
- Lower risk
- Higher Sharpe ratios

699

Alternative Investments

Hedge Fund Performance Biases

- **Cherry Picking** → reporting selected results
- **Non-market valuation** → smoothes results, reduces reported risk
- **Survivorship bias** → poor performers disappear, biases mean return upward, risk downward
- **Asymmetrical returns** → standard deviation can be a misleading risk measure

700

Alternative Investments

Closely Held Company Valuation

- The replacement **cost approach**
- **The comparables approach**
- **The** (NPV of) **income approach**

701

Alternative Investments

Valuation Discounts and Premiums

Note that discounts and premiums are relative to characteristics of the company or shares used for the comparable value/benchmark value

- **Discount** for lack of liquidity/marketability compared to comparable publicly traded firm
- **Discount** for lack of control (i.e., minority interest) when comparable is the sale of controlling interest
- **Premium** for control/controlling interest when comparable is minority stake and subject company valuation is for a controlling interest

702

Alternative Investments

Investing in Commodities

- Investing in commodities gives an investor **exposure to** an economy's **production and consumption growth**
- When the economy experiences growth, the demand for commodities increases, and price increases are likely
- During recessions, commodity prices are likely to fall with decreased demand
- **Swings in** commodity **prices** are likely to be **larger** than changes in finished goods prices

703

Alternative Investments

Commodities Investing

Primary **motivations** for commodity investing:

- Inflation **hedge**
- **Speculation** on the near-term direction of commodity prices

Commodity-linked equity investments: Shares of commodity producing companies

Commodity-linked bonds: Provide income as well as exposure to commodity price changes

704

Alternative Investments

Collateralized Commodity Futures

- Enter into a futures contract
- Buy T-bill equal to contract value

Holding period returns are:

1. T-bill % returns (yield) +
2. Futures % return (change in contract value)

705

Alternative Investments

Spot Prices and Expected Future Prices

- **Contango**
  Futures price is **above** the spot price

- Long hedgers (users of the commodity) bid up the price of commodity futures—paying a premium for the hedging benefit from taking long futures positions

706

Alternative Investments

Spot Prices and Expected Future Prices

- **Backwardation**
  Futures price is **below** the spot price
- Dominant traders in a commodity future are **producers hedging** exposure to unexpected **price declines**
- Historically, backwardation has been the typical situation and is sometimes referred to as **normal backwardation**

707

Alternative Investments

Sources of Risk and Return

Risk

- Long exposure to a commodity price can be achieved through a derivative investment in forwards or futures
- Some physical commodities cannot be effectively purchased and stored long term
- Derivatives may be a more efficient means of gaining long exposure than purchasing the commodities outright and storing them

708

Alternative Investments

Sources of Risk and Return

Return

The return on a commodity investment includes:

- **Collateral yield**: the return on the collateral posted to satisfy margin requirements
- **Price return**: the gain or loss due to changes in the spot price
- **Roll yield**: the gain or loss resulting from re-establishing positions as contracts expire

Roll yield is **positive** if the futures market is in **backwardation** and **negative** if the market is in **contango**

709

Alternative Investments

A commodity index strategy is considered an **active investment strategy** because the manager must:

- decide **which maturities to use** for contracts
- determine **when to roll futures over** into new contracts
- **manage portfolio weights** to match those of the benchmark index
- determine the best choice of **securities to post as collateral**

710

Alternative Investments

Net Operating Income (NOI) – Solution

Apartment has 25 units, average rental $1,000/mo., Taxes are $70,000/yr., maintenance is $25,000/yr. Average vacancy is 5%, collection losses are 2% Calculate NOI.

$$(25 \times 1{,}000 \times 12)(1 - 0.05 - 0.02) - 70{,}000 - 25{,}000$$

$$= \$184{,}000$$

Required return is 10%,what is income approach value?

$$\frac{184{,}000}{0.10} = \$1.84 \text{ million}$$

711

Alternative Investments

Venture Capital NPV – Solution

Initial investment = $2 million, **req. return** = 20%

Estimated payoff after 3 years = $9 million

Conditional Failure Rates – given survival

Yr. 1 → 8%, Yr. 2 → 15%, Yr. 3 → 10%

Probability that venture survives for 3 years

(1 – 0.08)(1 – 0.15)(1 – 0.10) = 70.4%

$$\text{NPV} = \frac{0.704 \times 9 \text{ million}}{1.2^3} - 2 \text{ million} = \$1{,}666{,}667$$

712

CFA® LEVEL 1

3-Day Review Slide Workbook

FIXED INCOME

Fixed Income Investments

Fixed Income Investments - Book 5

Fixed Income Investments

Bond Indentures

A **bond indenture** specifies all the obligations of the issuer of a fixed income security

Covenants – protect bondholder interests

Negative covenants – prohibitions on the borrower

Affirmative covenants – promises by the borrower

714

Fixed Income Investments

Amortizing and Nonamortizing Bonds

- Nonamortizing securities pay only interest until maturity, then the par value is repaid
  - Coupon Treasury bonds
  - Most corporate bonds
- Amortizing securities typically make equal payments over the life of the bond, each consists of interest and principal

715

Fixed Income Investments

Bond Features

- **Face value, par value, maturity value**
- **Coupon rate, nominal yield**: Annual % of par value
- e.g., \$100,000 6½% semiannual-pay July 1, 2025—pays \$3,250 Jan 1 and July 1

716

Fixed Income Investments

Coupon Structures

- **Zero-coupon bonds**

  pure discount bonds, pay no coupon
- **Step-up notes**

  coupon rate increases over time
- **Deferred coupon**

  bond's coupons compound

717

Fixed Income Investments

Floating-Rate Securities

- **Coupon formula**

  Reference rate + margin
  - e.g., LIBOR + 1.5%, annualized rates
- **Cap**: Maximum on formula rate
- **Floor**: Minimum on formula rate

718

Fixed Income Investments

Accrued Interest

- Full price = clean price + accrued interest

$$AI = \frac{\text{days since last coupon}}{\text{days between coupons}} \times \text{coupon payment}$$

719

Fixed Income Investments

Call Provisions

- Issuer can redeem bonds prior to maturity
- Call protection for some period

Call prices typically decrease over time (e.g., 15-year bond: callable after 5 years @ 102 and callable after 10 years @ par)

720

Fixed Income Investments

Prepayment Option

- On an amortizing security, such as a mortgage
- Prepayments are repayment of principal **in excess of scheduled principal payments**

721

Fixed Income Investments

Sinking Fund

- **Sinking fund** redemptions are calls of a portion of an outstanding bond issue, typically at par
- **Premium bonds**: Cash paid to trustee, bonds to be retired chosen by lottery
- **Discount bonds**: Bonds can be purchased and delivered to trustee to be retired

722

Fixed Income Investments

Redemption Prices

- Call prices are regular redemption prices
- Sinking fund redemptions and redemptions under other provisions are special redemption prices

  (e.g., redemptions due to forced asset sales)

723

Fixed Income Investments

Embedded Options

- Options that **benefit the issuer/borrower** – lower bond values/increase yields
- Options that **benefit the holder/lender** – increase bond values/decrease yields

724

Fixed Income Investments

Embedded Options

Option Type	Benefits the…
Call Provision	Issuer/Borrower
Prepayment Option	Issuer/Borrower
Caps	Issuer/Borrower
Put Provision	Buyer/Lender
Conversion Option	Buyer/Lender
Floors	Buyer/Lender

725

Fixed Income Investments

Margin Buying and Repurchase Agreements

- **Margin buying:** Borrowing funds to purchase securities. The securities are the collateral for the margin loan
- **Repurchase agreement:** An institution sells a security with a commitment to buy it back at a specified higher price
- Most bond-dealer financing is achieved through repurchase agreements rather than margin loans

726

Fixed Income Investments

Bond Discounts and Premiums

- Yield = coupon rate → bond price at par
- Yield < coupon rate → bond price over par bond priced at a premium
- Yield > coupon rate → bond price under par bond priced at a discount

727

Fixed Income Investments

Price/Yield for an 8% Bond

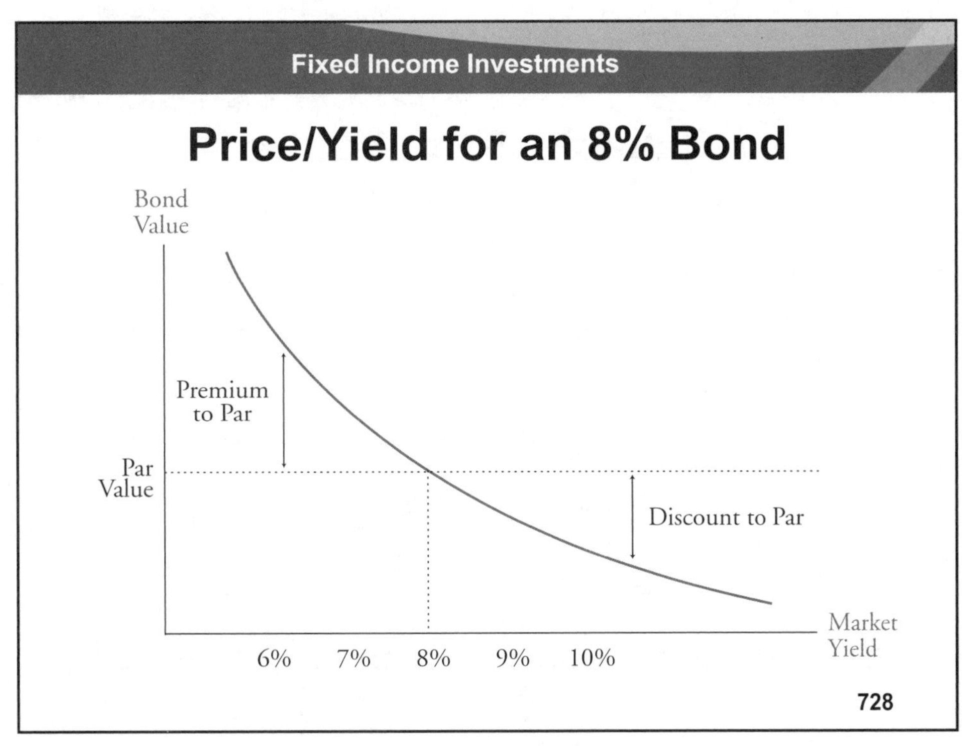

728

Fixed Income Investments

Factors Affecting Interest Rate Risk

- Longer maturity → higher interest rate risk
- Higher coupon → lower interest rate risk
- Higher yield → lower interest rate risk
- Call option → lower interest rate risk
- Put option → lower interest rate risk

729

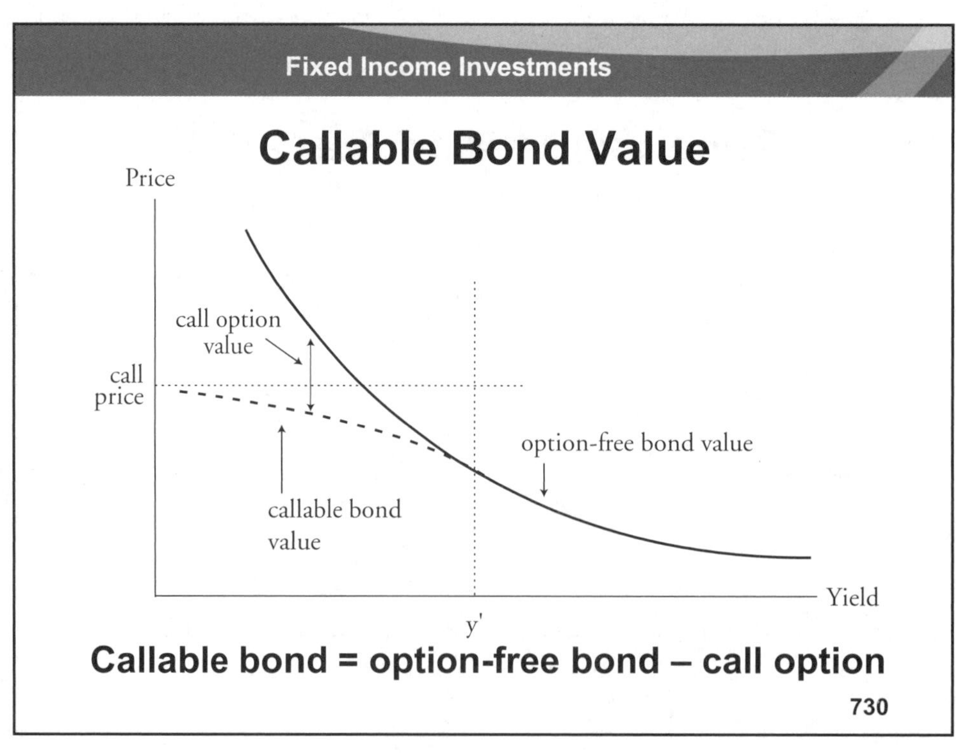

Fixed Income Investments

Floating-Rate Securities

- **Coupon is periodically reset** based on a reference rate (plus a fixed margin)
- Has **interest rate risk** between reset dates
- Price may **differ from par at reset** if:
  - Credit quality of issuer changes after issuance
  - Margin over reference rate no longer appropriate

731

Fixed Income Investments

Measure Interest Rate Risk With Duration

Duration is the approximate percentage price change for a 1% change in yield

$$\text{duration} = \frac{\text{price w/yield decline} - \text{price w/yield increase}}{2 \times \text{initial price} \times \text{decimal change in yield}}$$

If market yield goes up 0.5% bond price goes from 980 to 960, if yield goes down by 0.5% price goes to 1,002

$$\text{duration} = \frac{1{,}002 - 960}{2 \times 980 \times 0.005} = 4.29$$

732

Fixed Income Investments

Price Impact of Yield Changes

Based on the duration of 4.29:

- If the yield goes **up** 0.25%, price goes **down** by 4.29 (0.25%) = 1.0725%
- For a bond valued at $2.5 million, a yield change of 0.25% leads to an approximate change in value of 1.0725% (2.5 mil) = $26,812.50
- **Dollar duration** of a bond is approximate change in value for a 1% change in yield, 0.0429 (2.5 mil) = $107,250

733

Fixed Income Investments

Duration and Yield Curve Risk

- Portfolio duration is an approximation of the price sensitivity of a portfolio to a **parallel shift** of the yield curve (yields on all the bonds change by the same percent)
- For a **non-parallel shift** in the yield curve, the yields on different bonds in a portfolio can change by different amounts
- **Yield curve risk:** The interest rate risk of a portfolio of bonds that is not captured by the duration measure

734

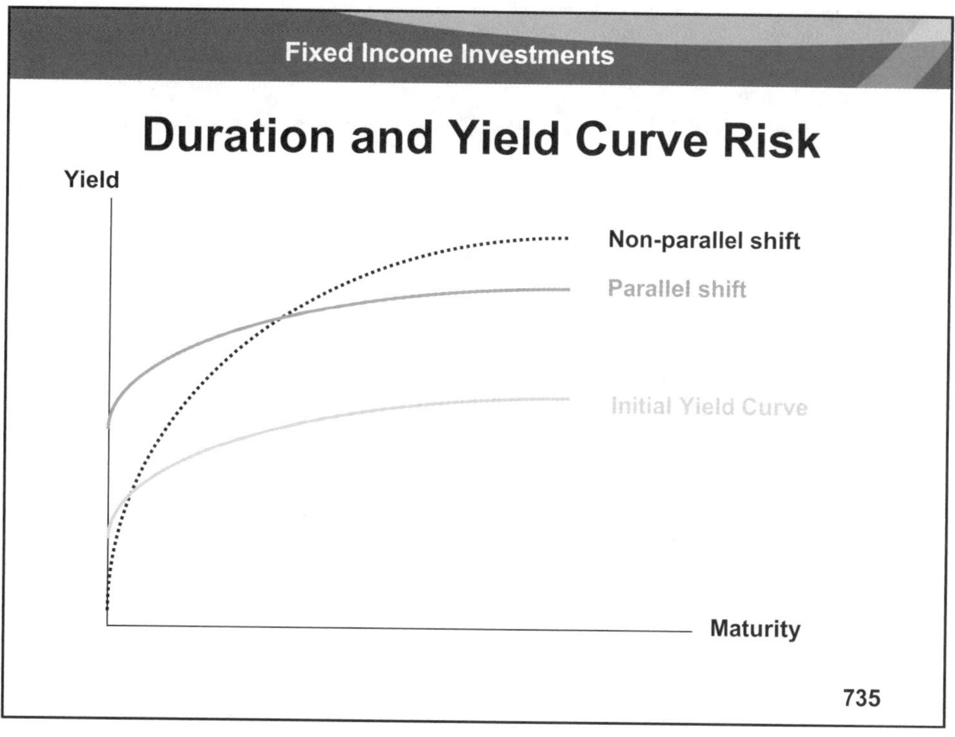

Fixed Income Investments

Callable and Prepayable Securities

- Callable securities are likely to be called when interest rates are low
- Principal repayment on prepayable securities is faster when interest rates are low
- Investors must reinvest principal when rates are low

736

Fixed Income Investments

Factors Affecting Reinvestment Risk

Reinvestment risk is **higher** when:

1. Coupon is higher
2. Bond has a call feature
3. A security is amortizing
4. A security contains a prepayment option

737

Fixed Income Investments

Forms of Credit Risk

- **Downgrade risk**: Probability of ratings decrease
- **Default risk**: Probability of default
  Bond ratings indicate relative probability of default
- **Credit spread risk**: Risk of increase in spread to Treasuries to compensate for default risk

The higher the rating (e.g., AA vs. A), the lower the market yield

738

Fixed Income Investments

Liquidity Risk

- Liquidity is high when there is a large amount of trades – can sell quickly at market price
- The **bid-ask spread** indicates the liquidity of the market for a security
- Even if an investor plans to hold the security until maturity, marking the security prices to market will result in lower returns when liquidity decreases (bids fall)

739

Fixed Income Investments

Inflation (Purchasing Power) Risk

Higher inflation decreases the amount of real goods and services that bond payments will purchase

Nominal rate = real rate + expected inflation

When expected inflation increases, nominal yields rise, values of debt securities fall

740

Fixed Income Investments

Effects of Yield Volatility

Increase in interest rate volatility increases option values

Increases **value of putable bond**

Decreases **value of callable bond**

741

Fixed Income Investments

Event Risk

- **Risk (to bond values) from other factors:**

Disasters

Corporate restructurings

Regulatory issues

742

Fixed Income Investments

Sovereign Debt

Bonds issued by central governments

- U.S. Treasury securities considered free of credit risk
- Sovereign debt of other countries considered to have varying degrees of credit risk

743

Fixed Income Investments

U.S. Treasury Securities

- **T-Bills**: Pure discount securities, less than one year maturity
- **Notes** and **bonds**: Semi-annual coupon interest, 2 to 30 years maturity
- **Treasury Inflation Protected Securities (TIPS)**

  Coupon **rate is fixed**

  Par value is **adjusted for inflation**

Semiannual payment = ½ coupon rate × adjusted par value

744

Fixed Income Investments

On- and Off-the-Run Treasuries

On-the-run issues: most recent, most liquid

Off-the-run issues: older issues

Stripped Treasuries: zero-coupon 'pieces' of Treasury notes and bonds, taxed on implicit interest

Agency securities: e.g. GNMA, FNMA, Sallie Mae, Freddie Mac, TVA

very little credit risk

745

Fixed Income Investments

Mortgage Passthrough Securities

- Percentage share of mortgage pool
- Interest, principal payments, prepayments
- Prepayment risk – rates down, prepayments accelerate

Collateralized Mortgage Obligations (CMOs)

- More complex cash flow claims – tranches
- Rearrange prepayment risk

Goal is always lower overall cost of funds

746

Fixed Income Investments

Municipal Securities

Tax-backed (general obligation) bonds

Revenue bonds – specific project

Insured bonds – higher rating, lower yield (cost)

Pre-refunded bonds – Treasuries deposited to fund payments

747

Fixed Income Investments

After-Tax Yield – Problem

Tax-free bond yields **7%** **Taxable bond** yields **10%**

Investor marginal **tax rate** is **35%**

Which bond will the investor prefer?

748

Fixed Income Investments

Corporate Bonds

Secured bonds – first claim against specific collateral (mortgage debt, collateral trust bonds)

Debenture bonds – unsecured bonds, no specific collateral (debentures)

Subordinated debenture bonds – lower priority claim

Commercial paper – 2 to 270 days, pure discount, not liquid

Medium-Term Notes (MTN) – Continuously offered by agent, best efforts, can customize, 9 months to 30+ years

Structured Notes – MTN combined with derivative to get equity or other exposure, “rule busters”

749

Fixed Income Investments

Other Debt Securities

Banks

Negotiable CDs

Days to 5 years, secondary market, typically LIBOR

Bankers acceptances

Short term, pure discount, few dealers, liquidity risk

Asset-backed securities

Issued by SPV which owns financial assets, e.g., mortgages, receivables, car loans, home equity loans

External Credit Enhancements

Corporate guarantees, Bank letters of credit, Bond insurance (insurance wrap)

750

Fixed Income Investments

Collateralized Debt Obligations

Pool of other debt obligations

(e.g., business loans, mortgages, asset-backed securities, other CDOs, bonds, etc.)

- **Balance Sheet CDOs**

  To reduce loans on balance sheet (banks)

- **Arbitrage CDOs**

  Profit from cash flow spread

- **Tranches**

  Created based on seniority of claims to cash flows from collateral

751

Fixed Income Investments

Yield Curve Shapes

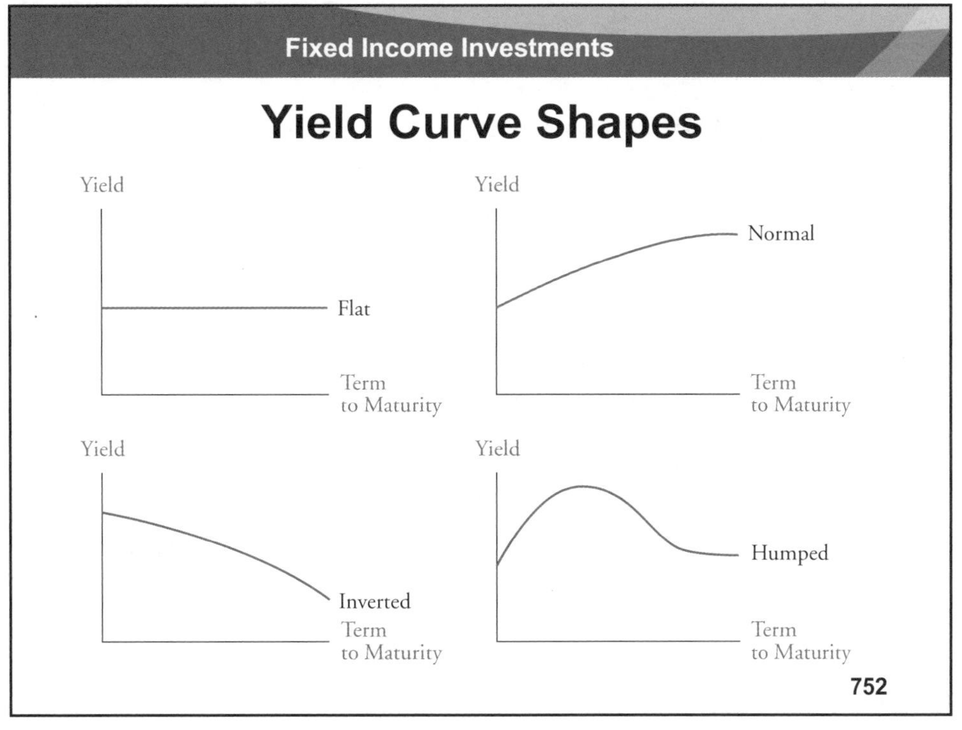

752

Fixed Income Investments

Term Structure Theories

1. Pure Expectations Theory

Yield curve shape determined by expectations about future short-term rates

2. Liquidity Preference (Premium) Theory

Greater premium (yield) required for longer maturities (includes expectations)

3. Market Segmentation Theory

Supply and demand for specific maturity *ranges* determines interest rates; any shape

753

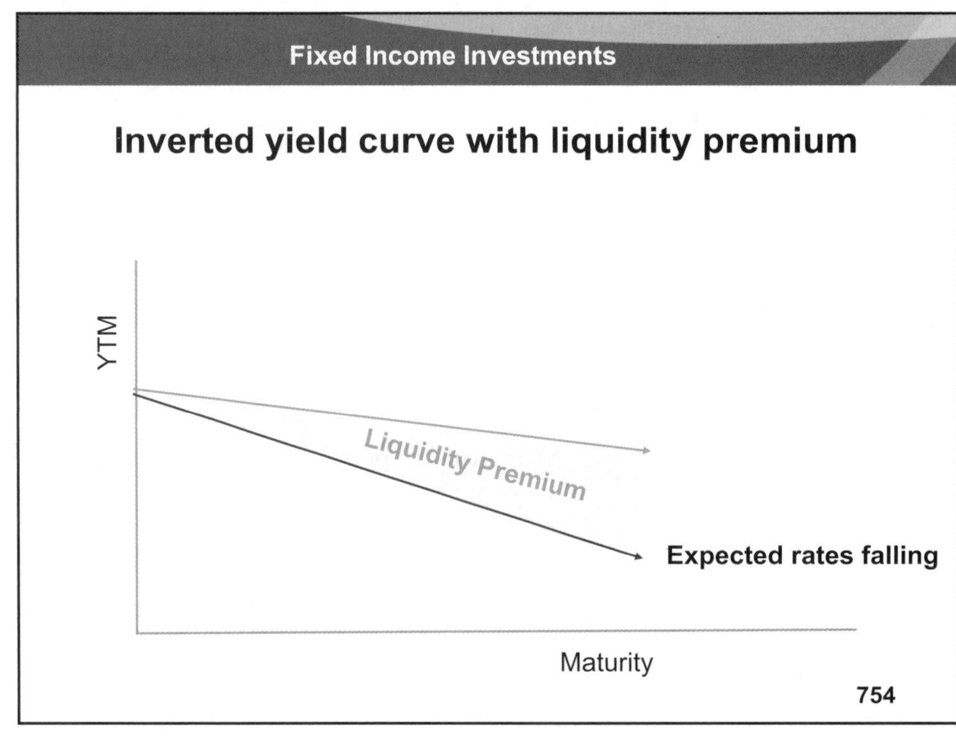

Fixed Income Investments

Treasury Spot Rates

- Conceptually like **zero-coupon** bond rates

755

Fixed Income Investments

Yield Spread Calculations

5-year Treasury yields 5% -Benchmark yield

5-year A-rated corporate yields 6.25%

absolute spread = 6.25 – 5.0 = 1.25%

$$\text{relative spread} = \frac{6.25}{5} - 1 = 1.25 - 1 = 25\%$$

$$\text{yield ratio} = \frac{6.25}{5} = 1.25$$

756

Fixed Income Investments

Credit Spreads

- Difference between yields of bonds that differ only in credit rating
- Often quoted as a spread to Treasuries
- Credit spreads narrow during expansions and widen during contractions/recessions

757

Fixed Income Investments

Embedded Options and Spreads

What is the effect of a call option on yield?

Including a **call option** increases required yield and **increases yield spread** relative to Treasuries

What is the effect of a put option on yield?

A put option is preferred by bondholders, yield and yield spread are decreased

758

Fixed Income Investments

Liquidity and Yield

- Investors prefer more liquidity so **less liquid** issues have **greater required yields** and **greater yield spreads** relative to Treasuries, which are very liquid
- **Larger issues** typically have **more liquidity** and therefore lower yields and lower yield spreads than otherwise identical smaller issues

759

Fixed Income Investments

Bond Valuation Process

1. Estimate cash flows
2. Determine the appropriate discount rate based on risk
3. Calculate present values of promised cash flows

Uncertainty about timing and amounts of cash flows makes valuation more difficult

760

Fixed Income Investments

Bond Value: 8% Coupon, 12% Yield

$$\frac{80}{(1.12)^1} + \frac{80}{(1.12)^2} + \frac{80 + 1{,}000}{(1.12)^3} = 903.927$$

N = 3; I/Y = 12; PMT = 80; FV = 1,000;

CPT PV = $903.93

761

Fixed Income Investments

Same (8% 3-yr.) Bond With a Semiannual-Pay Coupon

PMT = coupon / 2 = $80 / 2 = $40
N = 2 × # of years to maturity = 3 × 2 = 6
I/Y = discount rate / 2 = 12 / 2 = 6%
FV = par = $1,000

N = 6; I/Y = 6; PMT = 40; FV = 1,000;
CPT PV = –901.65

762

Fixed Income Investments

8% 3-Year Bond With Semiannual Coupon Payments, YTM = 12

YTM = 12%	**YTM = 8%**	**YTM = 4%**
N = 6	N = 6	N = 6
PMT = 40	PMT = 40	PMT = 40
FV = 1,000	FV = 1,000	FV = 1,000
I/Y = 12/2 = 6	**I/Y = 8/2 = 4**	**I/Y = 4/2 = 2**
CPT PV = 901.65	CPT PV = 1,000	CPT PV = 1,112.03

763

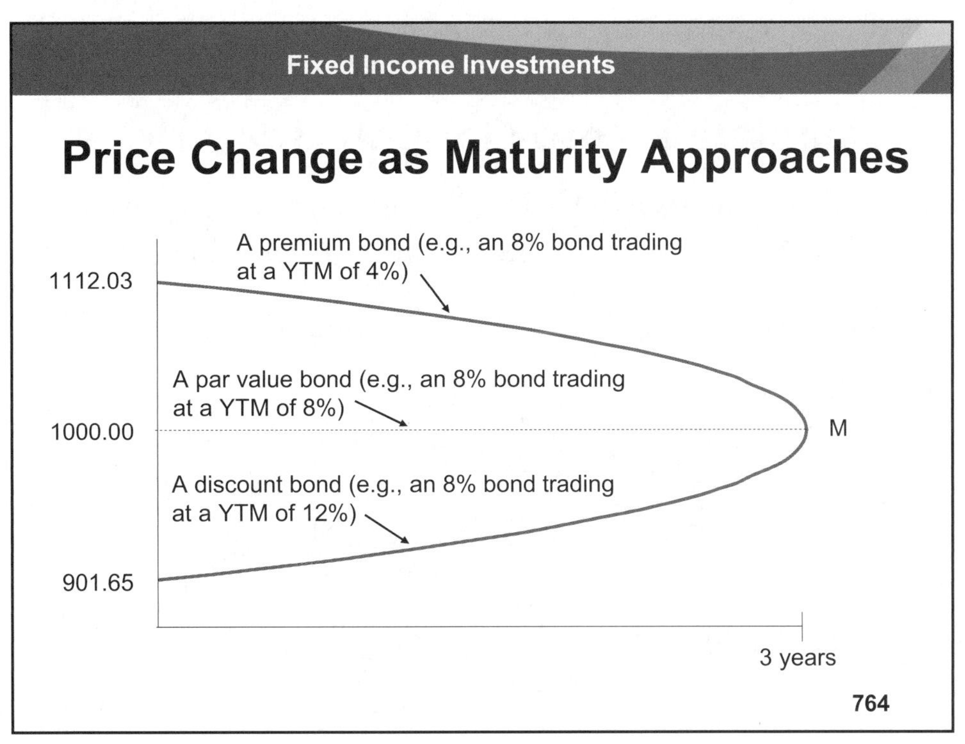

Fixed Income Investments

Value Change as Time Passes – Problem

6% 10-year semiannual coupon bond has a YTM of 8%

1. What is the price of the bond?
2. What is the value after 1 year if the yield does not change?
3. What is the value after 2 years if the yield does not change?

765

Fixed Income Investments

Calculate a Zero-Coupon Bond Price

$1,000 par value zero-coupon bond matures in 3 years and with a discount rate of 8%

Calculate BEY

TVM Keys:

N = 3 × 2 = 6, PMT = 0, FV = 1,000,

I/Y = 8 / 2 = 4 CPT PV = –790.31

Mathematically: $\frac{1,000}{(1.04)^6} = \$790.31$

766

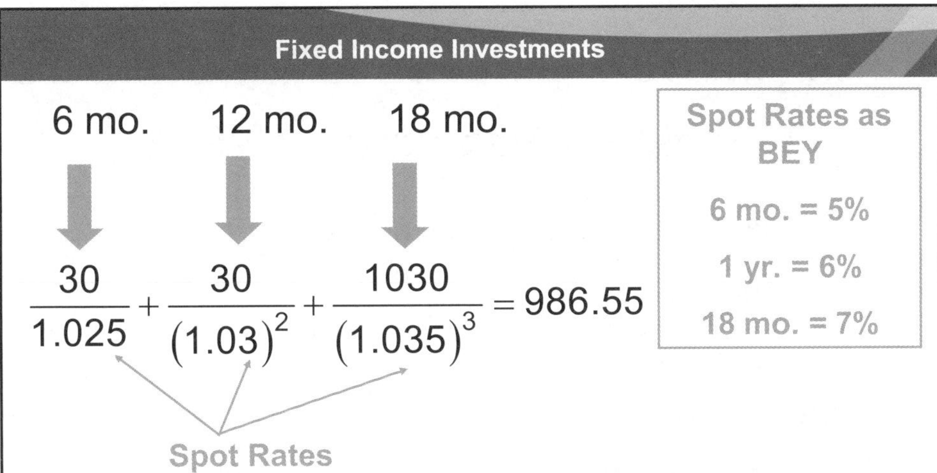

For arbitrage-free spot rates, 986.55 = mkt value

If mkt value = 984, buy bond, sell pieces

If mkt value = 986.55, buy pieces, sell bond

767

Fixed Income Investments

Sources of Bond Return

1. Coupon interest
2. Capital gain or loss when bond matures or is sold
3. Income from reinvestment of cash flows

768

Fixed Income Investments

Traditional Measures of Yield

Nominal yield (stated coupon rate)

Current yield

Yield to maturity

Yield to call

Yield to refunding

Yield to put

Yield to worst

Cash flow yield

→ IRR-based yields

769

Fixed Income Investments

YTM for an Annual-Pay Bond

Consider a 6% 3-year annual-pay bond priced at $943

$$943 = \frac{60}{(1+\text{YTM})} + \frac{60}{(1+\text{YTM})^2} + \frac{1060}{(1+\text{YTM})^3}$$

TVM functions: N = 3, PMT = 60, FV = 1,000,

PV = –943, CPT I/Y = 8.22%

Priced at a discount → YTM > coupon rate

770

Fixed Income Investments

YTM for a Semiannual-Pay Bond

With semiannual coupon payments, YTM is 2 × the semiannual IRR

$$\text{price} = \frac{\text{coupon 1}}{\left(1+\frac{YTM}{2}\right)} + \frac{\text{coupon 2}}{\left(1+\frac{YTM}{2}\right)^2} + \ldots + \frac{\text{coupon N + par value}}{\left(1+\frac{YTM}{2}\right)^N}$$

771

Fixed Income Investments

Semiannual-Pay YTM Example

A 3-year 5% Treasury note is priced at $1,028

N = 6 PMT = 25 FV = 1000 PV = –1,028

CPT I/Y = 2%   YTM = 2 × 2% = 4%

The YTM for a semiannual-pay bond is called a Bond Equivalent Yield (BEY)

Note: BEY for short-term securities in Corporate Finance reading is different.

772

Fixed Income Investments

Current Yield
(Ignores Movement Toward Par Value)

$$\text{Current yield} = \frac{\text{annual coupon payment}}{\text{current price}}$$

For an 8% 3-year (semiannual-pay) bond priced at 901.65

$$\text{Current yield} = \frac{80}{901.65} = 8.873\% \quad \text{YTM} = 12\%$$

773

Fixed Income Investments

Yield Measures – Problem

For a bond trading at a premium, order the coupon (nominal) yield, current yield, and YTM from smallest to largest.

774

Fixed Income Investments

Yield to Call – Problem

Consider a 10-year, 5% bond priced at $1,028
What is the YTM?

If it is callable in two years at 101, what is the YTC?

775

Fixed Income Investments

Assumptions and Limitations of Traditional Yield Measures

1. Assumes held to maturity (call, put, refunding, etc.)
2. Assumes no default
3. Assumes cash flows can be reinvested at the computed yield
4. Assumes flat yield curve (term structure)

776

Fixed Income Investments

Required Reinvestment Income

6% 10-year T-bond priced at $928 so YTM = 7%

1st: Calculate total ending value for a semiannual compound yield of 7%, **$928 × (1.035)^{20} = $1,847**

2nd: **Subtract total coupon and principal payments** to get *required reinvestment income*

$1,847 – (20 × $30) – $1,000 = $247

777

Fixed Income Investments

Factors That Affect Reinvestment Risk

Other things being equal, a coupon bond's **reinvestment risk** will *increase* with:

- *Higher coupons*—more cash flow to reinvest
- *Longer maturities*—more of the value of the investment is in the coupon cash flows and interest on coupon cash flows

778

Fixed Income Investments

Semiannual-Pay YTM to Annual-Pay YTM

Semiannual-pay YTM (BEY) is 8%, what is the annual-pay equivalent?

$$\left(1+\frac{0.08}{2}\right)^2-1=8.16\%$$

Annual-pay YTM is 8%, what is the semiannual-pay equivalent (BEY)?

$$\sqrt{(1+0.0816)}-1=4\%\times 2=8\%$$

Just like stated and effective rates with semiannual compounding

779

Fixed Income Investments

Theoretical Treasury Spot Rates

6-month T-bill price is 98.30

1-year 4% T-note is priced at 99.50

6-month discount rate is 1.73% $\quad \frac{1{,}000}{983}-1=1.73\%$

BEY = 2 × 1.73 = 3.46%

$$\frac{20}{1.0173}+\frac{1{,}020}{(1+?)^2}=995 \quad 995-\frac{20}{1.0173}=975.34=\frac{1{,}020}{(1+?)^2}$$

$$?=\sqrt{\frac{1{,}020}{975.34}}-1=2.26\%,\quad \text{BEY}=2\times 2.26=4.52\%$$

Could now use these rates and price of 18 mo. Treasury to get 18 mo. Spot rate

780

Fixed Income Investments

Nominal spread is just difference in YTMs

Zero-volatility (ZV) spread is the (parallel) spread to Treasury spot-rate curve to get PV = market price

Option adjusted spread (OAS) is ZV spread with the effect of embedded option removed from yield/price

Option cost in yield% = ZV spread% – OAS%

Option cost > 0 for callable, < 0 for putable

Must use OAS for debt with embedded options

781

Fixed Income Investments

Forward Rates

Forward rates are ***N*-period rates** for borrowing/lending at **some date in the future**

$$(1+S_3)^3 = (1+S_2)^2(1+{}_1F_2)$$

$S_2 = 4\%$, $S_3 = 5\%$, calculate ${}_1F_2$

$$\frac{(1+S_3)^3}{(1+S_2)^2} - 1 = {}_1F_2 \text{ so, } \frac{(1.05)^3}{(1.04)^2} - 1 = 7.03\%$$

Approximation: 3 × 5% – 2 × 4% = 15% – 8% = 7%

782

Fixed Income Investments

Forward Rates From Spot Rates

$S_2 = 4\%,\ S_4 = 5\%$, Calculate ${}_2F_2$

$$\sqrt{\frac{(1+S_4)^4}{(1+S_2)^2}} - 1 = {}_2F_2 \text{ so, } \sqrt{\frac{(1.05)^4}{(1.04)^2}} - 1 = 6.01\%$$

Approximation: 4 × 5% – 2 × 4% = 20% – 8% = 12%

12% / 2 = 6%

${}_2F_2$ is an annual rate, so we take the square root above and divide by two for the approximation

783

Fixed Income Investments

Spot Rates From Forward Rates

Example: $S_1 = 4\%,\ {}_1F_1 = 5\%,\ {}_1F_2 = 5.5\%$

Find the 3-period spot rate

$$[(1.04)(1.05)(1.055)]^{\frac{1}{3}} - 1 = S_3 = 4.8314\%$$

Approximation: $(4+5+5.5)/3 = 4.833$

784

Fixed Income Investments

Valuing a Bond With Forward Rates

1-year rate is 3%, ${}_1F_1$ = 3.5%, ${}_1F_2$ = 4%

Value a 4%, 3-year annual-pay bond

$$\frac{40}{1.03} + \frac{40}{(1.03)(1.035)} + \frac{1{,}040}{(1.03)(1.035)(1.04)} = 1{,}014.40$$

$1+S_1$ $\quad (1+S_2)^2 \quad (1+S_3)^3$

785

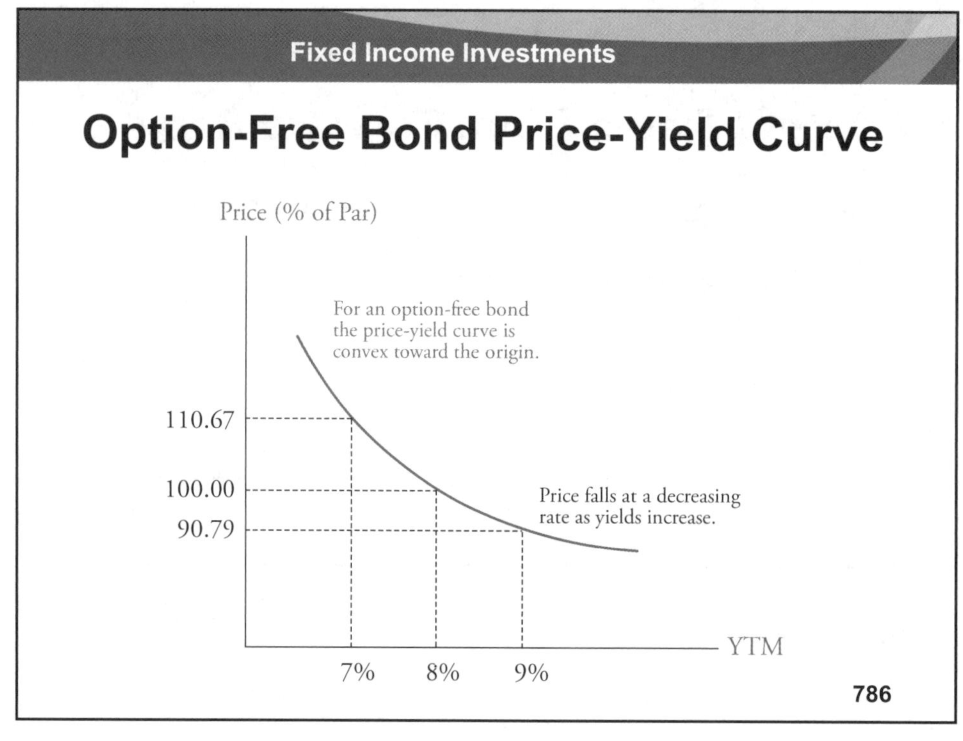

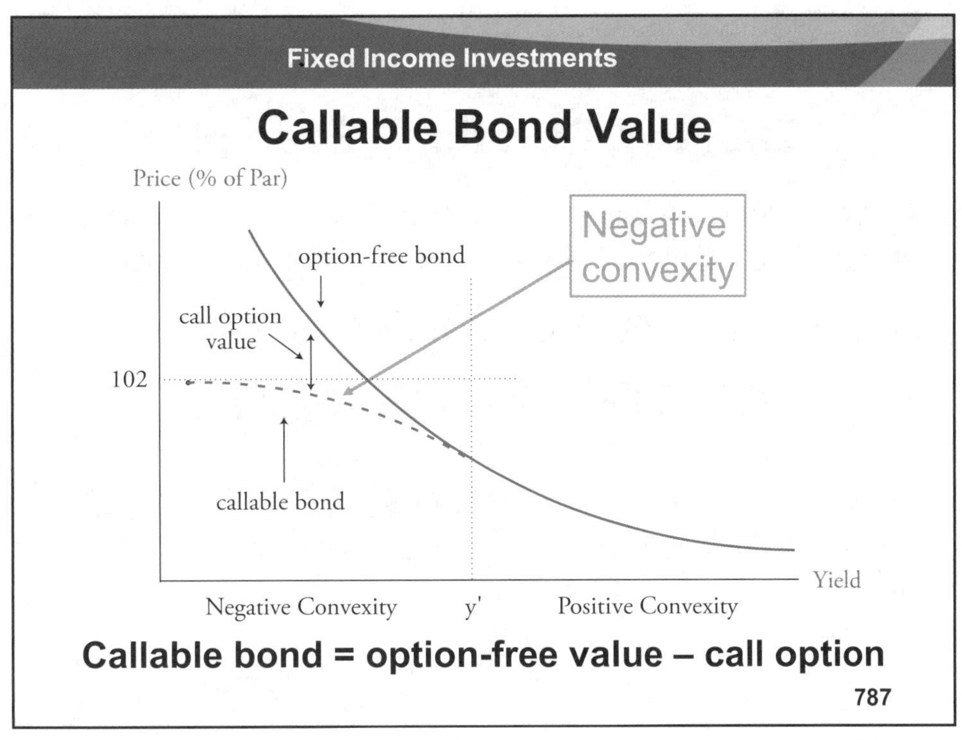
Fixed Income Investments
Callable Bond Value
Price (% of Par)
Negative convexity
option-free bond
call option value
102
callable bond
Yield
Negative Convexity
y'
Positive Convexity
Callable bond = option-free value – call option
787

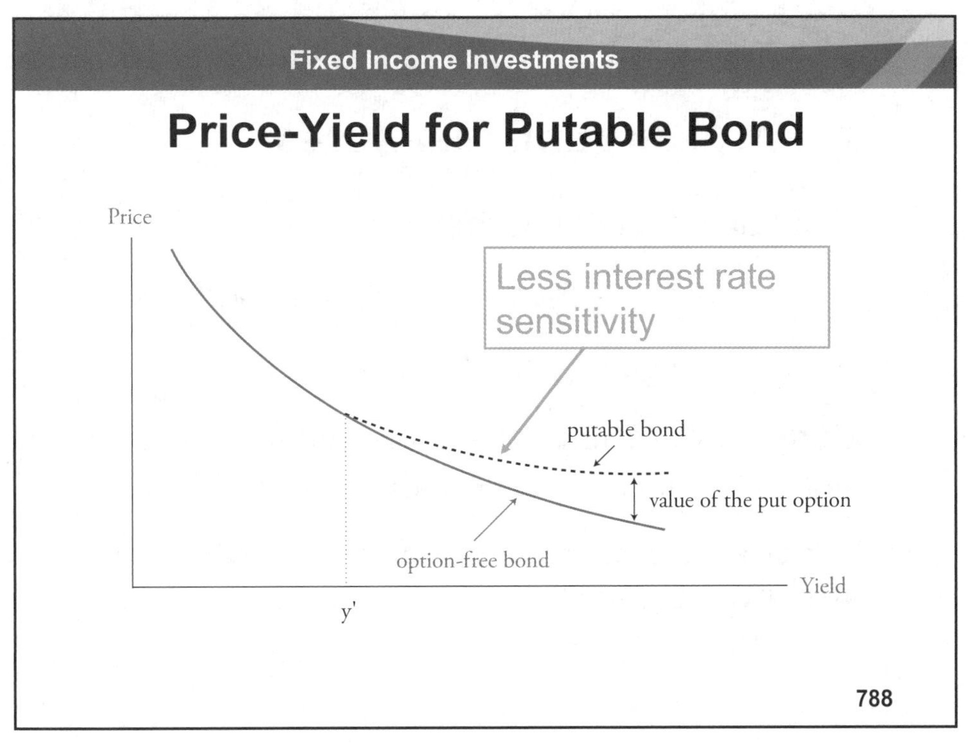
Fixed Income Investments
Price-Yield for Putable Bond
Price
Less interest rate sensitivity
putable bond
value of the put option
option-free bond
Yield
y'
788

Fixed Income Investments

Effective Duration - Example

15-year option-free bond, annual 8% coupon, trading at par, 100. Calculate effective duration based on:

Interest rates ↑ 50bp, new price is 95.848

Interest rates ↓ 50bp, new price is 104.414

Effective duration is: $\frac{104.414 - 95.848}{2 \times 100 \times 0.005} = 8.57$

V_- (104.414); V_+ (95.848); current price (100); 50 basis points (0.005)

789

Fixed Income Investments

Duration Measures

- **Macaulay duration** is in years
  - Duration of a 5-yr. zero-coupon bond is 5
  - 1% change in yield, 5% change in price
- **Modified duration** adjusts Macaulay duration for market yield, yield up → duration down
- **Effective duration** allows for cash flow changes as yield changes, must be used for bonds with embedded options

790

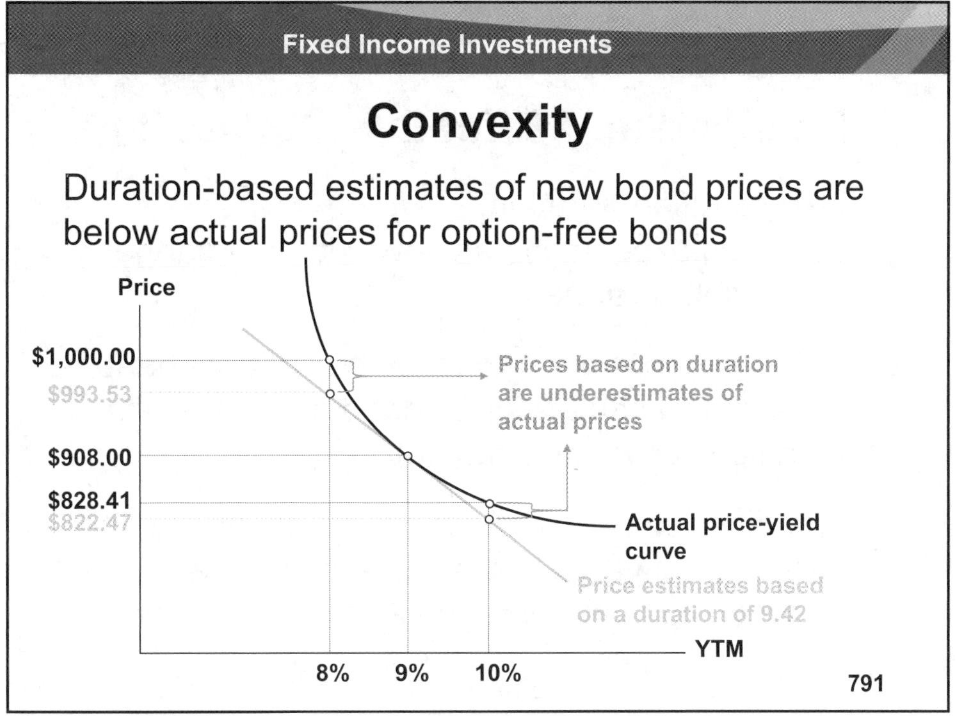

Fixed Income Investments

Using Duration and Convexity

A bond has a duration of 8.5 and convexity of 52.4, estimate price change for a 0.5% increase in yield.

Duration: $-D \times \Delta y = -8.5 \times 0.005 = -4.25\%$

Convexity:

$$+ C (\Delta y)^2 = 52.4(0.005)^2 = 0.00131 = +\ 0.131\%$$

$$-4.119\%$$

792

Fixed Income Investments

Modified and Effective Convexity

- Like modified duration, modified convexity assumes expected cash flows do not change when yield changes
- Effective convexity takes into account changes in cash flows due to embedded options, while modified convexity does not
- The difference between modified convexity and effective convexity mirrors the difference between modified duration and effective duration

793

Fixed Income Investments

Price Value of a Basis Point

- A measure of interest rate risk often used with portfolios is the **price value of a basis point**
- PVBP is the change in $ value for a 0.01% change in yield
- Duration × 0.0001 × portfolio value = PVBP

Example: A bond portfolio has a duration of 7 and value of $900,000

PVBP = 7 × 0.0001 × $900,000 = $630

794

Fixed Income Investments

After-Tax Yield – Solution

Tax-free bond yields **7%** **Taxable bond** yields **10%**

Investor marginal **tax rate** is **35%**

Which bond will the investor prefer?

---

after-tax yield = 10% × (1 – 0.35) = 6.5%

$$\text{taxable-equivalent yield} = \frac{7\%}{(1-0.35)} = 10.77\%$$

The municipal bond is preferred

7% > 6.5% and 10% < 10.77%

795

Fixed Income Investments

Value Change as Time Passes – Solution

6% 10-year semiannual coupon bond has a YTM of 8%

1. What is the price of the bond?

   N = 20, PMT = –30, FV = –1,000, I/Y = 4% **PV = 864.10**

2. What is the value after 1 year if the yield does not change?

   N = 18, PMT = –30, FV = –1,000, I/Y = 4% **PV = 873.41**

3. What is the value after 2 years if the yield does not change?

   N = 16, PMT = –30, FV = –1,000, I/Y = 4% **PV = 883.48**

796

Fixed Income Investments

Yield Measures – Solution

For a bond trading at a premium, order the coupon (nominal) yield, current yield, and YTM from smallest to largest.

$$\text{Current yield} = \frac{\text{annual coupon}}{\text{bond price}}$$

For premium bond, price > par

Current yield is less than coupon rate

YTM takes account of negative movement toward par value – must be less than current yield for premium bond

797

Fixed Income Investments

Yield to Call – Solution

Consider a 10-year, 5% bond priced at $1,028 What is the YTM?

N = 20 PMT = 25 FV = 1,000 PV = –1,028
CPT → I/Y = 2.323% × 2 = **4.646% = YTM**

If it is callable in two years at 101, what is the YTC?

N = 4 PMT = 25 FV = 1,010 PV = –1,028
CPT → I/Y = 2.007% × 2 = **4.014% = YTC**

YTC may be less than YTM for premium bond

798

Notes

Notes

Notes